W9-DHM-520

MONTGOMERY COLLEGE LIBRARY
ROCKVILLE CAMPUS

SHAKESPEARE AND DECORUM

Shakespeare and Decorum

T. McAlindon

BARNES & NOBLE
BOOKS
10 East 53d St., New York 10022
(a division of Harper & Row Publishers, Inc.)

T. McAlindon 1973

All rights reserved. No part of this publication may be
reproduced or transmitted, in any form or by any means,
without permission.

First published in the United Kingdom 1973 by
THE MACMILLAN PRESS LTD

Published in the U.S.A. 1973 by
HARPER & ROW PUBLISHERS, INC.
BARNES AND NOBLE IMPORT DIVISION

ISBN 06 – 4946 77 – 0

Printed in Great Britain

mc 77 -1424

Your crown's awry;
I'll mend it and then play.
(Antony and Cleopatra, V ii 316–17)

Contents

Acknowledgements

This book develops an approach to form and meaning in Shakespeare's plays which I first employed in articles on *Troilus and Cressida* (*Publications of the Modern Language Association of America*, LXXXIV, 1969; LXXXVII, 1972) and *Hamlet* (*Shakespeare Studies*, V, 1970). Much of the material of the *Hamlet* article is incorporated in Chapter 3 below; I am grateful to the editor of *Shakespeare Studies* for permission to reproduce it.

I am happy to record a debt to Mr D. J. Palmer and Mr P. A. Hepton, two long-suffering friends who read each chapter as it was written, gave 'an attent ear' to more than a few fervent monologues, and offered many useful criticisms.

T. McA.

N.B. Except where otherwise indicated, all citations of Shakespeare are from *The Complete Works*, ed. Peter Alexander (Collins, London and Glasgow, 1951 ; repr. 1966).

1
Words, Deeds and Decorum

On the night she is to be murdered by Othello, Desdemona makes a stray remark to Emilia which a modern audience would regard as of little or no significance. Having told Emilia of the maid Barbary who died for love, and before she actually sings Barbary's song, Desdemona momentarily recalls the man whom she and her husband have just entertained to dinner :

> *Emil.* Shall I go fetch your nightgown ?
> *Des.* No, unpin me here.
>   This Lodovico is a proper man.
> *Emil.* A very handsome man.
> *Des.* He speaks well. (IV iii 33–6)

Concerning Lodovico, the proper man, this is all Desdemona has to say : that he speaks well. It seems a trivial observation, serving no other purpose than to enhance dramatic realism by its inconsequential nature. However, like many stray remarks uttered at a time of emotional crisis, it is an oblique allusion to something that matters profoundly. It is given significance by a dramatic context in which murder – involving the destruction of marriage, friendship and social order – is effected in large measure by imperfect communication :

> Upon my knees, what doth your speech import?
> I understand a fury in your words,
> But not the words. (IV ii 31–3)

Moreover, the dramatic context of imperfect communication, as well as the complimentary 'He speaks well', derive intense significance from a particular system of education, indeed from a whole culture.

Everyone in Shakespeare's audience who had acquired the basic assumptions of contemporary education would have known that to describe Lodovico as a good speaker was equivalent to saying that he was wise, self-controlled, judicious. They would have inferred that he was well fitted to the task of separating truth from lies and ambiguities, seeing justice done, and bringing back to the Venetian senate a clear report of the dark and barbarous events which took place at Cyprus. The literate Elizabethan spectator would have shared our enthusiasm for the superb self-expressiveness of Othello and of Shakespeare's other heroes; but in contemplating the miseries which these men bring upon themselves and others, the Elizabethan would – unlike us – have had in mind the kind of solemn warning which Lear gives Cordelia as they both stand on the threshold of tragedy: 'Mend your speech a little,/ Lest you may mar your fortunes' (I i 93–4).

As is well known, the grammar-school education which moulded the Elizabethan mind was essentially rhetorical. Its purpose was to give the student a thorough training in the so-called arts of language – grammar, logic and rhetoric. A concomitant aim was to inculcate moral principles and an interest in debating moral issues. This, however, like the teaching of grammar and logic, was looked on as an integral part of rhetorical education rather than as an adjunct : Cicero and Quintilian, the two rhetoricians most admired and studied in the Renaissance, had laid it down as a first principle that no one could be a master of eloquence unless he was a virtuous man and a sound thinker in the moral as well as the logical sense.

In Shakespearean studies, familiarity with the Elizabethan grammar-school curriculum and general consciousness of its rhetorical nature have resulted mainly in close and respectful attention to the texture of thought and expression in the plays. There has been a great increase in critical sensitivity to Shakespeare's skill in dramatising debate, reflection and reasoning. His obviously conscious use of syllogism, enthymeme, and the logical fallacies is often noted. Above all, we have come to realise that the astonishing richness and vitality of his language was greatly dependent on his trained facility in using the numerous figures of speech classified in rhetorical tradition.[1] But Shakespeare acquired from this tradition considerably more than an analytical grasp of the techniques of reasoning and expression. He inherited from it a clearly articulated philosophy of language. And he inherited, too, a sane and subtle doctrine – that of decorum – governing the arts of expression and persuasion at every point. It is part of my intention in this book to show that these two intimately related and basic constituents of rhetorical tradition contributed a great deal to the meaning and design of Shakespeare's plays.

The doctrine of decorum, however, was as much a part of moral as of rhetorical tradition and was applied to non-verbal as well as to verbal behaviour. My interest in decorum, in fact, is not purely rhetorical; almost nothing, for example, is said about verbal style in the chapters on *Macbeth* and *Antony and Cleopatra*. My primary purpose rather is to show how deeply Shakespeare's understanding and representation of human behaviour – of words and deeds – was affected by this comprehensive doctrine of decorum and, in the process, to illuminate the meaning and form of individual plays. Nevertheless, since speech was regarded as the most characteristic form of human behaviour, and since social behaviour in general – 'civil conversation' as it was so often termed – was itself thought of as an elaborate form of self-expression and communication, language and style will necessarily claim a great deal of my attention.

II

The Renaissance philosophy of language (and rhetoric) can quickly be reduced to a few basic tenets acquired mainly from Cicero and Quintilian. Speech, it was asserted, is what distinguishes us from the beast and so is 'the fairest gift of providence to man'. It is also, as Ben Jonson put it, 'the Instrument of *Society*', since through rational persuasion men were encouraged to leave the predatory solitude of the wilderness and establish communities, cities and laws. In fact, the archetypal founder of society was held to be an orator : a heaven-sent man whose well-tuned and enchanting words drew men away from demonic chaos into a rational and harmonious order – an Orpheus, a Mercury, a prophet of the Word.[2]

If eloquent men alone could create society it follows that those who protect and guide it must be eloquent too. As the wonder-working oratory of such stage heroes as Tamburlaine the Great and Henry V might suggest, even military leaders were reminded of this.[3] But for rhetoricians and humanists alike, the military role of eloquence was naturally of far less importance than its strictly political one; their emphasis on the *bloodless* nature of military conquests achieved through eloquence – in parleys and the like – suggests that the proper function of the word is to render the sword unnecessary. Universal assent was given to Cicero's insistent claim that rhetoric and political science are more or less synonymous. 'Honest and eloquent Orators,' wrote Henry Peacham in *The Compleat Gentleman* (1622), are 'props to uphold a State, and the onely keyes to bring in tune a discordant Commonwealth', oratory being 'a principall meanes of correcting ill manners, reforming lawes, humbling aspiring minds, and upholding all vertue'.[4]

As the title of Peacham's work might recall, the worship of eloquence had an enormous effect on ideals of nobility and gentility during the Renaissance. The medieval type of complete man, who found all his fulfilment in the restricted milieu of tourneys and baronial wars, gave way (much as Hotspur does to Hal) to one who was trained both in 'arts and martial exercises' (*II Henry IV*, IV v 74); and those arts were the arts of language and of 'civil conversation'. For this reason we will probably gain most insight into the Renaissance regard for communicational skill from the so-called courtesy books, where the broadly social as distinct from the political life of the ruling class is considered; and of those from Castiglione's *The Book of the Courtier* (1528, tr. 1561) and Guazzo's *Civile Conversation* (1574, tr. 1581) in particular. Castiglione's dialogue on the perfect courtier is modelled (as its Tudor translator duly noted) on Cicero's *Orator*, a treatise on the perfect orator; and the influence of the model is apparent not only in the arts of the courtier but in his social function as well. As defined by Castiglione and elaborated by his successors, the ultimate purpose of all the courtier's graceful attainments is to enable him to delight his lord and prince, secure his favour, and thereby be in a position to 'enforme him frankly of the truth of every matter meete for him to understand . . . to disswade him from every ill purpose, and to set him in the way of virtue'. This is the art of rhetoric in a new guise, the well-known purpose of that art being to delight, to instruct and to persuade with a view to virtuous action.[5]

Humanist thought seems thus to have been in complete sympathy with the claim of the classical rhetoricians that eloquence is a moral virtue. For theological reasons, however, acceptance of this view was tacit rather than stated. But the almost equally bold rhetorical maxim that speech is the image of mind and soul was habitually affirmed.[6] By extension, too, language was thought to mirror the political and even the moral condition – good or bad – of a nation.[7] Indeed, in their own way humanist thinkers went even further than Cicero in sanctifying language. They conflated the myth of the orator rescuing mankind from barbarism with the biblical Fall and Redemption;[8] and they conceived of eloquence as proceeding from and upholding the divinely appointed order of things in much the same way as Christ, the Word, expressed and confirmed the attributes of the Creator: 'The order of God's creatures in themselves is not only admirable and glorious, but eloquent...'[9]

However, just as eloquence might decay in a corrupt society, so in turn it might be used to corrupt and destroy: 'Much hurt it may doe, if like a mad man's sword, it be used by a turbulent and mutinous orator'.[10] This uncomfortable truth had to be faced if only because it formed the basis of the general condemnation of rhetoric made by Socrates and his like. In refuting the Socratic argument, the rhetoricians made a distinction between the art itself and those who misuse it. But they took occasion also to emphasise that, precisely because of its harmful potentialities, rhetoric should never be detached from logic and ethics. In this way they turned the argument against the anti-rhetorical philosophers, making them responsible for the rise of unscrupulous and eloquent hypocrites. Originally (goes the argument) the teacher of philosophy and of rhetoric were one and the same, but Socrates 'separated the science of wise thinking from that of elegant speaking' and so encouraged 'the absurd and unprofitable and reprehensible severance between the tongue and the brain'.[11] Yet it was never forgotten by the champions of eloquence that the fearful successes of brilliant but unscrupulous persuaders were in themselves testaments to the might and importance of the tongue.

In consequence of these assumptions, there was no strict distinction between moral and rhetorical considerations in the evaluation of oral or written speech. This is especially apparent in the procedural method adopted by the courtesy writers in dealing with the nature and the laws of speech, for they move systematically from a consideration of truthfulness and the vices opposed to it (these vices cover almost all the moral abuses of language) to an application of the basic principles of rhetoric to conversational speech. The moral vices of language, which were formulated almost as precisely as the rhetorical vices, were lying and railing, boasting and idle swearing, flattery and slander (or 'ear poisoning').[12] In a society where advancement depended so much on acquiring a good name, slander was regarded as an especially vicious crime. And since flattery frequently involved a complaisant attitude to the sins of the great it was thought to be scarcely less dangerous. As for boasting and swearing, one is given the impression – by secular and religious moralists alike – that Renaissance society was filled with swaggering fellows who thought that the surest way to pass for a gentleman was (as Sir Thomas Elyot put it) to adorn their speech with oaths much as an oration is with figures.[13] Criticism of this fashionable vice, however, was prompted not simply by considerations of restraint and reverence. Behind it was the fear that casual swearing may beget casual forswearing or commit one to a rash and immoral course of action. Behind it, too, was the conviction that the whole order of society – justice and law itself – rests on respect for oaths and promises, for the solemn word.[14] In the oath, the word's essential function as a bond is confirmed by civil and divine law.

III

Obviously, then, Thomas Nashe believed he was expressing everything of importance concerning the right use of language when he wrote :

> Perswade one point thoroughlie rather then teach many things scatteringly; that which we thinke let vs speake, and that which we speake let vs thinke; let our speache accorde with our life.[15]

This remark, however, is characteristic of its age not only in its refusal to separate eloquence from virtue but also in its appeal to what Nashe's contemporaries accepted as the fundamental norm, both rhetorical and moral, for all good speech : there must be a harmony between thought and word, between word and deed. The sign, the sensible impression of such harmony was decorum, or what the Elizabethans – preferring native or native-sounding words – variously referred to as comeliness, seemliness, fitness, decency, meetness, propriety, grace.

Although every possible device which might produce effective and pleasing utterance was systematically studied in the five parts of rhetoric (invention, arrangement, style or ornament, delivery or 'action', and memory), it was continually stressed that the techniques of verbal art are neutral instruments which assist the speaker only if he has acquired the discretion to use them when and where they are appropriate. Decorum was thus a creative concept utilised in every conscious search for the right thing to say and the right way to say it; and in turn it provided the aesthetic philosophy and the critical method which operated in every evaluative response to a speech, sermon, play, or poem. But Cicero claimed in his *De Oratore* that decorum is 'the universal rule' in life and in oratory alike; and in his treatise on moral duty (*De Officiis*) – the most important single text for the study of moral philosophy during the Renaissance – he elaborated this idea at great length. Throughout the Renaissance, when, if ever, life itself was an art, this claim met with universal acceptance. Thus, in the forty-page discussion of decorum at the end of *The Arte of English Poesie* (1589), George Puttenham observes that poets, like orators, should 'know the comeliness of an action as well as of a word', draws all his exemplary material from social and political situations, and gives judgement on verbal and non-verbal problems of propriety alike. Likewise in *The Courtier* one whole book out of four (Bk II) is given to a dialogue on 'fitness' on the ground that all the courtly qualities and attainments discussed therein are of no advantage unless employed in the appropriate manner.

The reason for the dual role of decorum as a behavioural and as an oratorical law is that it was a concept of philosophical origin. Its roots are in the teachings of Plato and Aristotle, and it was even affected by Stoic thought. In its fully developed form – as presented by Cicero and Quintilian, and by Renaissance writers – it is manifestly a synthesis of some of the most fundamental notions in the moral and aesthetic theory of classical antiquity.

The essentially aesthetic attitude of the Greek philosophers towards human conduct is apparent in the doctrine generally and operates particularly in the axiom that decorum proceeds from harmony and proportion.[16] The ubiquitous warning that a reasonably sustained decorum is impossible without 'a learned and experienced discretion' [17] goes back to the Platonic and Aristotelian view that virtue cannot be attained without practical sagacity or prudence – the ability to discern what is right in the given circumstances. From Aristotle, too, came the core of the doctrine : the belief that moral and aesthetic virtue both reside in the mean; that the mean is not mediocrity but an ever-moving, elusive point of natural perfection situated between extremes of excess and deficiency.[18] The Peripatetic equation of the mean and the appropriate obviously accounts too for the belief that 'in Temperance man may behold . . . how to frame all things according to that which the Latines call Decorum'.[19] And since decorum was essentially a doctrine of adjustment and relationships, it easily assimilated the Stoics' hostility to cloistered wisdom, their insistence that the purpose of all knowledge is to make men citizens of the world and to confirm the bonds of humanity. Lastly, because it signified harmony and proportion on the one hand, and social adjustment on the other, decorum coalesced with the mighty concept of world order and in particular with the notion that Nature's order rests on degree. As Elyot explained in his famous account of order, superior and inferior things alike are useful and pleasing when functioning in the place 'appropered unto them by God', useless, 'uncomely' and 'unseemly' when not. In effect, decorum was thought to be natural order as perceived by the senses or the aesthetic imagination.[20]

IV

According to a formula which every schoolboy had engraved on the tables of his memory, one achieved decorum by considering the thing said or done, the end in view, the persons involved, the time and the place – that is, 'the circumstances'; and it was probably felt that in behaviour generally most of the problems of decorum relate to the circumstances of person and time.

The circumstance of person requires in particular an awareness that things essentially distinct in nature must not be confused or allowed (in Guazzo's phrase) to 'degenerate . . . from their kinde'.[21] One must never act in obedience to mere impulse or passion since that is not consonant with man's superiority to the rest of the animal creation;[22] rashness of any kind, therefore, is antithetical to decorum. The sexes, too, must not be confused :

For as it is seemly for him to shew a certaine manlinesse full and steadie, so doth it well in a woman to have a tendernesse soft and milde, with a kinde of womanlye sweetness in every gesture of hers, that . . . may alwaies make her appeare a woman without anye likenesse of a man.[23]

Age also has to be considered : thus, amorous and sporty old gentlemen who put out the banner of youth (one thinks of Sir John Falstaff) are held to be particularly graceless.[24]

Considerations of class or office similarly enforce the lesson that 'what may well become one man to do may not become another'.[25] Indeed, the relationship between man and name or title was treated as a very fundamental question of decorum, closely akin to the first principle of linguistic decorum, that of 'calling things by their right names'.[26] Like the relationship of words and matter, too, it was customarily expressed in terms of the imagery of dress. There are those whose inherited cloak of nobility simply brings ridicule upon them, despite all its glittering splendour ; forgetting that 'the name of a sovereign or ruler without actual governance is but a shadow', they 'wear it not comely and as it appertaineth'. Conversely, there are the social upstarts whose noble name hangs loose upon them, like giant robes upon a dwarfish thief.[27]

The analogy of unsuitable or borrowed robes came naturally to the mind of any Elizabethan concerned with the discrepancy between name and man, since dress was one of the most familiar items in the whole question of personal decorum. Seen as having a semantic function, it was expected, like language, to be suited to and indicative of time, place, personality, office and – above all – social class. Both in England and in France there had for centuries been laws designed to uphold this kind of decorum. They were re-promulgated in Tudor England in response to an epidemic of sartorial gorgeousness and eccentricity which affected European society from top to bottom. Courtly and religious writers joined forces to condemn these extravagant deviations in costume from 'honest comelinesse', the beauty 'which becometh Christians'.[28]

The most testing requirement in decorum of person, it was stressed, lies in adjusting one's behaviour to the needs and nature of other people. Fitness of this kind underlines the relativistic character of decorum and brings to mind Quintilian's remark that propriety demands above all else 'a wise adaptability'. A complete gentleman needs 'a good judgement' and 'a knowledge in so many thinges' because he must 'varie his conversation' and 'never want good communication and fitte for them hee talketh withall'.[29]

The seventeenth-century panegyrist who described Sir Thomas More as 'a man for all seasons' obviously saw him in just this light : as a man who could suit times and places and accommodate himself to persons of all sorts. But the panegyrist allowed the circumstance of time to do duty for the others; and this was quite common, since an act described as timely or seasonable is usually one that is proper in every respect. In fact, timeliness was conceived simply as decorum itself, though with one of its conditions emphasised.[30] All investigations of the time 'theme' in Shakespeare's plays which do not take this into account are, in consequence, seriously incomplete.

There were, of course, other reasons besides its inclusive potential for the special importance of time in the doctrine of decorum. The conception of world order as measure and harmony predisposed men to believe that Nature's first law is to 'keep time in all' (*Othello*, IV i 92). Timeliness, moreover, had a long and independent life of its own in moral thought, learned as well as popular, the philosopher's interest in the concept of εὐκαιρία (the opportune moment) being as old as Plato. But the moral philosopher who taught the Renaissance most about *opportunitas* – the author of *De Officiis* – identified it with the prudential aspect of decorum; and that is how it always appears in Renaissance literature : as 'the knowledge of opportunity of things to be done or spoken, in appointing and setting them in time or place to them convenient and proper'; as an exquisite 'mean between two extremities wherein nothing lacketh or exceedeth'.[31]

One must, of course, distinguish in Renaissance literature between the philosophical attitude to time and the lyrical; according to the latter, time is simply a malicious spirit who accelerates and retards his pace to the disadvantage of lovers, and abruptly terminates all men's enjoyment of youth and beauty. But at their most ambitious – as for example in *Romeo and Juliet* and *The Rape of Lucrece*, in Spenser's 'Epithalamion' and Chapman's part of *Hero and Leander* – Elizabethan poets were liable to bring together the lyrical and the philosophical attitudes to time and to allow the second to eclipse the first. The infinite sadness of queens and ladies dying young and fair, and the sheer perversity with

which Time seems to smash our plans for happiness, are duly recognised; yet we are led to believe in the end that Time is the cause
of unhappiness only when men forget that 'ripeness is all'. The
natural tendency to blame Time is made quite explicit in *Lucrece*
when the heroine declaims lengthily against him (and Opportunity) for conniving at the bestial act which brings married happiness to an abrupt end and compels her to take her own life; but
it has already been made clear that the sole cause of her tragedy is
'the untimely thought' and 'all-too-timeless [untimely] speed' of
the rash and lustful Tarquin (ll.43–6).

As the other three of the Elizabethan works I have just mentioned will show, the concept of timeliness is very often bound up
with that of ceremony or ritual order: the tragedy of 'hastie
accidents' ('Epithalamion', l.429) in young love is equivalent to a
rejection of the ceremonious pace of ideal life as it is acted out in
public courtship and the marriage rite. Ceremony – the quality
proper to a rite or ceremony – is so closely associated with decorum
(especially decorum as seasonableness) as to be almost synonymous
with it: in Chapman's poem, for example, 'Ceremonie', 'Comelinesse' and 'Time' are allied divinities opposed to 'marriage violence' of any kind. But ceremony is not decorum. It is, rather, the
kind of decorum which inheres in those stereotyped patterns of
verbal and non-verbal behaviour that are accepted by society as
solemn signs of good intent towards others or towards agreed
values, codes and duties. Because of their grave and traditional
nature, ceremonies constitute that area of speech and action where
propriety is most expected; they are formal orderings of speech
and gesture, of costume and movement, in which departures from
accepted style are instantly perceptible and either offensive or
ridiculous.

Ceremonies are also reminders that all the world's a stage on
which every man must accept his part and play it with the maximum of propriety. This is a Stoic conception of life and one which
was transmitted to the Elizabethans mainly through the *De
Officiis*, where it is used to delineate the virtue of constancy (*con-
stantia*). Constancy is of great importance as being one of two
related virtues which serve to correct any tendency in the pursuit
of decorum to obscure the need for sincerity and individuality.
Rightly understood, decorum implies that just as the individual
or 'proper' perfection of a man depends on his correct functioning

within a complex whole, so, too, the proper functioning of the whole is disturbed as soon as the individual ceases to do or be what is proper to him alone. Hence the need for constancy, which entails perfecting one's own gifts rather than copying those of others, discerning and adhering to one's role or duties, and imposing order and consistency on one's life as a whole.[32] 'O heaven, were man but constant, he were perfect!' – it is Shakespeare's belief,[33] it is Castiglione's, and certainly it is Cicero's and Seneca's. Yet in the Renaissance as a whole, respect for this ideal of truth to self showed itself principally in a very vocal hatred of affectation or 'curiousness'. There was complete agreement with Quintilian's insistence that affectation is the quickest way to destroy decorum and the most insidious of all vices for those in search of cultivation. However, the virtue opposed to it sprang not from moral but from rhetorical tradition : it was *sprezzatura*, the artful naturalness which conceals care and premeditation.[34] The perfect orator, actor or gentleman – and in the Renaissance all three might be one – never oversteps the modesty of Nature.

v

For rhetorical decorum, or eloquence, the first requirement was held to be proper diction. Words should 'express well and clearly the conceits of the minde', 'properly agree vnto that thing which they signifie', and be chosen with due regard for contextual fitness.[35] It was mainly through study of the classified vices of language that the different ways in which words – and figures – could be improperly used were impressed on the mind.

Since moral and social faults are involved in such vices as cacemphaton (words with an obscene sense) and tapinosis ('such wordes and termes as do diminish and abbase the matter . . . imparing the dignitie, height, vigour or maiestie of the cause'), these were severely condemned.[36] Yet the faults in diction which provoked most attention and contempt in the Renaissance were those which proceed from a desire to impress the audience or reader rather than to express the matter clearly, and so result in affectation or obscurity ('darkenesse'). These were indentifiable as pleonasmus (too many words), macrologia (superfluous clauses and sentences), cacozelia ('when we affect new wordes and phrases' or 'coigne fine wordes out of the Latin'), and soraismus (the unnecessary use of words from divers languages, hence called 'the mingle-mangle').[37] The last two vices relate to the great sixteenth-century debate on what Roger Ascham called 'strange and inke-horne' as distinct from 'proper and commonlie used wordes'. All I need say here on this subject is that the use of neologistic and archaic words was always viewed by the most distinguished contributors to the debate (both on the continent and in England) as an intrinsic part of the complex issue of rhetorical decorum, and that those who adopted a progressive attitude were just as hostile as the conservatives to the use of strange words which manifestly do not denote 'propriety rather than affectation' or serve to enhance 'the decorum and coppy [copiousness] of our tongue'.[38]

That affectation and obscurity were the faults in diction most strenuously condemned during the Renaissance is a fact which needs emphasising, for it is still widely assumed that adverse criticism of stylistic ornateness in the sixteenth century indicates a growing minority reaction against 'the rhetorical spirit' of the times. The truth of the matter is that the most scathing attacks on verbal exhibitionism came from those most completely dedicated to the proposition that eloquence is the dyke between civilisation and barbarism. For them rhetorical affectation was not merely repellent but dangerous, being the false, gaudy art which brings true art into disrepute. All their advice therefore on 'true diction' is accompanied by contemptuous blasts at the folly of the speaker or writer who 'in busying his braine about the vain pompe of wordes . . . doeth not conceive the matter so well, nor contrive it in such order, as he ought to doe'.[39] And when at times they express a preference for honest plainness they are reacting not against ornament but against affectation and excess in ornament. 'I would rather have a plaine downright wisdom than a foolish affected eloquence' – this expresses no dislike of true rhetorical art.[40]

Whereas proper diction was deemed the foundation of eloquence, figurative language was held to be its distinguishing characteristic. It was recognised, however, that figures are departures from ordinary and straightforward modes of expression and arrangement and that there may be therefore no essential difference between them and some of the vices of style. Unlike the deviant character – the 'noueltie and strange maner of conueyance' – of cacozelia and the like, that of the figures is agreeably surprising and effective and thus serves to make the style 'nothing the more vnseemely or misbecoming, but rather decenter and more agreeable to any civill eare and vnderstanding'.[41] The principle involved here underlies the familiar classical and humanist argument that art is not at variance with Nature but is rather its coadjutor, an extension of Nature's own art; it could be used, too – and this is of great importance for the present study – to justify any deviation from what would conventionally be thought natural and proper: some rare individuals can make defect perfection. Nevertheless, the proximity of virtue to vice in art was generally held up as a warning that figures or ornament can, when indiscreetly used, produce an effect exactly opposite to the one intended, bringing ridicule rather than admiration and persuasion.

In considerations of the proper relationship between subject-matter and style, indecorum was usually perceived in one of two guises (each of which can involve the other): either as a discordant combination of things unlike – an 'evil mixture' – or as a flight from moderation to extremes. The grossest errors were undoubtedly of the first kind. They consist chiefly of the application of a high style to a low or trivial subject and – a kind of sustained tapinosis – of a base style to a high or noble subject; and they seemed all the worse in that they so often involved a patent disregard for degree. Closely related to such errors is that vice which has become embalmed in literary history as the mingling of comedy and tragedy, of clowns and kings – the use of a light and jesting tone in serious matters.[42]

However, since distinction in style was usually thought to be dependent on amplification through 'increasing' and 'diminishing' (in practice one had to specialise in exaggerating and belittling, praising and dispraising, accusing and exonerating), the commonest danger in the path of the good speaker or writer was felt to be that of overstepping or not reaching the relevant mean. The ideal set before him therefore was that of a 'well tempered style'.[43] As in decorum of general conduct, infinitely more attention was given to excess than to deficiency, it being at once more tempting and more likely to disgust. The two vices of excess were periergeia ('overlabour'), which proceeds from an inordinate desire for refinement of expression, and bomphiologia – using 'such bombasted wordes, as seeme altogether farced full of winde, being a great deale too high and loftie for the matter'.[44] The more famous instances of adverse criticism aimed at Elizabethan writers by their own contemporaries are attacks on these two vices of style.

In delivery ('the language of the body'), as in diction and ornament, extremes were treated as the principal danger; 'comely moderation' became almost a catchphrase. Again, too much was thought to be vastly more offensive than too little; indeed, for classical rhetoricians the noisy and fiercely gesticulating speaker – often compared to the bad actor – was the nightmare image of a great art hideously debased. Hamlet's Termagant actors who thrill the groundlings and grieve the judicious are descended not only from the medieval stage but from the pseudo-orators who bellow and dash about, stamp their feet, gesticulate 'with all the frenzy of a lunatic' and generally 'confer the title of force on that which is really violence'.[45]

VI

In view then of what has been recalled so far in this chapter, it should not seem unreasonable to suggest that decorum might have been uppermost in Shakespeare's mind when he set about dramatising the disorders which bring misery or ridicule into the lives of the nobility, or even when he thought of composing a speech for an actor on a stage. But there is one more reason why decorum could have engaged his thoughts from the outset of his career; and I have left it to the last, not because I believe it is the most important reason, but because it relates specifically to the drama.

The new drama created in the sixteenth century was felt by all the educated to be defective in one outstanding respect: its violation of decorum.[46] Nurtured on a dramatic tradition – that of the Middle Ages –which was characterised by an arresting amalgam of the sublime, the homely and the grotesque, the Elizabethan audience would have had no patience with plays written in accordance with the classical separation of social and aesthetic categories. The dramatists, therefore, had to accept that 'my lord fool' – so Chapman called him – was almost the most important member of the cast. They had often to crowd major events together without due regard for time and place and to neglect a number of minor refinements usually thought appropriate for the staging of high and tragical events. Contrary, however, to what is often suggested, they did not cheerfully ignore the charge of gross indecorum, since it was based on principles which they had obviously no inclination to challenge. For the most part, they admitted – sometimes resignedly and sometimes bitterly – that their better judgement had bowed to the taste of 'the uncapable multitude' and 'these jig-giuen times'.

It has been remarked, therefore, that although the dramatists were articulate for a century and a half on the question of mixing comedy with tragedy, they still produced no higher aesthetic principle in its defence than that the audience demanded it.[47] But Shakespeare and at least one of his contemporaries are, I believe, clear exceptions to this generalisation. Following a path indicated to him by the author of *The Spanish Tragedie* (whose inventiveness I can do no more than refer to here), Shakespeare resolved the problem of enforced indecorum and even made it the source of enormous artistic gain. Yet his solution to the problem is not based on the aesthetic theory which is now an intrinsic part of our critical response to his most daring work – the theory that a vein of comedy can greatly enhance tragic effect, and that a play which combines the domestic and the grand, the laughable and the terrible, is a truer image of nature than 'pure' tragedy. It is even possible that he would have rejected this view. For instead of attempting to undermine the orthodox belief that the new mixtures were grotesque rather than natural, Shakespeare accepted them as improper and made them his subject, or an aspect of his subject. Wherever in his plays the improper occurs, it is generally a means whereby he registers upon the aesthetic sense of the judicious an intense visual or auditory perception of those defects, lapses or perversions of judgement which are the source of tragic or comic action.

Shakespeare was thus able to draw the formal disorders of the new play into a controlled and significant vision of disorder on the stage of life. And having evolved this 'strange maner of conueyance', he set about abusing dramatic decorum with a force and consistency which made his contemporaries (including Kyd) look timid. He gave the stage its greatest 'fool and jester' (*II Henry IV*, V v 49); but as all the world knows, that fool is an elderly knight, one who not only (as Sir Philip Sidney would say) 'plays a part in maiesticall matters, with neither decencie nor discretion',[48] but actually comes near to ousting the Lord Chief Justice and becoming the king's mentor. In *King Lear* the matching of 'vile russettings . . . with monarchs and with mighty kings' (I now quote from Hall's satire on the stage) is carried to the extent that the king is the fool and the fool is the man of good counsel. Even in his comedies, in order to effect a more daring fusion of meaning and form, Shakespeare provokes us into accusing him of having produced a discordant mixture of the kinds. *Love's Labour's Lost*, for example, ends not in marriage but in funeral gloom, boldly imaged on the stage in the black-clad figure of Marcade – a parting sign of the improprieties which have dominated the action throughout; while the thoroughly inept title of *All's Well That Ends Well* underscores the tragic seriousness of the comic action and the unsatisfactoriness of the marriage denouement for which a decent girl has indecently schemed. Confronted with such mixtures and extremes, we are forced to ask, as Theseus does when confronted with Bottom's play (a tragedy offered to celebrate a marriage and replete with 'very tragical mirth', a production in which 'there is not one word apt, one player fitted'): 'How shall we find the concord of this discord?' And the only answer to such a question is in 'concordant discord' or 'decorous indecorum'.[49]

'Quite athwart/Goes all decorum' (*Measure for Measure*, I iii 30–1): such then was the plan. And as I have implied, the use within the play itself of plays, masques, rites and the like is a principal clue to this plan. Shakespeare's drama-within-drama does, of course, merit attention for quite other reasons: it contributes enormously to theatrical effectiveness by obscuring the division between nature and art, audience and actor (thus intensifying the illusion of reality), and by providing tense and spectacular scenes. But the semantic function of Shakespeare's microcosmic dramas remains all-important. Precisely because they are defective dramatic forms in which is crystallised all the confusion of the society which produces them, they serve to remind thoughtful spectators that the loss of decorum is more a subject than an attribute of the macrocosmic play which contains them.

VII

Since I wish to show that Shakespeare's concern for decorum affects the meaning, organisation and texture of his plays, my intention for the rest of this book is to devote each chapter to the analysis of a particular play in the light of the ideas sketched in the preceding pages. The plays chosen have been selected partly because of their popularity and complexity, and partly because they enable me to prove that Shakespeare's preoccupation with fitness in word and deed is active in his approach to the most dissimilar characters and situations. Although they should corroborate and clarify one another, these critical chapters are independent studies. Moreover, the nature of the play chosen is such that in each chapter a particular aspect of the subject is thrown into relief. The chapter on *Richard II*, like those on *Hamlet* and *Othello*, is much concerned with language and style; its principal concern, however, is the play's (much misunderstood) use of ceremony and ceremoniousness. In the *Hamlet* chapter the governing motive is the impact on the play of the notion of life as drama and as meaningful, harmonious form. *Othello* and *Macbeth* are both shown to explore in quite different ways the law that ripeness is all and to establish that this law is but an aspect of the comprehensive law of decorum; but *Othello* is treated primarily as the tragedy of the tongue and its terrible potency, *Macbeth* as the play which shows that fitness is simply naturalness. Finally, in the protagonists of *Antony and Cleopatra* we behold Shakespeare dramatising and questioning what he himself has practised all his life : the alchemic art of making defect (and excess) perfection.

2
Richard II

I

One of the most distinctive features of *Richard II* is its air of medievalism. In giving this character to the play, however, Shakespeare was not aiming chiefly at historical accuracy or the delights of period flavour; nor was he seeking to show that Richard is the last of an old race of kings compelled by historical necessity to give way to a new breed of efficient and prosaic rulers.

To understand the artistic purpose of the play's medievalism we have to bear in mind that it is conveyed to us entirely through the use of chivalric rites, ideals, and manners. The nobles who surround King Richard are knights rather than courtiers – men whose models are found in Malory and Froissart rather than in Castiglione and Guazzo. They are, nonetheless, the obvious progenitors of Renaissance gentlemen, and their declared values are an integral part of their descendants' view of life. They accept that a knight should be 'true' – should not lie, should keep his word, should be loyal. They believe that the proper end of military skill is to enable one to fight in the service of a noble cause. And they would agree that no man could win a finer eulogy than that accorded by the Bishop of Carlisle to Thomas Mowbray, Duke of Norfolk, who spent the last years of his life in the service of Christ and in the defence of truth itself against error and barbarism – 'black pagans, Turks, and Saracens' (IV i 92–100). But the whole point of Carlisle's beautifully evocative panegyric is that true knighthood has vanished from England. For although they give many impressive signs to the contrary, Richard and his divided followers are a collection of talkers, flatterers, liars, slanderers, and 'recreant traitors'. The only war for which they become famous is not fought against the enemies of England, much less against black pagans and Turks: it is an unnatural conflict between Englishman and Englishman, cousin and cousin, father and son. And in the period covered by the play these knights do not even get beyond the battle of words to the clash of swords; the most important actions they are involved in are all anti-climaxes – more unfulfilled promises. 'Methinks King Richard and myself should meet', says Bolingbroke,

> With no less terror than the elements
> Of fire and water, when their thund'ring shock
> At meeting tears the cloudy cheeks of heaven. (III iii 54–7)

But victory in this elemental conflict of king and usurper is determined by the tearful verbalising of one man and the artful silence of the other.

Throughout *Richard II*, Shakespeare represents the actions which lead to or constitute civil war as departures from what is natural and customary and therefore becoming. Thus in one passage Bolingbroke is seen as an overflowing river which ignores natural bounds and as a leader who forces people to adopt attire and accoutrement, and modes of speech and behaviour, which are quite inappropriate to their age, profession or sex (III ii 106–19). Elsewhere attention focuses more narrowly on the unfitness of Englishmen fighting their compatriots instead of Frenchmen and Saracens, and committing atrocities which would move 'barbarism itself' to tears (V ii 36): 'Ten thousand bloody crowns of mothers' sons/Shall ill become the flower of England's face' (III iii 96–7; cf. I iii 125–8). But this in turn is narrowed down to a form of indecorum with which 'civil and uncivil arms' (III iii 102) are most continuously identified throughout the play: the spectacle of knights whose every word and deed is a betrayal of knighthood. The glorious England of John of Gaunt and the Black Prince 'hath made a shameful conquest of itself (II i 66, II iii 101).[1] It has done so because its knights have betrayed what they stand for, and because in so doing they have proved treacherous to one another. They have unlearned the wisdom uttered – improperly, of course – by a certain unprofessional fool :

> This above all – to thine own self be true,
> And it must follow, as the night the day,
> Thou canst not then be false to any man. (*Hamlet*, I iii 78–80)

II

No one, admittedly, would even begin to think of Richard as 'the prince of chivalry' (to borrow a phrase from *Troilus and Cressida*). But that itself is a point of dramatic significance; and it must be related to the larger truth that, although Richard suffers most from betrayal, he shares in the general failure to be true to himself and to others. His volatile shifting from confidence to despair and from arrogance to self-abasement, his painful self-consciousness, and his pathetic inability to keep a firm hold on his own identity, make him, like Hamlet and Lear, the kind of character from whom no spectator can ever really dissociate himself – thoroughly credible and human. Part of Shakespeare's considerable achievement in this play, therefore, is that the commonest moral blemish in the nation becomes a psychological reality in Richard and even accounts for his remarkable immediacy as a character creation. Coleridge has suggested that what individualises Richard is the consistent inconsistency of his behaviour. But the Elizabethans would probably have used the term inconstancy. This can imply not just an unwillingness to act in an orderly and consistent fashion, but disloyalty to others, disloyalty to self, and (cognate with this) an inability to confront the vicissitudes of Fortune without loss of dignity and self-control.[2] All these forms of changefulness are present in Richard and account in large measure for his downfall.

Richard's errors and failures are all accompanied by pointed reminders of the role or identity to which he should be faithful. While he is succumbing to the flat refusal of Bolingbroke and Mowbray to make peace at his request, he recalls almost wistfully that he was 'not born to sue, but to command' (I i 196). The dissident lords do not ascribe his wretched management of national affairs to any ingrained incompetence but to the fact that he has surrendered his will to others : 'The King is not himself, but basely led/By flatterers' (II i 241–2). And it seems that their intention in siding with Bolingbroke is not to unseat Richard but to 'make high majesty look like itself' (II i 295) by eliminating his flatterers. What turns them into usurping rebels is the way in which Richard disintegrates at the approach of merely seeming disaster. When he hears of Bolingbroke's return from banishment, he fluctuates repeatedly from excessive confidence to unwarranted pessimism, and finally subsides in total despair; his whole emotional condition is an image of absolute subjection to the inconstancies of Fortune's wheel. He is, of course, reminded that his gloom is both base and unjustified: 'Comfort, my liege; remember who you are' (III ii 82); but this simply provokes in him an absurdly bombastic strut which leaves him all the more vulnerable to the next piece of bad news: 'I had forgot myself; am I not King?/Awake thou coward majesty! thou sleepest' (III ii 83–4).

In the upshot Richard throws away his crown in what he considers to be a royal gesture of resignation to Fortune's cruelty: 'A king, woe's slave, shall kingly woe obey' (III ii 210). But the queen takes a different view of his abject submissiveness. For her it means that he has been transformed and deposed 'both in shape and mind' (V i 26–8), having forgotten that 'the king of beasts' paws in rage against its enemy and never fawns with 'base humility' (V i 29–34). Richard does, in fact, die like a lion, and with perhaps the most magnificent cry of rage in all Shakespeare: 'Go thou and fill another room in hell' (V v 107). It is an almost invariable rule in Shakespeare's history plays that nothing in the life of a fallen prince or nobleman becomes him like the leaving of it.

III

Richard is right in recalling that the self to which he should be true is located in the name of king – in what he has inherited 'by fair sequence and succession' (II i 199). But he makes the classic aristocratic error of assuming that a name or title has virtue irrespective of the behaviour of the person who carries it. Far from being – as W. B. Yeats imagined – the kind of too-perfect aristocrat who fails because he is not base enough to cope with the rough, middle-class mentality of men like Bolingbroke, Richard was conceived by Shakespeare as a prince who wantonly squanders inherited riches and sullies the glory of his family.[3] Throughout Act Two, Scene One, his uncles and the dissident lords unite in condemning him as a 'most degenerate king' (II i 262). In these criticisms his wasteful habits and his abuse of his own kindred are adroitly identified with his failure to live up to the reputation for chivalrous heroism won by his forebears. England, say his critics, is completely bankrupt – but not for the usual reason of excessive expenditure in wars, for Richard never warred at all; rather he 'basely yielded upon compromise/That which his noble ancestors achieved with blows', and even spent more in peace than they in wars (II i 173–83, 252–5). Although descended from 'royal kings/ Feared by their breed' and 'renowned for their deeds', Richard is therefore 'in reputation sick' (II i 51–3, 96). And so, in consequence, is his kingdom. Once 'dear for her reputation through the world', 'for Christian service and true chivalry', England is now reduced to a wretched farm from whose tenants money is continually extorted. The only name then which befits Richard's composition is 'Landlord of England . . . not King' (II i 73, 113).

Names function with exceptional prominence in *Richard II* as an index of value and order. This is partly because an anxious concern for rank, rights and responsibilities is proper in times of political and social upheaval, but partly too because the hallmark of a knight is an almost mystical obsession with honour and reputation. The play opens with Mowbray protesting that he is 'a loyal gentleman' and angrily rejecting the charge – which almost everyone else of importance will face sooner or later – that he deserves 'a foul traitor's name' (I i 44, 148). In pleading with the king for trial by combat, he explains that 'spotless reputation' is 'the purest treasure mortal times afford' and that without it 'men are but gilded loam or painted clay' – remove it from a man and he will cease to exist (I i 177–83). One of the ironies of this fervent speech is that it is addressed to someone who in effect has done far more than Bolingbroke to disgrace Mowbray's 'fair name' (I i 167) – for the murder of which Mowbray is accused is mainly Richard's crime. From the outset, therefore, it is apparent that Richard abuses not only the name of king but the names of other men as well. He finds it improper that the dying Gaunt should 'play so nicely' with his name; but Gaunt defends himself by presenting this as a bitter reaction to the banishment of his son and heir – an act which implies an attempt to destroy his family name : 'Since thou dost seek to kill my name in me,/I mock my name, great king, to flatter thee' (II i 86–7). Richard's subsequent seizure of all Gaunt's possessions completes the effect of banishment on Bolingbroke, reducing him to a bare, unaccommodated man without out a single sign of his noble identity (III i 24–7). And as York warned Richard, the unnaming of Bolingbroke is a fatal error, since it attacks the principle of temporal order and hereditary succession on which his own identity depends : 'Be not thyself' (II i

195–9). In the short term, it provides Bolingbroke with a good excuse for returning from exile and so initiates the chain of events which ends in Richard's deposition and death.

With the return of the banished man in search of a title, there is a rapid decline in social order marked by impropriety and confusion in the use of names and forms of address. Richard's emissary addresses Bolingbroke by his old title of Hereford and is told in effect that he must be talking to the wrong man (II iii 70–3). Later, Northumberland's communication with Bolingbroke is sharply interrupted when York rebukes him for omitting Richard's title : 'It would beseem the Lord Northumberland/To say "King Richard" ' – such impropriety would once have cost him his head, adds York (III iii 6–14). Yet Richard himself will soon be heard conniving at this very form of indecorum, for he addresses Northumberland with the half-mocking, half-defeatist question : 'Most mighty prince, my Lord Northumberland,/What says King Bolingbroke?' (III iii 172–3). This kind of speech prepares for the moment when Richard will volunteer to 'submit . . . and lose the name of king' – and will even call himself 'a traitor with the rest' (III iii 142, 144–5 ; IV i 247).

The renaming of Bolingbroke merely increases uncertainty and discord. When he offers to ascend the throne 'in God's name', and York cries, 'And long live Henry, fourth of that name!' (IV i 112–13), the Bishop of Carlisle protests : 'My Lord of Hereford here, whom you call king,/Is a foul traitor to proud Hereford's king' (IV i 134–5). But Carlisle himself is deemed to be the traitor and is arrested for 'capital treason' on the spot (IV i 151). This kind of stark disorder in the placing of names and words dominates the last scenes of the play – or the first phase of Bolingbroke's reign. It is caused mainly by reactions to the discovery that Aumerle and others are conspiring to kill the new king ; but it begins just before the actual discovery when York corrects his wife for referring to their son by his customary titles : 'Aumerle that was/But that is lost for being Richard's friend,/And madam, you must call him Rutland now' (V ii 43–5). This sounds like a courteous correction, yet it is as unbeseeming in York as the rude brevity which he once condemned in Northumberland. And it is not the only remark of its kind which he makes here. Not long ago he referred to Richard as 'my sovereign, whom both my oath and duty bids defend' (II ii 112–13) ; but now he is telling his wife that he is one of Bolingbroke's 'sworn subjects' and that he has pledged in parliament for his son's 'truth and lasting fealty to the new-made king' (V ii 39, 44–5). Not long ago, too, he rebuked the ingratiating Bolingbroke for addressing him as 'My gracious uncle!' (II iii 85): 'I am no traitor's uncle; and *that word grace* in an ungracious mouth is but profane' (II iii 88–9).[4] Yet when he finds that his son has sworn himself to a conspiracy against the usurper, he explodes with: 'Treason, foul treason! Villain! traitor! slave!' (V ii 72). The wild impropriety of these words in his mouth is greatly increased by the hysterical show of physical energy and moral enthusiasm which follows. Loftily brushing aside his wife's appeals ('Peace, foolish woman ... Thou fond mad woman'), he calls out repeatedly for his riding boots and then, although 'weak with age' and 'prisoner to the palsy' (II ii 83; II iii 104), gallops off to the new-made king to demand the instant execution of his 'disloyal' son. The climax of all this unseemliness occurs in the unctuous and bombastic outburst of the usurper:

O heinous, strong, and bold conspiracy!
O loyal father of a treacherous son!
Thou sheer, immaculate, and silver fountain,
From whence this stream through muddy passages
Hath held his current and defil'd himself!
Thy overflow of good converts to bad;
And thy abundant goodness shall excuse
This deadly blot in thy disgressing son. (V iii 59–66)

Himself the treacherous son of a loyal father, Bolingbroke (like York) can never again rebuke anyone of treachery or disobedience without his words turning instantly against himself. This is an irony of which superb use is made in *Henry IV*.

Too much emphasis, I believe, has been placed on Bolingbroke's pardoning of Aumerle and Carlisle. The remark of Aumerle's pleading mother that there is 'no word like "pardon" for kings' mouths so meet' (V iii 119) is perfectly correct. But it forces us to reflect that all the other words used by Bolingbroke and his associates after he becomes king are very unmeet. While news flows in about the businesslike beheadings of the other 'dangerous consorted traitors' who sought his 'dire overthrow' (V vi 15–16), and while King Richard is being brutally murdered in

his prison-cell ('What means death in this rude assault?' [V v 105]),
Bolingbroke ('Great King') and his supporters ('Kind uncle York',
'gentle Percy', etc.) courteously greet one another with gracious
words and titles which do not match their conduct.

On the other hand, Bolingbroke righteously refuses his 'good
word' and 'princely favour' (V vi 42) to the man whose hand has
put an end to Richard's life, and who now brings him news of the
deed. Yet this is no augury that words and titles will be rightly
bestowed in the future. Exton insists that the murder was but the
translation of Bolingbroke's words and thoughts into act: 'From
your own mouth, my lord, did I this deed' (V vi 37). But Bolingbroke knows that those words were cunningly 'dark' ('Have I no
friend will rid me of this living fear?' [V iv 2]), and now takes
refuge in the fact – thus perpetuating a divorce between thought,
word and deed. It bears recalling that when he took it upon himself to condemn Richard's favourites to death, he accused them not
just of destroying all the signs which told the world what he was,
but of having previously caused Richard to 'misinterpret' him
(III i 18). Now he hints at a similar charge of wilful misinterpre-
tation against the man who was so quick to discover the covert
meaning of his 'kingly doom and sentence' (V vi 23) on his cousin
and king; and at the same time clouds himself with more ambiguity. Dismissing Exton to wander with Cain through shades of
night, where he himself belongs, this guilty judge is inwardly
possessed by feelings of satisfaction and regret at the death of
Richard, and his divided heart can express itself only in the most
ambiguous fashion: 'Though I did wish him dead,/I hate the
murderer, *love him murdered*' [my italics] (V vi 39–40). The be-
getter of divided loyalties, Bolingbroke inevitably 'sets the word
itself against the word' (V iii 122). No one could ever interpret him
satisfactorily – and his reign will be one long twilight of moral
uncertainty and mutual misunderstanding.

IV

It should be apparent from what I have said so far that although
the misuse of names is of great importance in the design of *Richard
II*, it is only one part of a large and complex pattern of linguistic
disorders – moral, semantic and stylistic – which signal the decline of this other Eden and demi-paradise into an unweeded

garden.[5] It has, of course, been observed many years ago that Shakespeare was much concerned with language in *Richard II* – that 'tongue' is its key word.[6] So far as I know, however, no adequate explanation of this fact has yet been offered. To say that the youthful Shakespeare was delightedly and self-consciously exploring the musical potential of the English language, transferring this enthusiasm to Richard himself, and adroitly criticising his own exuberance in the process, is to touch on only a fraction of the truth and to obscure the immense sophistication of the play's dramatic art. Certainly the verse is wonderfully musical. Moreover, Shakespeare even allows his characters to talk about the harmonies of speech and to compare the tongue to musical instruments. But they also make remarks which suggest that 'linked sweetness long drawn out' is the least important of the harmonies associated with the instrument of speech. There is in the play an unremitting concern for 'the tongue's office' (I iii 256), for the relationship between tongue and heart, word and deed; and the verse itself seems most harmonious when – as in Gaunt's eulogy on the lost paradise, or Carlisle's on the redeemed Mowbray – the understanding tells the ear that the music in the words is an echo of the profound harmony of natural and moral order. It is less helpful to relate the obvious preoccupation with language in *Richard II* to the evolution of Shakespeare's poetic style than, say, to de la Primaudaye's chapter 'Of the tongue, and of the nature and office thereof', to his argument that 'the tongue is the best and worst thing that is', and to his long moral-allegorical passages on the tongue as a musical instrument from which 'there should proceed a good harmony and pleasant melody'.[7]

Since justice is the basis of social harmony, the words spoken by the king in his capacity of supreme judge and arbiter are the words which matter most in any realm. Accordingly, Richard's first failure in justice – his handling of the dispute between Bolingbroke and Mowbray – is continuously represented as part of his disrespect for and deficiency in good words. Unable at first to settle the quarrel by oral arbitration, he gives in to the two men's demand for the rougher method of trial by combat. But in the middle of this second trial he reverts abruptly to oral judgement, imposes a sentence of exile on both men, and offers no explanation whatever for the enormous disparity between the sentences: ten years for Bolingbroke, life for Mowbray. Mowbray's anguished res-

ponse to 'the hopeless word of "never to return"' (I iii 152) simultaneously suggests that Richard delivers the gravest of sentences in
a light and thoughtless fashion and that in so doing he is bent on
the destruction of speech itself – the quibble on 'sentence' neatly
associates judicial and rhetorical disorder :

> A heavy sentence, my most sovereign liege,
> And all unlook'd for from your Highness' mouth.
> A dearer merit, not so deep a maim
> As to be cast forth in the common air,
> Have I deserved at your Highness' hands.
> The language I have learnt these forty years,
> My native English, now I must forgo ;
> And now my tongue's use is to me no more
> Than an unstringed viol or a harp;
> Or like a cunning instrument cas'd up
> Or, being open, put into his hands
> That knows no touch to tune the harmony.
> Within my mouth you have engaol'd my tongue,
> Doubly portcullis'd with my teeth and lips ;
> And dull, unfeeling, barren ignorance
> Is made my gaoler to attend on me.
> I am too old to fawn upon a nurse,
> Too far in years to be a pupil now.
> What is thy sentence, then, but speechless death,
> Which robs my tongue from breathing native breath ?
>
> (I iii 154–73)

The hint that Richard utters grave sentences lightly is confirmed
by his curt and unfeeling reply to Mowbray, and by his sudden
reduction of Bolingbroke's sentence from ten to six years (on seeing
Gaunt in tears). Even Bolingbroke comments on the disorders in
Richard's sentencing (though he, too, will one day be exposed by
the nature and effects of his 'princely doom and sentence') :

> How long a time lies in one little word !
> Four lagging winters and four wanton springs
> End in a word : such is the breath of Kings. (I iii 213–15)

Despite the reduction of Bolingbroke's sentence, Gaunt is convinced – and rightly so – that the sentence of exile on his son will

have the effect of killing him, the father : 'Thy word is current with him [Time] for my death' (I iii 231). Moreover, in responding to Richard's tart remark that he himself was a party to the sentence on his son, Gaunt makes the further accusation that Richard, as well as disposing lightly of death-giving words, produces in others an unnatural and fatal divorce between the tongue and the heart. Mowbray's inability to do more than hint at the unfairness of the sentence passed on him, and Bolingbroke's inability to tell the whole truth about the murder of Gloucester, reflected ironically on Richard's grand claim that he allowed 'free speech and fearless' to those involved in the trial (I i 17, 123). So, in a different way, does this complaint of Gaunt's :

You urg'd me as a judge ; but I had rather
You would have bid me argue like a father.
O, had it been a stranger, not my child,
To smooth his fault I should have been more mild.
A partial slander sought I to avoid,
And in the sentence my own life destroy'd.
Alas, I look'd when some of you should say
I was too strict to make mine own away ;
But you gave leave to my unwilling tongue
Against my will to do myself this wrong. (I iii 237–46)

Richard's essential opposition to well-ordered speech, and his notable facility for delivering light and callous words at grave and painful moments, are exhibited again at the death of Gaunt. (The causal connection between the 'sentence' of exile and this event must not, of course, be forgotten.) Since Gaunt is his uncle and the most respected of his counsellors, Richard should receive his dying words with reverence and humility. To emphasise this, Shakespeare makes use of the traditional belief that God endows the last words of good men with special wisdom ; Gaunt feels himself to be 'a prophet new inspir'd' and recalls that 'the tongues of dying men/Enforce attention like deep harmony' (II i 5–6, 31). But after mustering a few light-hearted queries, the young king is enraged by Gaunt's solemn warnings and reacts by calling him 'a lunatic lean-witted fool' who deserves to be beheaded for speaking so disrespectfully to his king : 'This tongue that runs so roundly in thy head/Should run thy head from thy unreverent shoulders'

(II i 115, 122–3). A few moments after he leaves Gaunt, Richard is told by Northumberland that the 'prophet' has died, and the phrasing of the announcement is such as to suggest that Richard's unreverent words, added to his reckless sentence, have finally destroyed an antique and sacred instrument :

> *K. Rich.* What says he ?
> *North.* Nay, nothing; all is said.
> His tongue is now a stringless instrument ;
> Words, life, and all, old Lancaster hath spent. (II i 148–50)

v

Gaunt's character has indeed been of verbal significance from the start. In the opening lines of the play we learn that he has kept his oath and bond but that he has been unable to do more than 'sift' his son on his motives for bringing the charge of treachery against Mowbray. Implicit in this introductory exchange between the young king and his time-honoured uncle are a number of ideas about verbal behaviour which are of fundamental importance for the two trial scenes which follow, and indeed for the rest of the play. Oaths are important, and it is necessary for men to reveal their thoughts candidly at the right time – to 'be even and direct', as Hamlet puts it. But as soon as we pass from men like Gaunt – one of the last representatives of a noble age – we have no guarantee that men speak freely and truly and keep their word, or that they will allow others to do so. At first impressed by the vigour and solemnity with which the many oaths are uttered, one soon becomes uneasy and eventually concludes (if one reflects on them at all) that their principal effect is to make lies, slander, disloyalty and 'indirect crook'd ways' (*II Henry IV*, IV iv 185) all the more reprehensible. Largely through them, language is built up into an ostentatious covering for 'empty hollowness' (I ii 59) : 'hollow' is another one of the play's key words.

As soon as they confront the king, both Mowbray and Bolingbroke adopt the attitude that words cannot resolve their quarrel and that 'the bitter clamour of two eager tongues' is essentially effeminate (I i 46–50). Yet they show themselves to be very proficient in the effeminate mode of attack and retaliation and they ask all those who are present to attend carefully to every word they utter. This is especially the case with Bolingbroke, who in the first scene solemnises his repetitive speeches with no less than seven oaths and promises. In his opening speech he swears to the king that what he says is true ('heaven be the record of my speech' [I i 30]) and that it is motivated only by sentiments of love and obedience towards him; while in the same speech he swears to Mowbray that his deeds (at the lists) will attest the truth of his words. His second speech concludes with a grand vow 'by . . . all the rites of knighthood' (I i 76) that his arm will make good what he has spoken – an idea which is repeated at the beginning and the end of his third speech. His fourth is a reply to the king's command to withdraw the challenge; but its substance and its violent imagery could be interpreted as showing that he is a man who neither means what he says nor has any respect for speech in general, for he now equates obedience to the king's command with 'deep sin' (I i 187) and goes on to affirm that he would bite out his tongue 'and spit it bleeding . . . in Mowbray's face' rather than speak conciliatory words.

Bolingbroke's promise that at the lists his deeds will justify his words is, of course, frustrated by Richard's intervention. Yet there is as much emphasis in that scene on the discrepancy between words and thoughts as between words and deeds; and even more than in the first scene we are conscious that – as Richard hinted earlier (I i 25) – one of the two men must care nothing for truth. Full dramatic use is made of chivalric ritual in order to isolate the word 'true' and to magnify the importance of the oath. The series of questions put to appellant and defendant by the marshal of the lists enjoins them to 'speak truly', 'in God's name', and on the oath of knighthood (I iii 14, 34). In their responses, each of them swears to his own innocence and the other's guilt, seals his word with the name of God, and concludes with a variation of the marshal's truth-formula which constitutes a claim to truth in deed as well as word: 'And as I truly fight, defend me heaven' (I iii 25, 41).

An important part of Shakespeare's strategy in these two scenes is to put on stage a man known to have brought two centuries of chaos to England through his breach of the oath of fealty – and to have him do nothing else but proclaim that his word is sacred and that it betokens love and loyalty for his king.[8] In subsequent scenes, too, the unreliable nature of Bolingbroke's oaths and promises continues to be exposed. On returning to England he makes

humble and flattering expressions of gratitude to those who support him and, quite unnecessarily, enforces these with a promise –
uttered five times – of material reward. One has no need of prophetic powers (or a knowledge of *Henry IV*) to evaluate this promise : its unsolicited, repetitious and essentially ignoble nature
is sufficient to indicate that it will not be kept. But there is another
reason why Bolingbroke's followers might well treat this promise
with some scepticism : and it is ultimately connected with the oath
of fealty. 'Trust not him that hath once broken faith,' said Eliza-
beth in *III Henry VI* (IV iv 30); and in this play Bolingbroke
makes an oath before his new friends which they are soon to see
him break. It is his oath assuring York (as the king's deputy), and
later the king himself, that although he has returned prematurely
from banishment, he has no rebellious intentions whatever
– indeed his love and loyalty are undiminished. All Bolingbroke's assurances are either repetitious or inflated; this one is
both, and in the highest degree. It is first made on his behalf and
in his presence by Northumberland (II iii 148–51). Later he himself repeats it (with the confusing addition of a threat) when in-
structing Northumberland what to say to Richard (III iii 35–48).
And by the time it reaches Richard's ears it has blossomed into
an extraordinary piece of verbal fungus : a disturbing blend of
flattery and deflation, of reassuring self-abasement and menacing
royal pride, such as could issue only from Bolingbroke (III iii
103–20).

It is left to Richard to condemn Bolingbroke, and all Englishmen who side with him, for 'cracking the strong warrant of an
oath' and so breaking faith with God as well as man (III ii 101 ;
IV i 235). And he lives long enough to see that disharmony between
tongue and heart will afflict even good men when Bolingbroke is
king : 'What my tongue dares not, that my heart shall say', promises the faithful groom (V v 97). But such is Shakespeare's impartial distribution of responsibility that even Richard himself is
seen as a perjurer. In reducing Bolingbroke's sentence from ten
years to six, he breaks the vow of impartiality which he made to
Mowbray (I i 115–21). And by surrendering his kingship without
a struggle, he openly supports and participates in the sin of his
forsworn subjects : 'With mine own breath [I] release all duteous
oaths,/All pomp and majesty I do forswear' (IV i 210–11).
Richard's previous remark that 'the breath of worldly men cannot

depose/The deputy elected by the Lord' (III ii 56–7) offers the
best comment on this suggestion that with his own breath he can
undo promises made by others and himself to God.

VI

While chatting to Richard about the departure of Bolingbroke
into exile, Aumerle uses phraseology which carries over from the
previous scene the idea of desecrating what is sacred : 'My heart
disdained that my tongue/Should so profane the word' (I iv
12–13). Aumerle, however, is not talking about an oath but about
'the word "farewell" ' (I iv 16). He is moralising on the need to
avoid affected courtesy; and moralising with flippant insincerity,
too, for he goes on to boast that by counterfeiting the impression
of speechless grief he succeeded in avoiding the word 'farewell' :
'Words seemed buried in my sorrow's grave' (I iv 15).

The 'hollow parting' (I iv 9) of Aumerle and his banished
cousin is typical of its environment. There is in Richard's court
the appearance of a highly developed sense of propriety, expressed
in gracious and ceremonious manners. It is so prominent and so
skilfully expressed that it has led many to look on Richard as a
king of old-world courtesy – a 'sweet lovely rose' – whose refined
and touchingly fragile world is rudely shattered by a no-nonsense
politician and his train of brazen upstarts. Support for this view can
be found in some incidents which mark the rise of Bolingbroke :
'Rude misgoverned hands from windows' top/Threw dust and
rubbish on King Richard's head' (V ii 5–6); while news of his
downfall is conveyed to the gentle queen not by some well-born
and suitably eloquent ambassador but by 'the harsh rude tongue'
of an old gardener (III iv 74, 93). Yet this sort of social behaviour
represents only one of two objectionable extremes, and it is as
untypical of Bolingbroke as it is of Richard. The other extreme
is the kind of courtesy or 'courtship' which, instead of revealing a
gentle mind and a desire to cement human relations, is really the
instrument of self-interest, narcissism or ambition. This is the sin
against courtesy – the profaning of civil conversation – which
characterises Richard's court; and it is by no means confined to
the king and his favourites.

The most elaborately courteous speeches delivered or reported
in the play are all reinforced by formal gestures : by kissing and

embracing, by handshaking and removing the hat, and, above all, by bowing and kneeling. In a technical sense, therefore, they are 'ceremonies' and so have some of the sanctity of oaths – a point emphasised by the fact that they are often explicitly offered as expressions of reverence and duty and with the idea of degree in mind. This prevailing ceremoniousness of manner – this search for grace or graciousness – is an extension of the ritual character of the great scenes; and with them it combines to give the play a ceremonial quality which some critics, with considerable justification, have treated as a fundamental clue in the interpretation of its principal characters. Influenced in part by Walter Pater, W. B. Yeats argued that Richard has a deep and genuine love of ceremony; he thought that this reflects the imaginative richness of Richard's mind and the elegance of a medieval and aristocratic way of life which he personifies. E. M. W. Tillyard also saw Richard as a man in love with ceremony, and he, too, construed this as a sign that Richard stands for a medieval and unpractical view of life to which Bolingbroke's modern spirit is naturally antagonistic. Quite unlike Yeats, however, Tillyard believed that Shakespeare intended Richard's regard for ceremony to be taken as a fatal defect. The trouble with Richard, said Tillyard, is that he is always 'more concerned with how he behaves, with the fitness of his conduct to the occasion, than with what he actually does'. He and his friends are interested only in 'the sheer propriety' of what they say and do; they are 'mindful of propriety and . . . unmindful of nature', and so their behaviour always betokens 'ceremony, not . . . passion'.[9]

These remarks offer good material for a lesson on semantics and the history of ideas. That an Elizabethan scholar so knowledgeable and so intelligent as Tillyard could adopt this conception of decorum in the interpretation of a Shakespearian play – a modern conception, and one so debased and so unsubtle as to be virtually opposite in meaning to the original – makes it in no way surprising that Shakespeare's interest in decorum should have escaped notice for so long. Tillyard, of course, was right in relating ceremony to propriety; and Yeats, too, was right in assuming that for Shakespeare and his contemporaries ceremony was the ethical and aesthetic manifestation of life lived at its best. But both critics were quite wrong in assuming that Richard is identifiable with ceremony and propriety and that Bolingbroke is a pragmatic, modern spirit indifferent to it. The text makes it perfectly clear that Bolingbroke and Northumberland are at least as addicted to ceremonious courtesies as Richard and Aumerle, and that Bolingbroke can throw himself into ritual performances with histrionic zeal; while a knowledge of Renaissance ethical and aesthetic theory, together with the text, shows that the king and the usurper are alike corrupters of ceremony.

One kind of debased and apparent courtesy commonly referred to or represented in the play is flattery, the evil which traditionally threatens every king. Richard seems to show the right attitude towards it when he exclaims: 'He does me double wrong/That wounds me with the flatteries of his tongue' (III ii 215–16). But these words are simply one more instance of Richard's distressing habit of saying the right thing at the wrong time or in the wrong way, for they serve as a petulant response to sound and encouraging advice. The truth is that Richard's ears are so accustomed to 'flattering sounds' of all kinds that the words of good counsel which every true courtier should offer his king at opportune moments merely irritate him (II i 17–25, 101, 242; II ii 84).

It must be added, however, that although Shakespeare reproduces the chroniclers' conception of Richard as a king misled by flatterers, he does little to make this a dramatic reality: not once in the play is Richard flattered by any of his favourites. The real master of sweet words is Bolingbroke, the smooth politician who knows, like Claudius of Elsinore, that the way to control events is to flatter this man and slander that one – in general to pour poison in at the ear. His gracious protestations of respect and affectionate good-will towards Richard (dead and alive), towards the common people, towards his closest associates, towards the deposed queen, and towards the dead enemy whom he once described as 'the first head and spring' of 'all the treasons for these eighteen years/Complotted and contrived' in England (I i 95–7) – all these add up to a ceremonious manner which does not fit. York's tart criticism applies to every one of Bolingbroke's gracious speeches: 'That word grace in an ungracious mouth is but profane.'

The falsity of Bolingbroke's smooth style, too, is betrayed to us by the man who helps him to the throne – who acts as his spokesman and admires him so much that he becomes a kind of understudy reproducing the arts of his master in coarsened and obvious form. This aspect of Northumberland's relationship with Boling-broke is finely elicited at the very beginning of their first dialogue together on stage. Northumberland commences by praising Boling-broke's 'sweet' – presumably flattering – conversation, and Boling-broke responds with exactly the same compliment (though modi-fied by his characteristic show of gracious humility). Shakespeare directs our responses to this illuminating dialogue (or non-dialogue) by filling Northumberland's speech with tell-tale words and phrases and by allowing him to so overreach himself in flattery that his tedious and slight argument ends in contradiction (II iii 6–18). Bolingbroke's answer – 'Of much less value is my company/ Than your good words' – is a kind of parry which suggests that a master of flattery is always immune to the poison himself. It is also an invitation by the dramatist to evaluate what is being offered as 'good words'.

Unlike these, most of the sweet and protesting words which stamp Bolingbroke and Northumberland as hollow men are well embellished with formal gesture and movement. Before the trial by combat begins, Bolingbroke announces that he must 'take a ceremonious leave/And loving farewell' of his friends (I iii 50–1), and begins by kneeling to his king and cousin, kissing his hand, and embracing him. It might be too much to describe this as the kiss of Judas rather than a ceremony performed out of love and 'in all duty' (I iii 52). But it certainly has the ignoble distinction of being the first of a series of superficially graceful and essentially hollow farewells. Coming after this exhibition of overdone eloquence, Aumerle's purportedly eloquent speechlessness is merely tit-for-tat.

Moreover, Aumerle's account of his hollow parting from his cousin is followed immediately by Richard's account of their cousin's farewell to the common people. And in this we are given a graphic picture – later confirmed by York (V ii 18–21) – of Bol-ingbroke as a crafty politician who not only employs ceremonious behaviour for his own ends and reduces it to an empty show, but also breaks some of its most elementary rules as a result of his tendency to protest too much. Richard, Bushy, Bagot and Green all observed that in 'his courtship of the common people' he did 'seem to dive into their hearts/With humble and familiar cour-tesy' : he '*threw away*' [my italics] reverence and smiles on slaves and poor craftsmen, offered a brace of draymen 'the tribute of his supple knee', and doffed his bonnet to an oyster-wench (I iv 23–33).[10] Such behaviour offends not merely by its insincerity and affectation : it completely obscures distinctions of rank or degree, which ceremony should always uphold. This is a fine dramatic point and fits in well with the conception of Bolingbroke as a man whose courteous humility is an essential part of a plan – conscious or unconscious – to get to the pinnacle of pride (I iv 35–6).

As the action proceeds, Bolingbroke's ceremoniousness becomes more conspicuous and more patently false. Although he has disobeyed the sentence of exile, he is quick to show the suppleness of his knee when he encounters the king's deputy. But York acidly remarks : 'Show me thy humble heart and not thy knee,/Whose duty is deceivable and false' (II iii 83–4). When he later confronts Richard himself, he makes a great fuss to the effect that he and his followers should kneel and 'show fair duty to his Majesty' – and, as with York, he uses the word 'gracious' as if it were his alone (III iii 186–9, 196).[11] Richard reacts to this performance with a cunningly ironic comment on the difference between his cousin's visible courtesy and his invisible feelings, between his low knee and his 'high' heart.

Characteristically, however, Richard is critical of disorder and disorderly himself at one and the same moment, for he encourages Bolingbroke to ignore the ceremonious gestures which every subject owes his king (III iii 194). Earlier, when he heard that Bolingbroke had returned in arms, he showed in much more emphatic form, and untouched by irony, this defeatist inclination to make others treat him as an equal. Then he advised his remaining followers to cover their heads in his presence, to forget about 'solemn reverence', and to *'throw away* respect,/Tradition, form, and ceremonious duty' (III ii 171–3) [my italics]. Nevertheless, it is not in the sphere of manners but rather in the great ritual actions, or at essentially ritual and solemn moments, that Richard contributes most to the destruction of ceremony. These provoking invitations to others to 'throw away' reverence and traditional form in his presence are important only as echoes of his own public violations of ritual order and as premonitions of the moment when he will throw away his kingship and profane the coronation rite.

Although Bolingbroke is just as falsely ceremonious in the trial scenes as Richard, and although he participates in the sacri-

lege of the abdication, Richard comes off as the most blatant
offender against ritual propriety. The trials by arbitration and by
combat are judicial rites of a different kind; but in both of them,
Richard – enthroned on his chair of state and surrounded by his
counsellors – is at once the supreme judge and the embodiment of
formal order. Both rites are irremediably disordered from the start,
since Richard, being guilty of the crime of which the defendant is
accused, is utterly unfitted for the role of judge – a point which is
very deliberately brought to our notice by the dialogue between
Gaunt and the Duchess of Gloucester in the intervening scene.
Yet the fact that Richard cannot even qualify for the role of judge
does not have nearly so powerful an effect on an audience as the
inconstancy of purpose which prevents him from allowing either
rite to reach its proper conclusion. In the trial by combat – most
revered perhaps of the traditional 'rites of knighthood' (I i 75) –
his capricious reversal to the procedure which was proper in the
first trial constitutes a most unsettling breach of decorum. And it
is rendered all the more noticeable by his own solemn injunctions
that the rite should be conducted in an 'orderly' fashion, 'formally,
according to our law' (I iii 9, 29), by the sense of hieratic correct-
ness which prevails until the knights are about to charge, and by
the incomparably perverse timing of his decision to settle matters
in a different way.[12]

So the impression in these scenes (and it is quite a strong one)
that Richard likes things to be done in an orderly, traditional,
and formal fashion – that he will uphold ceremony at all costs –
is utterly misleading: as misleading as his physical resemblance
to the Black Prince. But perhaps it is the abdication scene which
offers the most plausible evidence for the view of Pater and Yeats
that Richard is deeply and nobly in love with ceremony: there
he could be said to supply a great ceremonial need and to invent
a rite for the solemn act of abdication when none already existed.
Yet, although Richard's performance at this point of his career
might well seem creative and imaginative to minds imbued with
fin de siècle aestheticism, it can only have seemed perverse and
destructive to Shakespeare's audience. This, after all, is where
Richard throws away his duties, and for that very reason his behaviour could not be deemed ceremonious or ceremonial in the
true sense. What Richard produces here for his own narcissistic
pleasure (hence the mirror) is a parody and undoing of the coro-

nation rite – a degrading and disgracing in which he 'undeck[s] the pompous body of a king' (IV i 250), denies his 'sacred state' (IV i 209), crowns a usurper, plays the part of 'both priest and clerk' (IV i 173), and confirms his sacrilege by resorting to mock-ritual language (IV i 204–21).[13]

Investigation of the moral and semantic aspects of speech in the play has necessarily involved incidental comment on verbal style as well. But this subject deserves special attention, not least because it is a tricky one and frequently gives rise to faulty interpretations and evaluations. In assessing the style of Shakespeare's early plays we cannot but be influenced by the knowledge that as he matured his use of language became more economical, more dramatic, less obviously literary. At the same time we have to be continually on our guard against assuming that every sign of rhetorical ostentation or verbal superfluity is proof that the exuberance of a youthful poet is conflicting with a specifically dramatic presentation of character and event. We have to recognise that since language (including style) is Shakespeare's subject as well as his instrument, he usually points to or hints at a mean which helps us to distinguish between the rhetorical defects of his characters and those features of style which he deemed acceptable before about 1598 but rejected or toned down thereafter. Another caveat is that the gradual chastening of his style may not be due *entirely* to an improvement in his dramatic sense. It may owe something to the fact that he exhaustively explored the dramatic potentialities of affected speech in his early plays and necessarily lost much of his interest in it later on.

The rhetorical or stylistic defects which Shakespeare makes dramatic use of in *Richard II* could be said to arise either from inconsistency or excess. They are closely related therefore to the conception of Richard as an inconstant and spendthrift prince. Of the two defects, excess is much the more noticeable, for it is by no means peculiar to Richard alone.[14] There are frequent allusions in the play to the evils of excess and to the decorous norm of measure and proportion: allusions, too, which often imply the belief that ethical and aesthetic, behavioural and stylistic considerations cannot be separated. York identifies Richard and his subjects with the 'base imitation' of Italian fashions in dress and manners (II i 21–3) – a remark which, for an Elizabethan audience, would suggest an addiction to affected elegance of speech as well. The uncontrolled self-pity which so strongly affects the style of some of Richard's more memorable speeches is indirectly criticised in the queen's remark that her 'poor heart no measure keeps in grief' (III iv 8; cf. II ii 1). On the other hand, the need to follow the mean and avoid extremes is clearly expressed by Mowbray and Ross, who present themselves as trying to steer a course between ignoble silence and dangerously liberal speech (I i 47–55; II i 228–9). But it is the gardener and his man who force us to reflect on the evils of excess and on the efficacy and beauty of the temperate mean. By pruning, binding and weeding, the gardeners manage to 'keep law and form and due proportion' (III iv 41) in their estate, whereas the royal guardian of 'this other Eden' so neglects his duties that the hedges are ruined (the usurper, too, will obliterate such natural divisions), the 'knots' or intricately patterned flower beds are all 'disordered', the wholesome herbs are swarming with caterpillars, and (since 'superfluous branches' are never lopped off) every tree 'with too much riches . . . [doth] confound itself' (III iv 45–64).

The allegorical garden scene has rightly been related to a long-established tradition of horticultural symbolism in political and moral writings.[15] It has been said, too, that a passage in the *Arte of English Poesie* on the relationship between art and nature – or some other such passage – may have inspired it.[16] This suggestion is apt, since it so happens that Puttenham's analogy between the artful activities of the gardener and those of the poet (whom he generally thinks of as 'playing the orator'),[17] is one of the great commonplaces of rhetorical tradition. It is used there to enforce the argument that spontaneous, natural utterance is generally inadequate and that control and cultivation are necessary if speech is to be fully effective and pleasing: 'Arte', as Puttenham says, 'is . . . an aide and coadiutor to nature'. But the imagery of pruning and weeding is also used to illustrate the idea that art itself must never become so luxuriant as to spoil nature;[18] and, in fact, Puttenham's passage occurs in the middle of that chapter whose whole purpose is to persuade the courtier that he must always dissemble his art and give the impression of graceful naturalness – in his writings and speech, as in his dress and in 'his ordinary actions of behauiour' (pp. 250–1). The symbolism of the gardeners' scene in *Richard II*, therefore, has considerable semantic resonance. It is an image of Richard's careless steward-ship of his realm, of his wasteful, self-indulgent and self-destructive habits, and of that extravagance and affectation which disgraces the speech, dress, and manners of himself and his subjects.

It is worth observing that the first signs of rhetorical inflation are to be found in the speech of Bolingbroke. It is true that on occasions he can be terse and business-like, or (which is more significant) silent or ambiguous; but the commonly held view that Shakespeare contrasts a talkative and lyrical Richard with a taciturn and prosaic Bolingbroke is quite erroneous. Bolingbroke is a man who swells 'high above his limits'; and from the beginning of the play to the end his speech betrays this fact. The dramatic irony and the hint of flattery in his very first sentence – 'Many years of happy days befall/My gracious sovereign, my most loving liege' (I i 20–1) – draw attention to the pleonastic character of each of the sweetly flowing lines. But this is a mere foretaste of the speech of accusation and defiance which follows. There Boling-broke protests his truth three times, protests his loyalty to the king three times, and twice accuses Mowbray of treachery; the key line of the speech is, 'Once more, the more to aggravate the note' (I i 43) – more and more means worse. Bolingbroke even adds a touch of 'sugar' to the 'hard' speech, for he amplifies his comment on the disgrace to Mowbray's lineage with a 'winter-starved' version of a familiar poetical image ('Since the more fair and crystal is the sky/The uglier seem the clouds that in it fly'), and so moves into rhyme in the last six lines. There is, of course, a lot of rhyme in the play, and for the most part it contributes to an impression of brittleness and a feeling that language is being over-burdened with the 'superfluous branches' of art. But we should note that it begins with Bolingbroke – and that it ends with him, too, in that most hollow and distasteful scene where York accuses his son of treachery to Bolingbroke, and Bolingbroke win-dily apostrophises the 'sheer, immaculate and silver fountain' of York's nobility.

Bolingbroke's speech, then, can be prolix (pleonasmus and mac-rologia), pompous and bombastic (bomphiologia), even 'curious' or over-refined (periergeia.[19] But when Richard's speech is marred by excess he is guilty above all things of the last of these vices –

of (as Puttenham would say) 'ouermuch curiosite and study to shew himself fine'. This weakness manifests itself chiefly in the pursuit of conceits to a point where the listener as well as the analogy itself is all but exhausted : 'I have been *studying* how I may compare . . .' (V v 1) [my italics]. One of the most 'curious' of his speeches is that in which he greets the English earth on disembarking after his voyage from Ireland, and likens himself to 'a long-parted mother' who 'plays fondly with her tears and smiles' in meeting her child (III ii 8–10). The circumstance of time alone makes this lingering and heavily figurative speech improper : as all his followers are uncomfortably aware, 'his designs crave haste' at this point (II ii 44). But it is, of course, the opening simile – reinforced with the extravagant gesture of getting down to weep over and caress the earth – which establishes the impropriety of the speech. The figure is thoroughly unfit because the weeping mother comparison does not suit a king at war with rebels at home and abroad ; and because, moreover, Richard cannot properly call himself either mother or father to a land which he has starved and stripped so as to feed his own 'insatiate' appetites (II i 38). His over-artful pursuit of a figure, therefore, has simply served to show that it was badly chosen from the start.

What distinguishes Richard from all other characters in the play is that inconstancy of attitude which reveals itself in a perpetual wavering between a high and manly style and a base and effeminate one. If one accepts that the turning point in his career is his parley with Northumberland at Flint Castle (before his descent into 'the base court'), then it will be seen that his downfall is the result of his complete uncertainty as to which style he should adopt. He begins with a magnificent rebuke of Northumberland for failing to kneel with due alacrity :

> We are amaz'd ; and thus long have we stood
> To watch the fearful bending of thy knee,
> Because we thought ourself thy lawful king ;
> And if we be, how dare thy joints forget
> To pay their awful duty to our presence ? (III iii 72–6)

And he goes on to promise 'scarlet indignation' and fierce war for all those who dare to threaten his crown. Northumberland is suitably subdued, and it is apparent that Aumerle is right in suggesting that the king can fight with words until friends lend swords (III iii 131–2). But Richard completely undoes the psychological effect of this majestic speech by his subsequent effusions – while Northumberland is still present – on the possibility of making 'some pretty match with shedding tears' or exchanging his 'large kingdom for a pretty grave,/A little little grave' (II iii 153–4, 165). When Northumberland returns to Bolingbroke, he is asked : 'What says his Majesty?' He replies that Richard has begun to 'speak fondly like a frantic man' (III iii 185) – which means that the king is doomed, and by his own sentences.

It is apparent from the very first scene that Richard can manage the royal style superbly. When he does, his rhythms are firm, his figures are apt and compressed ('lions make leopards tame'), he uses the high, royal 'we', and avoids rhyme. But he never sustains this style and will slip suddenly into tremulous, prettified and uncontrolled speech which debases majesty to the point of provoking laughter : 'Well, well, I see/I talk but idly, and you laugh at me' (III iii 171–2 ; cf. III ii 23). These transitions from the manly to the effeminate and the royal to the foolish are most discordant, and fully bear out the Ciceronian maxim that constancy is the essence of decorum.[21]

3

Hamlet, Prince of Denmark

I

In Shakespeare's great tragedies, as in his histories, the individual's loss of identity (or assumption of a false role) is the most emphatic sign of disorder and indecorum. But this phenomenon is much more intensively explored in the tragedies than in the histories since, in them, the fate of the individual rather than that of society or the nation is the chief source of interest. In *Hamlet*, the problem of lost and false identity is virtually identified with the loss or abuse of 'form'. Thus, in her moving but noticeably formalized lament for the man who was once his country's 'chiefest courtier' (I ii 117), Ophelia equates the true Hamlet with form itself: he was 'the glass of fashion and the mould of form', the 'unmatch'd form and feature of blown youth' (III i 153, 159). Hamlet's grievous 'transformation' (II ii 5), too, has been caused to a great extent by his horror at what can be called the violation of form around him: within two months of his father's death, his mother has married his uncle, and so a bed and a throne once occupied by a king of consummate grace and dignity – 'A combination and a form ... Where every god did seem to set his seal/To give the world assurance of a man' (III iv 61–3) – have been usurped by a satyr, a Vice, a king of shreds and patches.[1]

Hamlet, moreover, is called upon to correct the disorders which disgust him; and for the most part he is eager to do so – just as he is eager to reform the disorders in that art which he sees as the mirror of nature: 'O, reform it altogether' (III ii 36). But he is haunted by a spirit which assumes his father's 'fair and warlike form' (I i 47), has to contend with an opponent endowed with devilish skill 'in forgery of shapes and tricks' (IV vii 89), moves in a world where 'forms, moods, shapes' no longer 'denote' (I ii 82) what they should, and is unhealthily attracted by Death itself and its strange transformations. So the task proves too much for him. Not the first who, with best meaning, have incurred the worst, the prince reduces himself to an antic – half real, half false – and his world to a shambles before reformation can even begin. Not surprisingly, then, this tragedy exhibits a greater range and concentration of formal disorder than any other of Shakespeare's plays. Manners, dress, speech, 'action' (delivery), acting, drama, game and rite are all abused in it either by excess or deficiency, fraudulence or disarray.

II

Almost as important in *Hamlet* as the notion of form is that of duty. The relationship between the two notions in the philosophical structure of the play is partly determined by the fact that Hamlet has a duty which involves the restoration of true form in a world which is out of joint : the works of the crowned Vice must be exposed. But the connection between form and duty is not limited to the conditions of Hamlet's predicament : they have a kinship which is essential, each being indissolubly bound up with the idea of the proper and fitting. Whereas form is the proper combination or fitting together of parts, the apt relationship of substance and shape, of thought and expression, duty (as Cicero taught) arises from that which is proper in a given set of circumstances and so is indistinguishable from decorum. Richard II's collocation of 'respect, tradition, form, and ceremonious duty' is itself good evidence of the affinity between the two concepts in Shakespearian thought. And the epithet which intervenes between the two words in that phrase is also suggestive : just as Shakespeare conceives of ceremony as an ordered expression or 'formal ostentation' (*Hamlet*, IV v 211) of a sense of duty and respect, so too he often uses 'form' as a synonym for 'established practice, ceremony, ritual'.[2]

In *Hamlet* duty is first invoked in relation to fitness; both words are prominent in the play's vocabulary and are obviously deemed to be intimately related if not synonymous.[3] Almost every character in the play professes or shows an eagerness to do his duty; and some, too – including the ghost, Claudius, Gertrude, Laertes, Polonius and Hamlet – are quick to give others 'lecture and advice' (II i 67) on *their* duty. All of which should augur well for the moral health of Denmark. But apart from the fact that what passes for dutifulness may be only an adherence to outward

...ns (cf. *Othello*, I i 50–2), a willingness to do one's duty and to see that others do theirs is no guarantee that good deeds will be done and bad avoided. Since fitness depends on variable factors, there will always be occasions when only a man of exceptional judgement can determine what words and deeds are appropriate. 'Judgement', 'discretion', 'reason' and 'understanding' are words which keep recurring in the dialogue and monologues of *Hamlet*; but they serve principally to emphasise that no one of any importance in Elsinore knows what is fitting or can distinguish the true from the false in matters of form and duty. The most significant use of the word 'fit' occurs then in a speech where Claudius offers Gertrude a hypocritical explanation of his indulgent treatment of Hamlet: 'But so much was our love,/We would not understand what was most fit' (IV i 19–20). In the court of the fratricidal and incestuous usurper, men spy on their friends, come between lovers, 'loose' their daughters, eavesdrop, pretend lunacy, calumniate, murder well-meaning blunderers, bury the innocent with 'maimed rites', and tip unbated foils with poison in the execution of what they believe to be 'fitting our duty'.

Apart from showing itself negatively in his disgust at his mother's behaviour and in his hatred of the bibulous royal satyr, the prince's devotion to form and fitness becomes apparent when the unexpected arrival of old friends momentarily re-awakens his original self (I ii 159ff., II ii). His social inferiors by a long way, they address him always as lord: 'your lordship', 'my honoured lord', 'my most dear lord'; but they are continually reminded of friendship: they are his 'dear friends', his 'excellent good friends', 'good lads', and even – for Hamlet has the impressive humility of a true aristocrat – his 'masters'. By his modesty, vivacity and humour, by scrupulously attending to each person as an individual worthy of respect, Hamlet (as Castiglione would say) 'frames himself to the company' and puts his social inferiors at their ease. He is 'most like a gentleman' (III i 11), complies gracefully with 'fashion and ceremony' (II ii 367), is 'familiar but not vulgar', and remembers that a man's treatment of others (whatever their merits or demerits might be) should always agree with his 'own honour and dignity' (II ii 526). And far from being superficial and unreflecting, his courtesy is the expression of a profound concern for what gives human life its grace and dignity, raising it above that of the 'beast that lacks discourse of reason' (I ii 150).

So Hamlet reminds Polonius how he should treat the
and them how they should treat 'that lord' (II ii 538). Bu
ficant though they are, such remarks on manners and l
relationships tell us far less about his regard for form and propriety
than do his lecture and advice to the players on that art whose
purpose is to present a 'piece of work' which will 'show the very
age and body of the time his form and pressure' (III ii 23, 44).
From the praise which he bestows on one play in particular (II ii
428–43), we can infer his belief that the good play will appeal to
superior judgements rather than to the crowd. It is well 'digested'
or arranged in structure; and both in structure and in style it is
notable for its artful concealing of art, its unpretentiousness and
moderation ('modesty'). No attempt is made in it to render the
matter more attractive either by salacious quips or rhetorical
'affectation' : it is a 'wholesome' and 'honest' play, 'by very much
more handsome than fine'. Acting, too, Hamlet believes, is governed by essentially the same principles (III ii 1–44). The player
must on no account 'o'erstep . . . the modesty of nature' but must
cultivate temperance and exercise all his discretion in avoiding
the twin extremes of excess and deficiency – a style which is
'o'erdone' and a style which is 'too tame' or 'come tardy off'. Like
the dramatist, the player will find that the first of these extremes is
the more insidious; he will be tempted to bellow and strut and saw
the air with his hands, thus producing an imitation of humanity
so 'abominable' – that is, so far from the true character of *homo
sapien*s – that it will seem like the work of one of Nature's journey-
men rather than of Nature herself. Of course, histrionic bombast
may well – like the clown's gratuitous and distracting jokes –
delight the 'unskilful' and 'barren spectators'; but since it denotes
a loss of discretion and the triumph of passion over reason and
moderation, it 'cannot but make the judicious grieve'. The essence
of all this advice on acting is contained in that sentence which invokes the familiar doctrine that decorum is the chief consideration
in 'action' or delivery: 'Suit the action to the word, the word to
the action'.[4] Like the references to moderation and temperance,
the generalised phrasing of this precept has the effect of implica-
ting the wider stage on which Hamlet himself is an actor. The
spectators of *Hamlet* are here reminded that there are in the
Danish court a number of important people whose words and
actions have no fit relationship. Conveniently, the double sense of

the word 'action' pinpoints the analogy between life and drama which pervades the whole play.

III

Although Hamlet detests noisy acting and the intemperateness it denotes, he is nevertheless the First Player in a piece which – if properly acted and staged – does considerable violence to the ear. The original assault upon the ear, that from which all the others follow, occurs in the murder of the old king, poisoned in a manner which Shakespeare chose purely for its emblematic potential. Powerfully impressed on the mind by the ghost's speech and later by the dumb show (there is emblematic intention here, too), the act of killing through the ear lies at the centre of a whole network of images whose function is to suggest that the excesses and disorders which afflict Denmark are closely related to the abuse of speech, to what we hear. Speech is violent, frightening, poisonous – not calculated to enlighten and to elicit an intelligible and civilized response but to drive 'wonder-wounded hearers' (V i 251) into strange silence or passionate execration : 'I have words to speak in thine ear will make thee dumb' (IV vi 21).

The first instance of violence to the ear occurs when Hamlet and his friends are waiting for the ghost at midnight and the silence is suddenly shattered by the sound of trumpets, kettle-drums and cannon. In reply to Horatio's astonished question, 'What does this mean, my lord?' (I iv 7), Hamlet explains that such noise is the language of swaggering drunkenness and revelry whereby the king 'brays out' his bombastic drinking pledges (I iv 11–12). His claim that this has become the norm is confirmed in the last scene of the play (V ii 266–70) and, in fact, evidence for it has already been provided in the king's jovial assurance that he would 'grace' Hamlet's 'unforced' show of filial duty with re-sounding toasts (I ii 123–8) :

> No jocund health that Denmark drinks today
> But the great cannon to the clouds shall tell,
> And the King's rouse the heaven shall bruit again,
> Re-speaking earthly thunder. Come away.
>   *(Flourish. Exeunt all but Hamlet.)*

This association of Claudius with noisy self-expression may seem inconsistent, since as a speaker he is glib and oily rather than loud; a true 'politician', he never gives way to ranting passion. But the guns, drums and trumpets are carefully used by Shakespeare to suggest that the vulgar and bombastic mode of utterance, which ultimately disgraces the two most promising young men in Denmark, begins with him, the complacent cutpurse of the empire.

Just as it offends Hamlet to the soul to hear a bad actor 'tear a passion to tatters' so as to 'split the ears of the groundlings', so Pyrrhus, his counterpart, is suddenly rendered immobile and 'speechless' when 'the hideous crash' of falling Troy 'takes prisoner . . . [his] ear' (II ii 470–9). But after this paralysed moment of 'silence' and inactivity ('Did nothing'), Pyrrhus bounds to the opposite extreme and proceeds to wield his avenging sword with a noise more hideous than that of the Cyclops' hammers falling upon the armour of Mars (II ii 481–5). Similarly Hamlet, who so far has been taciturn and inactive ('Dull and muddy-mettled . . ./And can say nothing'), decides that if the player who recites the Pyrrhus–Hecuba speech had his 'motive and . . . cue for passion',

> He would drown the stage with tears,
> And cleave the general ear with horrid speech;
> Make mad the guilty and appal the free,
> Confound the ignorant, and amaze indeed
> The very faculties of eyes and ears. (II ii 555–9)

And so 'our chiefest courtier' proceeds to 'out-herod' Herod. The absent Claudius – 'Bloody, bawdy villain?/Remorseless, treacherous, lecherous kindless villain!' (II ii 575–6) – is the first victim of Hamlet's 'mouthing'. He is quickly succeeded by the gentle Ophelia – who hears 'sweet bells jangled, out of tune and harsh' (III i 158) – and then by Gertrude. It is with the queen that Hamlets's noise is at its worst: 'What have I done that thou dar'st wag thy tongue/In noise so rude against me?' (III iv 39–40; 'Ay me, what act,/That roars so loud and thunders in the index?' (III iv 51–2). Here too, as with Ophelia, his words are not only loud but savagely cruel –he does indeed 'speak daggers' to his mother (as he promised): 'O Hamlet, speak no more! . . . O, speak to me no more!/These words like daggers enter in my ears;/No more, sweet Hamlet . . . No more!' (III iv 88, 94–6, 102).

In noise, as in other respects, Laertes is Hamlet's counterpart. On his return to court from Paris he is heard even before he is seen. This is in no way surprising from a courtly point of view since he has joined forces with 'the rabble' who, crying stupidly like dogs on a 'false trail', applaud him to the skies as their chosen king (IV v 99–105). Raging for revenge, he brings them into the castle to the very door of the chamber where the king and queen are anxiously conversing. 'Alack, what noise is this?' (IV v 94), asks the queen; and while a gentleman explains, the tumult grows louder and the doors are crashed in : 'The doors are broke' (IV v 108). Since Ophelia is totally 'divided from herself and her fair judgment,/ Without the which we are pictures or mere beasts' (IV 82–3), she too is identified in this scene with meaningless sound and, like her brother, is introduced by noise.

> *A noise within:* 'Let her come in.'
> *Laertes.* How now ! What noise is that ? (IV v 149–50)

This deeply significant scene represents a recession to the language of primitive man : the spirit of Caliban and of Jack Cade is in the ascendant. Reason, 'antiquity' and 'custom' – 'the ratifiers and props of every word' – are 'forgot' or 'not known' (IV v 101–2) and the consequent decay of temperate and intelligible speech augurs the unmaking of civilization : 'As the world were now but to begin . . .'[5]

Because of Claudius' presence, one can sense even in this scene a distinction between speech which is noisy and confused and that which gives the impression of reason and moderation but gently enters the ear as an unsuspected poison. When the ghost warned Hamlet about the 'wicked wit and gifts' and the 'witchcraft' which enabled Claudius to seduce Gertrude and deceive the whole kingdom (I v 43–4), he was undoubtedly referring to his brother's verbal skill.[6] The first scene in which Claudius appears clearly establishes him as a man whose easy command of flattering, casuistical and bland speech enables him to smooth over unpleasantness, dissolve opposition, and move people in whatever direction he chooses; it is not in the least surprising that, through his 'forged process', 'the whole ear of Denmark/Is . . . rankly abus'd' concerning the true nature of the late king's death (I v 36–7). But his sinister use of the art of persuasion is not fully displayed until his handling of Laertes after the death of Polonius : by combining flattery with an appeal to filial love and duty, he shows how to 'infect' the 'ear with pestilent speeches' (IV v 87–8), 'envenom' it with thoughts of revenge and murder, and so plant in the unconscious mind of the listener the idea of poisoning an un-bated foil (IV vii 3, 103, 161).

Yet Claudius is not the only one whose verbal witchcraft in-flames the agitated mind and incites to murder. Nor is the power of persuasion limited to words and voice : as Antony proves so impressively in *Julius Caesar*, there is an appeal to mind and emotions through the eye as well as the ear. The mere sight of Ophelia distributing flowers in gentle madness all but overwhelms Laertes : 'Had'st thou thy wits, and didst persuade revenge,/It could not move thus' (IV v 165–6). And Hamlet is profoundly moved by the player's 'action', particularly its visual aspect (II 11 47–50). But the most eloquent and persuasive character is the ghost, whose power to bewitch both eye and ear is irresistible. The chief secret of his art is that he is so slow to speak. Rather like Antony in his refusal to read Caesar's will to the mob ('I must not read it . . . It will inflame you, it will make you mad'), he excites an overpowering desire to hear him utter what he alone knows. Being 'distill'd/Almost to jelly with the act of fear', Marcellus and Barnardo 'stand dumb and speak not to him' (I ii 204–6); nor does he speak to them. But the mere 'sight' of him is such that they 'assail' the 'ears' of Horatio (I i 25, 31) until he, too, becomes involved. Horatio's first appeal to the ghost to speak is vigorous enough : 'By heaven I charge thee, speak ! . . . Stay, speak, speak ! I charge thee speak !' (I i 49, 51). Perhaps because it has been adjured in the name of heaven, 'it will not answer' (I i 52). And yet, having disappeared, it returns tantalisingly to provoke Horatio's clamorous though unavailing appeals (I i 128–39). Later, Hamlet gives 'an attent ear' to Horatio's description of this 'dumb' ghost (I i 171 ; I ii 192) and shows a desire to hear it speak which will not be mastered by any consideration : 'I'll speak to it, though hell itself should gape/And bid me hold my peace' (I iii 245–6). And when he is confronted by the ghost, he presents the picture of a man so obsessed with a desire to know and listen that he has become a tool in the hands of the speaker even before a single word is uttered : 'I will speak to thee . . . O, answer me !/ Let me not burst in ignorance . . . why . . . why . . . what . . . Say,

why is this? Wherefore? What should we do?' (I iv 44–57).
What should he do? First, he must open his ears wide to an
astounding tale of poisoning through the ear : 'Mark me . . . lend
thy serious hearing/To what I shall unfold . . . List, list, O, list!
. . . Now, Hamlet, hear' (I v 2, 5, 22, 34). It is odd that the ghost
should tell Hamlet not to pity him since he goes on to make a long
speech whose tremendous effect on the mourning son depends
greatly on its appeal to his sensitive, sympathetic emotions : 'Alas,
poor ghost!'; 'thou poor ghost' (I v 4, 96). The ghost's initial 'pity
me not' (I v 5) is really a rhetorical trick which prepares the way
for that superbly artful use of the figure occupatio (paralipsis) :[7]

> But that I am forbid
> To tell the secrets of my prison house,
> I could a tale unfold whose lightest word
> Would harrow up thy soul, freeze thy young blood,
> Make thy two eyes, like stars, start from their spheres,
> Thy knotted and combined locks to part
> And each particular hair to stand an end
> Like quills upon the fretful porpentine.
> But this eternal blazon must not be
> To ears of flesh and blood. (I v 13–22)

The exclamation, 'O, horrible! O, horrible! most horrible!' (I v
80), which crowns the ghost's account of how he has been re-
morselessly sent out of life 'unhous'led, disappointed, unanel'd,'
with all his imperfections on his head, is another most impressive
use of a familiar figure; the functional equivalence of the two
figures is to be seen from the fact that each is followed immediately
by the same crucial injunction in the name of nature and filial
love : 'If thou didst ever thy dear father love . . . Revenge his foul
and most unnatural murder'; 'If thou hast nature in thee, bear it
not' (I v 24–5, 81). From start to finish, the ghost's speech is calculated to excite the kind of horrified pity which leads to rage and
vengeance. And his advice to Hamlet that 'howsomever' he pur-
sues 'this act' (that is, of vengeance) he must not taint his mind
(I v 84–5), seems rather similar in its context to the appeals for
moderation made by Antony and Iago to the men whom they
have just worked up into a frenzy of uncontrollable hatred (*Julius
Caesar* III ii 211; *Othello*, III iii 455).

IV

Given the emotionalism of Hamlet and Laertes, the hypocrisy and vulgarity of Claudius, and the absence of any deflating commentator such as Thersites or Iago, it is not surprising that the verbal style of the Danish court suffers a great deal from excess and hardly at all from undue diminishing; swollen and ulcerated, this social organism 'dies in his own too much' (IV vii 118). The first and most palpable sign of the overdone style is to be found in the comical prolixity of the chief counsellor. Polonius is one of those 'tedious old fools' who are identifiable with 'words, words, words' (II ii 192, 218); a 'foolish prating' counsellor, he acquires a becoming gravity and reticence only in death (III iv 213–15). Stupidly, too, he invokes the rules by which he stands condemned, reminding us that 'brevity is the soul of wit,/ And tediousness her outward flourishes', that figures of speech can be foolishly used, and that 'art' should be invisible and subservient to 'matter' (II ii 90–99).

Superfluity of words and sentences is not the only blemish on Polonius' style; cacozelia, or the affected use of Latinate and neologistic diction, is to be seen in his fondness for words like 'prenominate', 'videlicet' and 'effect defective'. Moreover, his oration to the king and queen on the theme 'I have found the very cause of Hamlet's lunacy' is marked by a cumbersome display of the machinery of 'invention' – division, definition, inquiry into cause and effect (II ii 49, 86ff.). And strange though it might seem at first, this abuse of rhetorical invention (or 'finding') is, in a way, intimately related to the cause of his own death and to the nature of his contribution to the larger tragedy. For the elaborate plotting which gets him killed – 'Thou find'st to be too busy in some danger' (III iv 33) – is nourished by his conviction that he can 'find/Where truth is hid, though it were hid indeed/ Within the centre' (II ii 156–8); and when he has failed, he leaves his master with the absurdly additional problem of how 'to find the body' (IV iii 31–5). If we bear in mind that Polonius probably goes through all the flourishes of rhetorical 'action', and that he is also an exhibitionist in memory ('these few precepts in thy memory/Look thou character') who is liable to wander from the point ('Where did I leave off?'), then it becomes apparent that throughout the play Shakespeare is using rhetoric and its parts – invention, ordering, style, action and memory – in the same way as he uses that art with which it overlaps – dramaturgy : that is, as a metaphor for the art of life itself, the discipline which gives meaning and form to experience.

The analogies between Osric and Polonius bear out this interpretation. In general, Osric does to 'the matter' what he does to his own diminutive figure : dresses it up in gorgeous, newfangled apparel for which it is quite unfitted.[8] He is the personification of elegant outward flourishes. But as Hamlet's exuberant parody makes abundantly clear, the speech in which he extols the son of Polonius is characterised in particular by an inordinate attention to 'golden words' and the topics of invention – 'to divide him inventorially would dozy th' arithmetic of memory' (V ii 114). The plot itself emphasises the ineffectualness of his ambassadorial art. While Hamlet is still in the act of equating his speech with mere wind, an anonymous lord arrives from the king to ask whether the prince is prepared to play now or later. Osric did not find all that he came for; he failed to keep clear in the tables of his memory what mattered most.[9]

The link between 'young Osric' and 'young Laertes' is apt. Laertes is 'newly come to court' (V ii 107) lacks the authentic refinement and the discrimination of a true gentleman. He is always properly conscious that he has some role to play; but even when he chooses the right one he so overacts as to give the impression of a man in borrowed robes. On his return from Paris, he is acutely aware of himself as a grief-stricken son and brother, whose family wrongs cry out to him for justice :

> O, heat dry up my brains ! tears seven times salt
> Burn out the sense and virtue of mine eye !
> By heaven, thy madness shall be paid with weight
> Till our scale turn the beam. O rose of May !
> Dear maid, kind sister, sweet Ophelia !
> O heavens ! is't possible a young maid's wits
> Should be as mortal as an old man's life ?
> Nature is fine in love ; and where 'tis fine
> It sends some precious instance of itself
> After the thing it loves. (IV v 151–60)

Laertes certainly has adequate cause for such grief and wrath. But his mode of expression, with its quantitive hyperbole (if we may so call it), pleonasm, laboured conceits and insistent exclamation, suggests that he is more concerned with himself as a figure of grief than he is with the pathetic object of his feelings : that he protests too much. Dr Johnson was right in describing these lines as 'obscure and affected', but wrong in saying that 'they could have been omitted in the Folio without great loss'.[10] We have been prepared to perceive their unfitness by the hypocritical remark of Claudius which immediately precedes them : 'Why, now you speak/Like a good child and a true gentleman' (IV v 144–5). Moreover, Laertes' speech here is of a piece with almost everything else he says and does : with his pompous moralising on maiden virtue and male lust as he sets out for Paris ('O, fear me not!'); with the 'giant-like' (IV v 118) bombast which he utters when he presents himself at the head of the rabble as heroic avenger and possible claimant to the throne ; and, above all, with the Herculean grief which he displays at the grave of Ophelia. His speech there reaches the ultimate in bombast (V i 240–8). Its hyperboles are more giant-like and quantitive than ever ('O, treble woe/Fall ten times treble . . .'). It is 'mouthed' (V i 277) in an accent such as to 'conjure the wand'ring stars and make them stand/Like wonder-wounded hearers' (V i 250–1). And it is reinforced with the extravagant 'action' of leaping into the grave to embrace and (he would have us believe) be buried with the dead girl. Such is Laertes' urge for expressional extremes that he abandons his proper role of bereaved brother for that of distracted lover : a strange echo of the incestuous love of the man who has become his tutor.

The behaviour of Laertes at the grave perfectly exemplifies what Hamlet so contemptuously rejected in those intemperate actors who are unable to impose a 'smoothness' on their style in 'the very torrent, tempest and . . . whirlwind of passion' (III ii 5–7). Yet Hamlet is so furious at being 'outfaced' (V i 272) in grief by Laertes that he stoops to a grotesque competition in bombast on the 'theme' (V i 260, 262) of love and grief : 'Nay, an thou'lt mouth,/I'll rant as well as thou' (V i 277–8). Not only does he surpass Laertes in the obvious inflationary device of quantitive hyperbole – 'forty thousand brothers/Could not, with all their quantity of love,/Make up my sum' (V i 263–6) ; he piles up those stale, amatory hyperboles (V i 268–70) which are cited in *Troilus and Cressida* as evidence that 'all lovers swear more performance than they are able' (III ii 74–82). His proclamation of royal identity, 'This is I,/Hamlet the Dane' (V i 251–2), simultaneously increases and clarifies the extreme unfitness of what he says and does; for the Hamlet we see here – to borrow a phrase from the hero of *Antony and Cleopatra* – is but 'a mangled shadow' of his royal self: 'But I am very sorry, good Horatio,/That to Laertes I forgot myself' (V ii 75–6).

'To thine own self be true' is, then, a moral of great relevance to Hamlet. His emotional distress and mental confusion inspire in him an instinct to imitate individuals whose style can only degrade him: he is impressed by 'examples gross as earth'. But it should be observed that this muddled admiration – or fascination – is apparent only in his response to violent grief and (a closely related phenomenon) violent action. Grief or mourning is, of course, a duty which has confronted everyone in Denmark for some time before the death of Ophelia; and it is a duty in which almost everyone failed. After the king's death, Gertrude acted 'like Niobe, all tears' (I ii 149). But apart from being a mere assumption of the outward forms of grief, her mourning (and so that of all the court) was of astonishingly short duration. Essentially, then, it was improper not because of excess (like Olivia's in *Twelfth Night*) but because of deficiency: it came tardy off. By way of revulsion, therefore, Hamlet is driven to admire the opposite extreme of overdone grief. This aberration in his judgement first occurs in his encounter with the players, a scene which deserves close attention since it is there, too, that he declines into noisy bombast and murderous passion for the first time.

As soon as the players arrive, Hamlet impetuously asks for a taste of their quality: 'We'll e'en to't like French falconers, fly at anything we see. We'll have a speech straight . . . come, a passionate speech' (II ii 424–6). Neither the choice of a passionate speech nor the falcon analogy are as innocent as they seem: Hamlet is soon to show (in his mother's closet) an inhuman, undiscriminating ferocity to which passionate speech – 'speaking daggers' – is seen as a natural accompaniment. The speech chosen here by Hamlet is doubly attractive to him, beginning as it does with the picture of a prince whose grief and wrath at the death of his father have driven him for revenge into the flames of Troy, and concluding with a widowed queen whose wild gestures and 'instant burst of clamour' at the death of her husband 'would have made milch the burning eyes of heaven,/And passion in the gods' (II ii 511–12). But these signs of immeasurable grief and wrath blind Hamlet to everything else in the speech. He seems in no way conscious that Pyrrhus' feelings have turned him into a tigerish (II ii 444), 'hellish', 'o'er-sized' murderer of an 'old grandsire' (II ii 456–8): this he might well have taken as a warning, since in the process of 'flying at anything we see' he, too, is to murder an old man – 'the *unseen* good old man' (IV i 12) – and, like Pyrrhus, become 'horridly trick'd/With blood of fathers' (II ii 451–2). But Hamlet's insensitivity to the style of the speech is much more illuminating. As a comparison with the corresponding passages in Virgil (*Aeneid*, ll 529ff.) and Marlowe (*Dido Queen of Carthage*, ll 505ff.) emphasises, the style – matching the 'o'er-sized' passions of Pyrrhus and Hecuba – is overdone in the extreme.[11] Hyperbolical conceits, moving into the grotesque and ridiculous rather than the obscure, prolixity, involved periphrasis, and an affectedly Latinate and archaic diction (even Hamlet is puzzled by 'the mobled queen') are all marshalled to produce an entirely spurious elevation of style; Polonius is perfectly right when he protests that it is too much. That Hamlet could ask for this speech, above all that he could introduce it as part of a play which is notable for its unaffected and wholesome style, shows just how much damage has been done to his judgement by grief and wrath.

The actor, too, admires the speech, surrenders to its emotionalism, and so prompts Hamlet to 'out-herod' Herod. The prince is momentarily disgusted with his own 'horrid speech', comparing himself (II ii 582) to a cursing whore who unpacks her heart with words. But there will be no such regrets after the outbursts against Ophelia and Gertrude. The ferocious verbal attack on his mother meaningfully coincides with the blind killing of Polonius: discretion has vanished, rashness is supreme. Gertrude describes this murder as 'a rash and bloody deed' (III iv 26), and Claudius calls it a 'vile deed', 'untimely done' (IV i 30, 40); but Hamlet places most of the blame on the 'wretched, rash, intruding fool' whom he admits to having killed in error, and maintains too that his own rashness is an instrument of divine providence (III iv 31–2, 175). He is thus well on the way to that point where he will turn the rule of reason and temperance upside-down : 'Rashly,/And prais'd be rashness for it . . ./Our indiscretions sometimes serve us well . . .' (V ii 6–8). If we consider the death of Polonius and its terrible consequences, and reflect that the (providential?) intervention of the pirates renders the murder of Rosencrantz and Guildenstern more pointless than ever, we might well ask whether rashness and indiscretion are ever beneficial, and remind the sadly confused prince of his sometime injunction : 'But let your own discretion be your tutor'. It is Hamlet's tragedy that, like almost everyone else in Denmark, he 'recks not his own rede' (I iii 51).

V

It is apparent in the closet scene that passion is responsible not only for noise and excess in speech but for a loss of meaning as well. Having bidden his mother good-night, Hamlet returns compulsively for 'one word more' (III iv 180) on the hateful subject of her relationship with Claudius. To her question, 'What shall I do?' (III iv 180), he answers with a speech of eighteen lines all but one of which (the first) are given to commands urging her to do precisely what he wants her not to do. The opening line is all-important in the logic of the speech; but its double negative and irregular rhythm prevent it from communicating its own meaning clearly, and its significant relation to the rest of the speech is lost in the vehement elaboration of the commands which follow (III iv 181–96). The bitter tone and the dramatic context enable us to 'ravel all this matter out' (III iv 186) and to overcome the momentary suspicion that Hamlet's thoughts have inexplicably changed their general direction, so we can here credit the dramatic poet with a thoroughly effective and decorous use of the satiric figure antiphrasis ('when we deride by plain and flat contradiction').[12] But in evaluating the speech of Prince Hamlet we must conclude that his wrath and disgust have well-nigh destroyed a basic process of rational communication – that of question-and-answer. This diagnosis can be supported by the fact that in the same scene his distemper has already produced a vivid instance of non-communication. In his direct manner, Hamlet has managed to voice – 'Ay, lady, 'twas my word' (III iv 30) – but not to transmit the most important fact in his life and his mother's : when he leaves her, Gertrude is still unaware that Claudius killed her husband – and Hamlet has proved that passionate outbursts do indeed 'confound the ignorant'.

As an omen and a cause of danger, 'dark' speech is no less important in Shakespearian tragedy than rash swearing and bombast. In different ways, Macbeth and Othello are enticed to their doom through 'the equivocation of the fiend/That lies like truth' (*Macbeth*, V v 43–4). As I have observed earlier, too, the twisted, uncommunicative language of passion helps to strangle Desdemona and so to make a terrible mockery of that justice which is purportedly being sought for. While in *Hamlet*, the destruction of the innocent together with the guilty is dependent upon the shrouding of truth in secrecy and the use of words as a disguise. One must admit, of course, that some of Hamlet's riddling manifests his fine sense of humour and his ready command of those 'privy nips' and 'merry conceits' which help to make the courtier a socially attractive person. Most of it, however, is a private language begotten by disgust and hatred; and it is intimately related to the secret justice (and therefore non-justice) of revenge. It must be considered, then, not only as a superb revelation of a penetrating, restless and unhappy mind, but as a sign of the isolation of the individual and the collapse of society.

Incest being the most fundamental disorder in human relationships, it is appropriate that the incestuous nature of his mother's second marriage should provoke Hamlet's most memorable riddles. The play thus provides striking literary evidence in favour of the anthropological theory that there is a correlation in mythic thought between incest and riddling.[13] The first two sentences uttered by Hamlet are exact verbal re-enactments of the bewildering confusion which incest produces in the mind : 'A little more than kin, and less than kind' (I ii 65); 'Not so my lord; I am too much in the sun' (I ii 67). The second sentence is Hamlet's answer to the first question that is put to him, and the questioner, Claudius, may not grasp its hidden meaning (cf. his 'I have nothing with this answer, Hamlet; these words are not mine' – III ii 93); but he can hardly fail to understand the pun in the very last sentence which Hamlet addresses to him : 'Here, thou *incestuous,* murd'rous damned Dane,/Drink off this potion. Is thy *union* here?' (V ii 318–19 [my italics]. Elsewhere the same close link between incest and riddling is apparent. When Hamlet begins to withdraw from his sometime friends Rosencrantz and Guildenstern into the language of 'mad north-north-west', his first perverse sentence is: 'But my uncle-father and my aunt-mother are deceived (II ii 372; cf. III iv 8–16). And the first bitter ambiguities (III i 95–148) which mark the end of his harmonious relationship with Ophelia (and the beginning of her descent into madness) are inspired with the feeling that marriage has become a state of corruption worse even than whoredom : to preserve her virtue, a maid must now go her ways to a 'nunnery' (that is, a brothel). 'This was sometime a paradox, but now the time gives it proof'; in an age of adultery and incest, paradox, equivocation and riddle are the norm.

Hamlet's rejection of normal verbal intercourse, his retreat from dialogue to monologue, is not idiosyncratic : it is part of a prevailing disease whereby words and thoughts, questions and answers are deprived of their pre-ordained natural relationships. Rosencrantz and Guildenstern may complain, 'I understand you not my lord' (IV ii 21) and righteously ask him to 'put ... [his] discourse into some frame' (III ii 300). But the reason for his refusal to give them 'a wholesome answer' (III ii 312) is that they have disregarded his solemn appeal to 'be even and direct' with him, that he has had to guess their thoughts from their blushes and to formulate for them the answer which they refused to give him (II ii 270–92). These two, however, are much less active than Polonius in depriving words of their semantic and social efficacy. The transformation of Hamlet's honey vows into bitter riddles begins with Polonius' claim that those vows are treacherous lies rather than sanctified bonds (I iii 115–31) and with his command that Ophelia should cease 'to give words or talk with the Lord Hamlet' (I iii 134), should 'repel his letters' (II i 109), 'admit no messengers, receive no tokens' (II ii 143). Polonius thus coins words which are socially destructive (slanders) and destroys those which are socially binding. But he also twists ordinary words to fit his own devious mind and so deprives them of their accepted meanings. In his thoroughly perverse endeavour to find the truth by telling lies ('Your bait of falsehood takes this carp of truth ... By indirections find directions out' – II i 62, 66), indeed, in the very process of slandering his own son ('these slight sullies – II i 39), he baffles Reynaldo by insisting that 'drabbing' and 'incontinency' are really quite distinct : 'That's not my meaning' (II i 26, 31–2). Ultimately, he gets lost in his own verbal labyrinth and has to call to his auditor for help : 'What was I about to say? By the mass, I was about to say

something; where did I leave?' (II i 51–2). This is a comic anticipation of the painful disjunction of words and thoughts experienced by Claudius when he discovers that no '*form* of prayer'
[my italics] can serve his turn : 'My words fly up, my thoughts
remain below./Words without thoughts never to heaven go' (III
iii 51, 97–8).

The disappearance of meaning is apparent, too, in the speech
of the lower orders. The rebellious people not only shout to the
heavens in senseless bestial noise, they are also 'thick and un-
wholesome in their thoughts and whispers' (IV v 79). The sexton
or first clown slips, by way of affectation, into the vice of acyron
and so produces meanings opposite to those intended ('salvation'
for 'damnation', 'se offendendo' for 'se defendendo' – V i 2, 10);
and his quibbling replies to Hamlet wilfully frustrate understanding.[14] Although amused, Hamlet is also quick to note that this
sort of affectation is a sign of social disorder :

> By the Lord, Horatio, this three years I have took note of it :
> the age is grown so picked that the toe of the peasant comes
> so near the heel of the courtier he galls his kibe. (V i 133–5)[15]

Indeed, the clown's speech prompts the musing Hamlet to
formulate a moral of pressing importance for himself and others.
Echoing his early request to Horatio and Marcellus that they
should utter no 'doubtful phrase', avoid all 'ambiguous giving
out' (I v 175, 178), he now concludes that 'we must speak by the
card, or equivocation will undo us' (V i 132–3).

VI

Since Hamlet does not realise the full truth of this remark, he is
hardly likely to suspect that unconscious equivocation contributes
even more to his own undoing than the conscious kind. Evident
more in his communings with himself than with others, fallacious
reasoning serves to gloss over the grave moral problem posed by
the situation which confronts him ; it is his 'imposthume .../That
inward breaks, and shows no cause without/Why the man dies'
(IV iv 26–8).

From the beginning of his career, Shakespeare frequently made
good use of sophistry and unconsciously fallacious reasoning as
vehicles of deception and self-deception and as pointers to moral

and psychological confusion. Of particular interest in relation to
Hamlet are those noblemen whose judgement is clouded by passion, an over-active imagination, a thirst for revenge, and a muddled devotion to honour. Characters such as these are liable to
plunge themselves and others into destruction after making some
memorable speeches which suggest that Shakespeare's much
praised skill in portraying the passions is not to be distinguished
from his ability to represent with the utmost naturalness every
kind of logical disorder in speech. Hotspur comes instantly to mind
here; but Troilus and Paris are more useful examples, since their
question-begging, self-contradiction, defective analogies and re-
liance on hidden false assumptions are exhibited in extended debate and exposed to a form of biting, intellectualised criticism
which makes it impossible for an audience to miss the connection
established by the dramatist between psychology, logic and morality (II ii 163–73).[16]

But it is not only the plays written before or at about the same
time as *Hamlet* which justify the assumption that any sign of
fallacious reasoning in the hero's thought must be considered to
have dramatic significance. Distinguished as it is by continual
reference to reason, judgement and understanding, the play itself
invites this approach. Moreover, although Claudius argues that
Hamlet's attitude to his dead father shows 'an understanding
simple and unschool'd' and is 'to reason most absurd' (I ii 97,
103), it is perfectly clear that the prince has an excellent understanding of the rules of formal logic : a fact which makes the overthrow of his 'noble and most sovereign reason' (III ii 157) all the
more noticeable and tragic. When Hamlet says to himself, 'I'll
have grounds/More *relative* than this' (II ii 599–600) [my italics],
he uses a technical term from formal logic with complete precision
and thereby emphasises his determination to proceed in a thoroughly rational manner to decide on the nature of the ghost and
the guilt or innocence of Claudius.[17] It is the logician in him who
responds with 'Nay, that follows not' to Polonius' hypothetical
syllogism : 'If you call me Jephthah, my lord, I have a daughter
that I love passing well' (II ii 406–8). And it is the same mocking
logician who remarks, 'I do not well understand that', when the
embarrassed Guildenstern hides behind this tortured, hypothetical
proposition : 'O my lord, if my duty be too bold, my love is too
unmannerly' (III ii 339–41). Musing in the graveyard, Hamlet

deliberately constructs a sorites or chain of syllogisms in order to prove to Horatio that his generalisation on the base uses to which we may return is not the fruit of morbid imagining but has been arrived at 'with modesty enough, and likelihood' (V i 200–6). This sorites echoes his reaction to the clown's equivocations. When he says, 'How absolute the knave is!' (V i 133), he once more employs with noticeable exactness a term from formal logic: he perceives that the devious clown has resorted to the fallacy of *secundum quid*, 'taking in an absolute sense a word uttered in a qualified sense'.[18] Hamlet's comments on the sexton's reasoning derive extra force from the fact that the sexton has been dazzling his companion with his logical expertise before Hamlet arrived. In 'debating the question' of Ophelia's death and burial he has resorted, in the best traditions of logical and rhetorical method, to an 'inventive' division of his subject: 'It argues an act; and an act hath three branches . . .' (V i 11–12). He has also made it as clear as his malapropian and question-begging manner will allow that when he employs the syllogism he does it wittingly:

> If the man goes to this water and drown himself . . . he goes
> . . . but if the water come to him and drown him, he drowns
> not himself. Argal [*ergo*], he that is not guilty of his own death
> shortens not his own life. (V i 15–20; cf. V i 12, 48).

The rest of the dialogue between the two clowns consists of riddling questions ('cudgel thy brains') whose casuistical answers depend on the fallacy of verbal equivocation.

In Hamlet's handling of the questions which vex his mind so profoundly the chief source of error is the hidden, false assumption – he can 'sweep' to conclusions in much the same way as he can stab a man to death from the wrong side of an arras. It is noticeably in relation to the ghost that this fault first shows itself. When Horatio warns him not to follow the ghost, Hamlet replies:

> Why, what should be the fear?
> I do not set my life at a pin's fee;
> And for my soul, what can it do to that
> Being a thing immortal as itself? (I v 64–7)

The most effective way of objecting to this would be to point out that murderers can send the souls of men to the 'sulphurous flames' of purgatory ('not shriving time allow'd') and that revengers often do their best to ensure that their victims are damned forever in hell. Hamlet has here implied that what endures forever cannot be harmed – an error which finds support in an equivocal use of the word 'immortal'.

A kindred fallacy occurs in an argument which Hamlet expresses in the form of an abbreviated hypothetical syllogism (an outstanding feature of the play's mode of reasoning): 'If his occulted guilt/Do not itself unkennel in one speech,/It is a damned ghost that we have seen,/And my imaginations are as foul/As Vulcan's stithy' (III ii 78–82); 'If 'a do blench I know my course' [and the ghost is not a spirit who] 'abuses me to damn me' (II ii 593–4, 598). In this argument it is assumed that spirits which tell the truth are necessarily good and that evil spirits always tell lies. Such an assumption completely ignores one of the most fundamental and best known axioms in Christian teaching – patristic, medieval and reformation – on the 'discretion' (that is, discrimination) of spirits: that evil spirits invariably moralise and tell some truths in order to betray us in deepest consequence. If, however, the ghost really is from purgatory much the same sort of objection arises: one has no reason to assume that the 'dread command' (III iv 108) of a spirit which is still so obviously unpurified of its sins and passions has any binding force than that of a living creature similarly affected. As Horatio says to Barnardo when Hamlet (waxing desperate with imagination) warns them not to follow: ' 'Tis not fit thus to obey him' (I iv 88).

But an even more palpable – indeed an astonishing – error of this kind lies in the argument that if the king blenches at the play he must be guilty of murdering his brother. Since the Player King is killed by his nephew and not his brother, those who do not know that Claudius is guilty (that is, everyone on and off stage) must recognise that two antithetical and therefore useless inferences can be made from his fright at false fire: (1) he did kill his brother and is terrified by Hamlet's knowledge of the fact; (2) he did not kill his brother and is filled with rage or fear at what he takes to be a crudely disguised threat of murder from his insulting and deranged nephew. Hamlet automatically makes the first inference and the court (no less automatically) makes the second. The judicious spectator will at least suspend his judgement until he overhears Claudius confessing his guilt in the prayer scene (a confession which Hamlet does not hear) – though the fact that Hamlet has been making hints about his own dissatisfied ambition, and that Claudius is not in the least perturbed by the dumb-show's image of ear-poisoning, might well incline such a spectator to feel that the court's interpretation has more probability. At any rate, no reliable conclusion whatever about Claudius' innocence or guilt can be drawn from the fact that he blenches.

Virtually inseparable from these errors is Hamlet's failure to specify and test the assumption that private revenge is right and proper : if Claudius killed his brother then he undoubtedly deserves to be punished; but 'if 'a do blench I know my course' – 'Nay, that follows not'. Events happen to unfold in such a way that Claudius' wickedness is brought into the open and he can be killed in a manner which amounts to a public execution. This is fortunate for Hamlet, since his determination to kill the king privately, with no more evidence to offer the world than the word of a secretive ghost, and to kill him in such a way as to ensure his damnation, is tragically at variance with the character of a noble prince who holds reason and religion in the highest regard. But although he escapes the role of merciless and calculating avenger, the price paid for his initial commitment to revenge and secrecy is very high indeed : Claudius the guilty is only one of eight people who lose their lives in a sequence of closely connected events set in motion by antic behaviour and the thrusting of a rapier through a screen. It can, of course, be argued that since there is no allusion whatever to the moral problem of revenge, we must simply ignore it; and that for a similar reason we must ignore Hamlet's obliviousness to the teaching that evil spirits can tell the truth. This would be a valid argument if Hamlet were presented as an unsophisticated hero in a barbarous or pagan setting; if Shakespeare and his contemporaries were indifferent to the serious implications of revenge; and if the truth-telling of treacherous spirits was an unfamiliar notion. The facts being otherwise, the argument seems to me to be unacceptable.[19] Hamlet's failure to question his assumptions about ghosts and revenge must have been intended as an indication of the extent to which 'the poison of deep grief' (IV v 72) – and the poison of hatred – can break down 'the pales and forts of reason' (I iii 28). In the Shakespearian canon, it is a new and subtle way of showing that 'revenge' has 'ears more deaf than adders to the voice of/Any true decision' (*Troilus*, II ii 172–3).

Polonius, Rosencrantz and Guildenstern are the most obvious victims of Hamlet's passion and of his commitment to quick revenge. Panic and impetuosity help to palliate the impression of these killings; but the self-righteous and specious arguments with which Hamlet justifies them do not. His contention that the death of Polonius fits into the scheme of divine providence is true in a strict theological sense, but is a point of which every murderer could avail himself. And Hamlet's promise (to his mother) that he 'will answer well' the death he has given Polonius (III iv 176–7) is eventually kept thus :

> What I have done
> That might your nature, honour, and exception
> Roughly awake, I here proclaim was madness.
> Was't Hamlet wrong'd Laertes? Never Hamlet.
> If Hamlet from himself be ta'en away,
> And when he's not himself does wrong Laertes,
> Then Hamlet does it not, Hamlet denies it.
> Who does it, then? His madness. If't be so,
> Hamlet is of the faction that is wrong'd ;
> His madness is poor Hamlet's enemy. (V ii 222–31)

'If't be so' indeed. Is it unfair to recall that when Hamlet promised Gertrude to 'answer well' for Polonius' death he also urged her most vehemently to confess herself to heaven and not to cover up her sins with the flattering and entirely erroneous belief that her moralising son was mad?

Hamlet is equally evasive and even more self-righteous concerning the deaths of Rosencrantz and Guildenstern :

> Why, man, they did make love to this employment ;
> They are not near my conscience ; their defeat
> Does by their own insinuation grow :
> 'Tis dangerous when the baser nature comes
> Between the pass and fell incensed points
> Of mighty opposites. (V ii 57–62)

Again, he protests too much : the leap into magniloquence in the last three lines seems designed to compensate for the flimsiness of the assumption that his victims were aware of Claudius' intentions. It is noticeable that Hamlet carries on immediately in the

same vein of moral certainty edged with protestation to assure
Horatio that Claudius must undoubtedly be murdered too :

> . . . is't not perfect conscience
> To quit him with this arm? And is't not to be damn'd
> To let this canker of our nature come
> In further evil? (V ii 67–70)

Morally neutral to a fault on such issues (but at least neutral),
Horatio makes no attempt to answer this (rhetorical) question. He
might well have observed, however, that the canker in human
nature is more likely to grow than to diminish when knavery is
answered with knavery. The way in which Hamlet introduces
ideas about conscience and damnation would certainly prompt
the scrupulous to think twice on the matter.

What Hamlet says to his mother and to Laertes concerning
his madness is one of several indications that his 'discourse' – his
speaking and reasoning – on fundamental issues has a strong element of self-contradiction, ambivalence, and ambiguity which,
in turn, emphasises the presence of unquestioned assumptions and
dubious conclusions. In his first soliloquy he rejects suicide because
it is condemned by divine law, but in his second he accepts revenge
although it, too, is condemned by divine law. In his third soliloquy
he assures himself that he is prompted to revenge 'by heaven and
hell' (II ii 580) : a most improbable liaison. And his final soliloquy
(prompted by Fortinbras) is one long tangle of contradictory argument, in which most of the errors of reasoning that have dogged
him since the appearance of his father's form coalesce and demand
scrutiny (IV iv 24–66).

Fortinbras' mighty expedition to seize a patch of ground not
worth the farming, at first provokes in Hamlet an attitude of complete disapproval : he sees it as the sign of a hidden moral ulcer
in the society from which it emanates. This is a reliable judgement,
for it corresponds with Horatio's picture of Fortinbras as a crude
strong-arm impatient to lead his makeshift army of 'lawless re-
solutes' into any enterprise that has a spice of adventure about
it (I i 86–100). But as soon as Hamlet begins to 'debate the issue'
of his own behaviour as well as Fortinbras', a change in his attitude towards the Norwegian prince begins to emerge ; and with
this change other uncertainties appear. Contrasting Fortinbras'

energy with his own apathy, and seeing in Fortinbras a spur to revenge, he then goes on to define the purpose of man's existence and to distinguish it from that of the beast: whereas the beast need only sleep and feed, man must use his God-given power of reasoning, his capacity for 'looking before and after', for perceiving causes and consequences. In the middle of this sequence of thought Hamlet's argument has moved in the wrong direction: the second contrast (man–beast) does not truly elaborate and reinforce the first one (Fortinbras–Hamlet); rather, it confuses and weakens it. Energetic action is undoubtedly antithetical to sleeping and feeding but it is not equivalent to the use of God-like reason; and failure to act energetically is not the same as allowing one's reason 'to fust . . . unused'. Once the notion of *homo sapiens* is introduced, Fortinbras becomes more liable to the charge of 'bestial oblivion' than Hamlet and ceases to have any value as a spur to right action.

In his next sentence Hamlet makes the remarkable admission that he does not know whether his inaction has been caused by too much or too little thinking. He then returns immediately to his confused use of Fortinbras as a spur to action and does so with a sentence in which verbal ambiguity serves to guide our response to the ensuing argument: 'Examples gross as earth exhort me.' By 'gross', Hamlet means 'obvious' or 'palpable'; but the other meaning (as in 'things rank and gross in nature') is necessarily operative in the context, since Fortinbras, instead of 'looking before and after' like a creature of reason,

> Makes mouths at the invisible event,
> Exposing what is mortal and unsure
> To all that fortune, death, and danger, dare,
> Even for an egg-shell. (IV iv 50–3)

Hamlet's phrasing here would encourage few rational men to emulate Fortinbras (it recalls the description of that other prodigiously active young man – Hotspur – who 'with great imagination/ Proper to madmen, led his powers to death,/And, winking, leapt into destruction'). But it is not intended by Hamlet to belittle Fortinbras; for as a result of taking Fortinbras as a model and a stimulus for action, Hamlet has moved for the moment into an attitude of unqualified approval and represents him in this same

sentence as 'a delicate and tender prince' inspired by 'divine ambition'. In thus exalting Fortinbras and depreciating himself,
Hamlet exhibits essentially the same kind of moral, logical, and
rhetorical confusion as is evident in Henry IV's praise of Hotspur
and dispraise of Hal (*I Henry IV*, III ii).

After he has spoken about Fortinbras' divine ambition, Hamlet
composes a definition of true greatness which is itself a memorable
epitome of the confusion that pervades the whole monologue:

> Rightly to be great
> Is not to stir without great argument,
> But greatly to find quarrel in a straw,
> When honour's at the stake. (IV iv 53–6)

The most acceptable reading of these lines seems to be: One
cannot achieve greatness in quarrelling over a straw except when
honour's at the stake. Such a notion is comprehensible enough at
first sight; but it has an inherent weakness which is greatly emphasised by the construction and phraseology of Hamlet's sentence.
'Rightly to be great is *not to stir* without great argument' [my
italics] can stand alone, and wins so much assent that we feel
compelled to ask for a definition of this 'honour' which allows a
great rule to be broken for a triviality. And the reduction of honour
in the next sentence to 'a fantasy and a trick of fame' makes such
a definition all the more necessary: in its context, honour is an
equivocal term. If, however, one ignores the fantasy and the trick
and supplies the orthodox Renaissance definition of honour as the
reputation for virtue or greatness, then one finds that Hamlet is
saying something like this: 'Rightly to be great is not to stir without great argument except when the reputation for greatness is
at the stake'; which differs very little from that other conspicuous
attempt to illuminate through definition: 'For, to define true
madness,/What is't but to be nothing else but mad?' (II ii 93–4).
It should be recalled that definition was a much prized logical
and rhetorical tool and that the qualities universally expected of
it were such that the unsatisfactory aspects of Hamlet's definition
could not have escaped notice. A definition, said Thomas Wilson
in *The Rule of Reason*, should contain no more than it defines;
it should express the very nature of the subject; it should contain
no ambiguity; and it should contain no obscurity.[20]

In listening to Hamlet's soliloquies, we, the theatre audience, cannot but be as puzzled as the stage audience which eavesdrops on his fourth soliloquy (III i 55) and attends to his every word and gesture in an effort to 'frankly judge' (III i 34) his mind. This phenomenon of puzzling speaker and puzzled audience is discussed, and its full implications explained, in a dialogue which follows immediately upon Hamlet's last and most confusing soliloquy. It introduces a scene in which dark speech combines with other abuses of the word to make manifest the coming disintegration of society : with the blank refusal of the frightened to speak and to listen ('dumbness'), the noise of the rabble, the rant of the avenger, and the ear-poisoning of the Machiavel. In terms of plot, this dialogue could easily be dispensed with ; but it greatly illuminates the form and meaning (and non-meaning) of the play, and it serves as an oblique but lucid and dispassionate comment on the words of the man who has just left the stage :

> *Queen.*   I will not speak with her.
> *Gent.*   She is importunate, indeed distract.
>   Her moods will needs be pitied.
> *Queen.*   What would she have?
> *Gent.*   She speaks much of her father ; says she hears
>   There's tricks i' th' world, and hems, and beats her heart ;
>   Spurns enviously at straws; speaks things in doubt,
>   That carry but half sense. Her speech is nothing,
>   Yet the unshaped use of it doth move
>   The hearers to collection ; they yawn at it,
>   And botch the words up fit to their own thoughts ;
>   Which, as her winks and nods and gestures yield them,
>   Indeed would make one think there might be thought,
>   Though nothing sure, yet much unhappily.
> *Hor.*   'Twere good she were spoken with ; for she may strew
>   Dangerous conjectures in ill-breeding minds. (IV v 1–15)

VII

A dialogue on the relationship between speaker and audience such as this fits easily into a play profoundly affected by the use of drama-within-drama. Although 'The Murder of Gonzago' and its preliminaries constitute the most striking feature of the play's dramatic content, this nevertheless is made up of ritual and theatrical ingredients in fairly even proportion. And the relationship between these two forms of the dramatic is finely established, too : the first allusion to acting occurs in Hamlet's comments on mourning and funeral, while in the fencing 'play' (IV vii 105 ; V ii 191, 199 etc.) – as in many formalised games – there is a distinct fusion of the theatrical and the ritual.

Ceremonies are abused in *Hamlet* from (literally) the first line to the last. The action commences with a breach in military rite, the nervous, oncoming guard challenging the man he is about to replace (I i 1–2); and it closes with the rite of a soldier killed on the field being given to a prince who has been poisoned at court in a game of foils : 'such a sight as this/Becomes the field, but here shows much amiss' (V ii 393–4). This blending at the close of two ceremonial disorders (the military and the funeral) is wonderfully artful, for it allows Shakespeare not only to echo the first words of the play but to sustain to the last the basic ritual disorder of the action : the individual violation, and the confusion, of funeral and marriage. The funeral rite at the close is improper not merely because it is unfitted to person and place; it should not have occurred at all : it is a mistake for a marriage.

The clash of funeral and marriage is visually defined at the beginning of the play by the melancholy figure of the hero dressed in a suit of solemn black amid a gay assembly of courtiers robed for marriage and coronation. Subsequently, Hamlet's mourning garb will be in complete disarray and it will be impossible to determine from it whether he is a grief-stricken son or a distracted lover. But here – contrary to appearances – his dress is what it should be and shows that he is the only one at court with a true sense of what is fitting. Although Claudius adroitly seeks to assure everyone that the style which he and Gertrude have encouraged agrees with decorum and that Hamlet's does not, the patronising concessions which he makes to Hamlet's interpretation of what is correct merely serve to damn the matrimonial mode in the eyes of any discreet observer :

Though yet of Hamlet our dear brother's death
The memory be green; and that it us befitted
To bear our hearts in grief, and our whole kingdom
To be contracted in one brow of woe ... (I ii 1–4 ; cf. I ii 87–8,
  90–1)

Insisting in deceptively smooth phrases that 'discretion fought with nature' (I ii 5) to demand that sorrow give way to joy, mourning to marriage, Claudius involves himself in a form of contradictory thought which leads inevitably to his glib approval of something so unnatural as 'mirth in funeral and . . . dirge in marriage' (I ii 12).

Claudius' allusion in these opening speeches to 'our sometime sister, now our queen' (I ii 8), and to 'my cousin Hamlet, and my son' (I ii 64), further emphasises that the marriage now being celebrated is one in which categories that are totally distinct in nature have become indistinguishable. But the untimeliness of the marriage is of greater importance in the total design of the play than its incestuous nature; for the haste with which Claudius and Gertrude unite necessarily involves an abuse of two ceremonies. The last line of Claudius' opening speech is, then, an omen of what is going wrong: 'Farewell; and let your haste commend your duty'; Claudius rules over a nation where haste is intimately related to a failure in the performance of duty. We have had hints of this even in the opening scene of the play, hints too which show that serious violations of time lead naturally to a confusion in ritual order: the impetuous Fortinbras' contempt for law and heraldry and his military threats have caused 'poste-haste and romage in the land', 'sweaty haste' which 'doth make the night joint-labourer with the day', and which, moreover, makes it impossible to 'divide the Sunday from the week' (I i 76–8, 107). Such remarks fall into a significant pattern when we hear Hamlet's most bitter comments on the marriage now being loudly celebrated:

> But two months dead! Nay, not so much, not two . . .
> O, most wicked speed to post
> With such dexterity to incestuous sheets!
> It is not, nor it cannot come to good. (I ii 138–58)

From Gertrude's 'original sin' other ceremonial disorders follow and, as a result, a history which begins with a marriage that has displaced a funeral concludes with funerals that have displaced marriage: such is the symmetry of tragic justice. The love of a Hamlet and Ophelia, we learn, has been sealed with all the solemnity of a betrothal ceremony; he has importuned her 'with love/ In honourable fashion' and 'given countenance to his speech . . ./

With all the holy vows of heaven' (I iii 110–11, 113–14). By hastily concluding that these 'sanctified and pious bonds' (I iii 130) are a mere 'rhapsody of words', Polonius destroys in its infancy the marriage of his daughter and the prince. In so doing, he accelerates a sequence of violent events which includes his own murder in circumstances requiring that he be buried 'hugger-mugger' (IV v 81). Echoing Hamlet, Laertes rages against the impropriety of his father's funeral rites :

> His means of death, his obscure funeral –
> No trophy, sword, nor hatchment o'er his bones,
> No noble rite nor formal ostentation –
> Cry to be heard, as 'twere from heaven to earth,
> That I must call't in question. (IV v 209–13)

But the ritual impropriety here is almost inoffensive in comparison to that which prevails at the funeral of the bride-to-be. Not only does the church curtail that ceremony on the debatable assumption that Ophelia committed suicide; the conduct of her lover and her brother ensures that it suffers from monstrous excess as well as deficiency.

The multiple improprieties of the scene are initiated by the first clown, a 'rude knave' who chats familiarly with the prince, sings discordantly in the grave, and knocks on the sconce with his 'dirty shovel' the probable remains of courtier, lady and lawyer (V i 95–6). It is ludicrously to the point that the grave-digger should sing a song so much concerned with what is 'meet' (V i 64, 94, 117), for he himself shows a conspicuous want of respect for person, time and place. But his indecorum is really the grotesque indecorum of 'the antic Death' himself, who grinningly reduces Alexander the Great and imperious Caesar to such base uses as loam for stop-gaps and beer-barrel bungs (V i 198–210).

Hamlet (as audience) introduces the funeral as one performed with 'maimed rites' – dubiously inferring that this really 'doth betoken' suicide (V i 213–14). What focuses all our attention on the ritual defects of the funeral, however, is the outraged questioning of Laertes : 'What ceremony else?' (V i 217); 'What ceremony else?' (V i 219); 'Must there no more be done?' (V i 229). An impression of even greater impropriety than actually occurs is induced by means of the 'churlish priest', who insists that in addition to being denied requiem music (V i 231–3), Ophelia should also have been buried in unsanctified ground and denied a final prayer : indeed, 'for charitable prayers,/Shards, flints, and pebbles, should be thrown on her' (V i 224–5). The discordant character of these words brings to mind the noise of kettle-drums, cannon and upspring reels which grated on the ear of Hamlet as he mourned for his father; and it anticipates further discord in requiem harmony at the close of the play.

The ranting and wrestling match on the coffin between the two chief mourners is the very nadir of ritual indecorum. At such a time, noise and violence would appal even the most uncultivated sensibility. But the offensiveness of Laertes and Hamlet here is intensified for more sensitive minds by the touch of insincerity and egotism in their conduct and by the confusion in roles and relationships : who is the distracted lover? Moreover, just as lover and brother are confused, so are marriage and funeral. Both forms of confusion, it should be noted, have been finely foreshadowed in the mad speech of Ophelia herself. When she sang : 'Larded with sweet flowers;/Which bewept to the grave did not go/With true-love showers' (IV iv 36–8), it was apparent that her mind would always be haunted by, but would never distinguish between, sorrow for a lost lover and a dead father. Rosemary is for remembrance (IV iv 172), but who was remembered? Correspondingly, this 'rose of may' (IV iv 154) did not know for certain – unlike Perdita (*Winter's Tale*, IV iv 127–34) – whether the flowers she carried were for Whitsun Pastorals and the rites of spring or for the burial of the one she loved. Now, at her own burial, the churlish priest unconsciously draws attention to a love–death, wedding–funeral confusion by reminding her brother that she was at least 'allow'd her virgin crants [garlands],/Her maiden strewments and the bringing home/Of bell and burial' (V i 226–8). As the Clarendon editors observed :

> In these words reference is . . . made to the marriage rites, which in the case of maidens are sadly parodied in the funeral rites . . . As the bride was brought home to her husband's house with bell and wedding festivity, so the dead maiden is brought to her last home 'with bell and burial'.[21]

But we are not entirely dependent on the alertness of two nineteenth-century editors for an understanding of Shakespeare's intentions here. Explicitly, and with ironic appropriateness, Gertrude herself comments on the ceremonial confusion as she scatters her flowers in the grave :

> Sweets to the sweet; farewell !
> I hop'd thou shouldst have been my Hamlet's wife;
> I thought thy bride-bed to have deck'd, sweet maid,
> And not have strew'd thy grave. (V i 237–40)

We are reminded here of the last four scenes of *Romeo and Juliet*, where the rosemary intended for the hastily arranged marriage of Paris and Juliet is placed on Juliet's body as she is carried (on the morning of the proposed wedding) to the vault, and where, at the end, the vault containing the disarrayed bodies of bride, groom and intended groom is strewn – literally and metaphorically – with broken flowers. Like Juliet, Ophelia is an almost child-like victim of that violent acceleration in the rhythm of nature caused by human rashness. She, too, is 'the sweetest flower of all the field' blasted by 'an untimely frost' (*Romeo and Juliet*, IV v 28–9); and it is cold comfort to be told that 'from her fair and unpolluted flesh' violets will spring (V i 233–4).

Claudius, Gertrude and Laertes being dead, the last moments of Hamlet are necessarily less discordant than Ophelia's; but the tragic cycle of ritual confusion is not yet complete – and besides, the first rash youth is still alive. As Hamlet lies dying in the arms of Horatio, speaking now some of the quietest and most beautiful verse he has ever spoken, his words are suddenly drowned in the tread of soldiers' feet and the crash of cannon : 'What warlike noise is this?', he asks – and then dies, with words of marvellous aptness : 'The rest is silence' (V ii 341, 350). However, although he has escaped from noise at last, the mourners and '*mutes* or *audience* to this act' (V ii 327) [my italics] have not. Horatio prays that angels will sing the prince's requiem, and in effect proceeds to do so himself. But what might have become a noble panegyric is lost in the clatter of kettle-drums, reduced to a dozen words, 'maimed' :

> Now cracks a noble heart. Good night, sweet prince,
> And flights of angels sing thee to thy rest ! [*March within.*]
> Why does the drum come hither?

It is, of course, the drum of the delicate and tender prince who, for the sake of an eggshell, will send twenty thousand men to their graves as if to their beds. Being so happily a soldier, he confidently orders a soldier's funeral for Hamlet, thinking it would be appropriate. But is it? Even he has enough wit to almost suspect that it is not – but no more:

> . . . and for his passage
> The soldier's music and the rite of war
> Speak loudly for him.
> Take up the bodies. Such a sight as this
> Becomes the field, but here shows much amiss.
> Go, bid the soldiers shoot. [*Exeunt marching; after the
> which a peal of ordnance are shot off.*] [22]

After which – possibly – the rest *is* silence.

Moving from rite to play, from form as social morality to form as entertainment, we begin to see in perspective Shakespeare's magnificent conception of his art as one which mirrors disorder in the drama of life and so achieves decorous indecorum. The crisis of the tragedy is caused by one kind of play, the catastrophe by another. Both plays are prepared for and staged with great deliberation. But the purpose for which they are presented is utterly at variance with the customary and natural end of all organised 'pastime' (III i 15; IV vii 33). On the sacrilegious principle that 'no place . . . should murder sanctuarize' (IV vii 128), they are designed not as joyous social events but as death traps. Their words and actions, therefore (like those in the burial of Ophelia), do not 'betoken' their true meaning; in fact, as each producer realises, only a bad performance can reveal the truth (III ii 137; IV vii 151). Moreover, both of these plays collapse before their natural conclusion, leaving the audience bewildered, horrified, 'mute': in each of them 'the mould of form' is 'blasted'.

The essential indecorum of the two plays is elaborated in detail. Prolix and bombastic, a laborious metrical sing-song, 'The Murder of Gonzago' is remote from the standards of literary excellence defined by Hamlet. Its actors, too, disregard their producer's advice. He has condemned dumb shows, but they insert one, and in such a way as to threaten his plan; he has also condemned over-acting, but now has to interrupt the performance to exhort the murderer to leave his damnable faces and begin (III ii 247). And, of course, his own antic disposition before and after the performance of the tragedy introduces a discordantly comic note : 'For if the king like not the comedy,/Why, then, belike he likes it not, perdy' (III iii 287–8). There is a deliberate and meaningful echo in this couplet of an analogous situation in *The Spanish Tragedie* :

> Now shall I see the fall of Babylon
> Wrought by the heavens in this confusion.
> And if the world like not this Tragedie,
> Hard is the hap of olde *Hieronimo*. (IV i 194–7)

Hieronimo is referring here to the tragedy which he plans to put on during Belimperia's wedding celebrations – a play which has been criticised as inappropriate for the occasion and which, like 'The Murder of Gonzago', constitutes 'poison in jest' (*Hamlet*, III ii 299).[23]

The preliminaries of the fencing 'play' serve to throw its impropriety into bold relief, Osric the gentleman on Laertes the gentleman being a superb lesson on the corruption of true courtliness : on what ought to be and is not. But more guidance than this is given before the unusually ritualistic game begins. Hamlet may be ironic when, in response to the messenger lord's comment – 'The queen desires you to use some gentle entertainment to Laertes before you fall to play' (V ii 197–9) – he remarks : 'She well instructs me'. His sentiment, however, is just, since the play in which he is about to perform is the last of the rites of chivalry : it is a 'brother's wager' (V ii 245) in which specifically 'gentle' virtues – courtesy, fair-play, magnanimity and the like – are publicly exhibited. But although both men recover their proper nobility in death, each of them embarrasses us before the end with words and gestures which are painfully unbecoming. Shaking hands with Laertes, and apologising for the murder of Polonius ('But pardon't, as you are a gentleman' – V ii 219), Hamlet exonerates himself completely in that speech, the stilted style and insincerity (or self-delusion) of which are worthy of Laertes at his worst. To the ignorant ear, Laertes' reply is as noble and courteous as Hamlet's apology : 'I do receive your offer'd love like love,/ And will not wrong it' (V ii 243–4); but as Guildenstern remarked on another occasion, 'Nay, good my lord, this courtesy is not of the right breed' (III ii 306–7).

VIII

My primary concern so far has been with form. As I have suggested, however, at the beginning of this chapter, and as becomes apparent whenever we examine speech which (in Claudius' phrase) 'lacks form a little', form itself is the revelation of meaning. It is to be hoped, therefore, that my analysis of (significant) formal disorder in *Hamlet* has helped to clarify not only the dramatic techniques of the play but also the ideas which it was intended to express. Indeed, the nature of my approach is such that an attempt to answer the evergreen question – What is the secret meaning of *Hamlet*? Why does it baffle? – is the next logical step. The attempt may, of course, seem as pretentious as it is logical, but it will at least have the virtue of brevity; for the answer I propose to give has been implied in almost everything I have already said.

In trying to answer this question, it is first of all necessary to bear in mind that similar questions are asked throughout the play itself : 'What may this mean . . .?' (I iv 52); 'What means your lordship?' (III i 106); 'What means this my lord? . . . Belike this show imports the argument of the play . . . Will 'a tell us what this show meant?' (III ii 133, 135,137); 'There's matter in these sighs, these profound heaves,/You must translate; 'tis fit we understand them' (IV i 1–2); 'What dost thou mean by this?' (IV iii 29); 'Alas, sweet lady, what imports this song?' (IV v 27); 'Pray you, let's have no words of this; but when they ask you what it means, say you this' (IV v 44–5); 'This nothing's more than matter' (IV v 171); 'What should this mean? . . . Or is it some abuse and no such thing?' (IV vii 48–9). But to all such queries in Elsinore there are no really satisfactory answers. The subjects of Claudius live in 'a strange-disposed time' when (to quote Shakespeare's Cicero) 'men may construe things after their fashion,/Clean from the purpose of the things themselves' (*Julius Caesar*, I iii 33–5); judgement being impaired or perverted, the signs are improper and meaning is necessarily elusive. And so with *Hamlet* and us. It has an enigmatic quality, not because its author or protagonist discovered that life is meaningless or absurd or that certain moral questions are inherently unanswerable; it is enigmatic, rather, because it is the sum total of all the imperfect signs, rites and plays which it contains and so – with daring logic – has been made to share in their indirect and reluctant surrender of meaning. Given a protagonist who swears his friends to silence, who talks mostly to himself and renounces dialogue on major issues, whose 'discourse of reason' is seriously flawed, and who cannot so much as formulate (though he *may* sense) what every rational Elizabethan would have considered to be his chief moral problem – given all this, the audience is compelled to rely on far more conjecture than would normally be required of it, and to be on its guard against grave misinterpretations: 'And you, the judges, bear a wary eye' (V ii 271). *Hamlet*, then, has been so written that the experience of the audience on the stage (which includes *all* the *dramatis personae*) is shared by that in the theatre. An exceptionally mimetic play, it enacts its own meaning, exemplifies its own moral. It is what it is about.

4

Othello, The Moor of Venice

I

When the urbane Lodovico comes to Cyprus on his diplomatic mission, he is soon caught in a social situation where his embarrassment quickly gives way to horror and incomprehension. The valiant general, who could impress the Venetian senate as much by his aristocratic bearing as by his military capabilities, rants and swears in public at his gentle bride, strikes her on the face, and coarsely dismisses her from the company. And when urged by Lodovico to call her back, he does so only to offer her mockingly to his guest in the manner of a procurer accommodating a client. Alone with the general's ensign, Lodovico asks :

> Is this the noble Moor whom our full Senate
> Call all in all sufficient? Is this the nature
> Whom passion could not shake, whose solid virtue
> The shot of accident nor dart of chance
> Could neither graze nor pierce? (IV i 261–5)

To which Iago truthfully responds : 'He is much chang'd'. A leader of rare dignity and self-control, a man whose nature is constant, loving, free and open, Othello has become 'eaten up' (III iii 395) with the violence and obscene suspicions of sexual jealousy – 'a passion', as Iago drily observes, 'most unsuiting such a man' (IV i 77).

Othello is another unique exploration of lost identity and transformation ; and also of false identity or assumed form. And in no other Shakespearian play are these cognate phenomena represented with such intense particularity. The political implications of the action being much slighter than in the other tragedies, the outlines of individual personality and the quality of personal experience are more sharply perceived. In the fall of Othello, Shakespeare finds a fable which allows him to narrow the focus of his dramatic imagination until it isolates the radical paradox of fallen human nature, the contradiction to which most of life's strange mutations can be traced. It is summed up in one memorable sentence in *The Rape of Lucrece* : 'In men, as in a rough-grown grove, remain/Cave-keeping evils that obscurely sleep' (ll 1249–50). God-like and bestial, Othello epitomises the Janus-like constitution of postlapsarian man. Even the title of the play suggests that he is irresolvable contrariety itself : he is 'all of the past trying to forget itself in a moment; he is Africa trying to breathe in Venice'.[1]

But however brilliantly individualised, Othello alone could not fully disclose the paradox of 'nature erring from itself' (III iii 231); to be complete, the picture needs Iago, the apparently average, decent man. It is not enough to show that a figure of Phidian grandeur and dignity can be metamorphosed into a beast almost in the twinkling of an eye; one must also confront the depressing truth that the final effect of centuries of civilised living – with all its art, its discipline and its cultivation of social feeling – may be to make the unreclaimed wilderness seem a kind and wholesome place. It is the discovery that 'there's many a beast . . . in a populous city/And many a civil monster' (*Othello*, IV i 63–4) which turns the bounteous and convivial Timon into the solitary Misanthropos who heaps scorching curses on mankind and its greatest city :

> Let me look back upon thee. O thou wall
> That girdles in these wolves, dive in the earth
> And fence not Athens. Matrons, turn incontinent.
> Obedience fail in children ! . . . Piety and fear,
> Religion to the gods, peace, justice, truth,
> Domestic awe, night-rest, and neighbourhood . . .
> Decline to your confounding contraries
> And let confusion live . . .
> Timon will to the woods where he shall find
> The unkindest beast more kinder than mankind.
> (*Timon of Athens*, IV i 1–4, 15–21, 35–6)

Lucrece confronts this same paradox when she finds that within the walls of Rome and her own house she is no better off than a white hind pleading 'in a wilderness where are no laws/To the

rough beast that knows no gentle right' (*Lucrece*, ll 543–5).
She perceives that 'outward honesty' and 'inward vice', honourable name and bestial behaviour are irreconcilables which are
often conjoined with the most disastrous results for men and cities :
as Tarquin to her, so Sinon to Priam and many a Trojan lord and
lady :

> Such devils steal effects from lightless hell ;
> For Sinon in his fire doth quake with cold,
> And in that cold hot burning fire doth dwell ;
> These contraries such unity do hold
> Only to flatter fools, and make them bold ;
> So Priam's trust false Sinon's tears doth flatter
> That he finds means to burn Troy with his water. (*Lucrece*, ll
> 1555–60).

Although akin to Lucrece in several respects, the gentle Desdemona does not arrive at this insight ; she dies understanding neither
the noble barbarian who murdered her nor the barbarous Venetian who tricked him into doing so. Honest, honest Iago is the
ultimate expression in Shakespeare of civil monstrosity and artful
barbarism.

II

'Perjur'd Sinon' deceived 'credulous old Priam' with 'an enchanting story' ; 'his words, like wildfire, burnt the shining glory/Of
rich-built Ilion' (*Lucrece*, ll 1521–4). The instrument which
Iago, like Sinon, borrows from civilisation in order to attack its
very foundations is verbal art. Considered as a whole, *Othello* is
arguably Shakespeare's most impressive tribute to the power of
speech and its importance in human life. Its hero 'commands/Like
a full soldier' (II i 34–5); and he does so because – whether he
addresses himself to judging senators, armed enemies or brawling
soldiers – he is a master of apt and arresting speech. His most
precious weapon is not a sword of Spain, the ice-brook's temper,
but shining words tempered to an exquisite proportion :

> Keep up your bright swords, for the dew will rust them.
> Good signior, you shall more command with years
> Than with your weapons. (I ii 59–61)

But Iago's magical transformation of Othello to beast, of love to hatred, and of harmony to discord means the reduction of eloquence to gibberish; so the most important (if not the most lasting) perception concerning the nature of speech which we acquire from this play is its treacherous and destructive potential. 'I had rather ha' this tongue cut from my mouth/Than it should do offence to Michael Cassio', protests Iago (II iii 213–14); and one cannot but reflect what a richer place the world would have been if that simple piece of surgery had been accomplished in time. Shakespeare, however, does not encourage such speculations, for they are at variance with his belief that the process of tragic causation is very complex indeed; more concretely, they would prevent us from recognising that Othello and Iago, although very different, are as closely related as two sides of one coin, and that Othello's own speech can be very dangerous even when it seems most spell-binding and sincere. In the end one can only say with security that *Othello* magnificently corroborates the Renaissance conviction that 'the tongue is the best and worst thing that is'.

Like that other Shakespearian Colossus, Julius Caesar, Othello 'hath the falling sickness', a fact which has obvious symbolic significance. His spiritual fall is physically enacted in the epileptic seizure brought on by an explosion of jealous passion. The immediate cause of this explosion lies in the staccato sequence of questions and non-answers which immediately precedes it:

> *Oth.* Hath he said anything?
> *Iago.* He hath, my lord; but be you well assur'd
> No more than he'll unswear.
> *Oth.* What hath he said?
> *Iago.* Faith, that he did – I know not what he did.
> *Oth.* What? what?
> *Iago.* Lie –
> *Oth.* With her?
> *Iago.* With her, on her; what you will.
> *Oth.* Lie with her, lie on her? We say lie on her
> when they belie her. Lie with her. Zounds,
> that's fulsome. (IV i 29–35)

Just before he becomes incoherent, Othello exclaims: 'It is not words that shake me thus' (IV i 42). But it is just that which shakes him so violently, nothing more substantial: a lie, an incomplete

sentence, and an equivocation. Flourished by the clown as well
as by the 'murderous coxcomb' (V ii 236) who shares his unamus-
ing sense of humour, 'lie' is for obvious reasons that most conspicuous quibble in a play about groundless sexual jealousy.[2] Whereas
lies and slanders seem to germinate everywhere in the rotten state
of Denmark, here they are incarnate in the person of Iago. His
identification with hell and devilry is apt not only because his
malevolence is joyful and unlimited but also because 'the father
of lies' is one of the oldest of Satan's titles. Iago resembles his
mythological prototype, too, in that he is an instinctive parodist,
mimic and arch-mocker – a perverted artist of the tongue whose
sole function is to discredit the Word.

The foundation of all Iago's achievements as a liar – his greatest
lie – is to convince the world that he is a personification of the
quality invoked at the start of the play by the deluded Brabantio :
'honest plainness' (I i 98). Throughout the play, no one is readier
than he to affirm the need 'to speak the truth', 'to be direct and
honest' (II iii 215; III iii 384), and to deal 'most directly' in the
affairs of a friend (IV ii 208). Privately, however, he conceives of
himself as a dark apothecary who pours poison into the ears of
trusting fools; and when he observes his poisonous medicine begin
to burn like mines of sulphur he watches the torments of his
victim with artistic satisfaction : 'Work on/My medicine, work.
Thus credulous fools are caught . . .' (IV i 44–5). There is probably
no greater testimony to the virulence of his poison than the way
in which it continues to affect Desdemona even after she has been
murdered. Her last words consist of a lie (or ambiguity) intended
to conceal Othello's guilt from Emilia; and Othello interprets
them as a sign that she is 'double damn'd' – 'a liar gone to burning
hell' (IV ii 39, V ii 132).

However, Iago's are not the only lies in the complicated web
of deceit which finally destroys himself, Emilia and Roderigo as
well as Othello and Desdemona. Out of loyalty to her husband,
and with little sign of being troubled by a sense of divided duties,
Emilia lies to her mistress about the lost handkerchief (III iv 20–1).
Later in the same scene she is present when Othello delivers his
cloudy warning to Desdemona about the importance of the handkerchief to their happiness. Yet when the distressed Desdemona
says : 'Sure there is some wonder in this handkerchief ;/I am most
unhappy in the loss of it', Emilia takes refuge in indignant general-

isations on the baseness of men (III iv 103–7; cf. III iv 156–63) – thus behaving exactly as her husband would in the same situation.

Emilia's awareness that the loss of the handkerchief and the estrangement of her lord and lady are connected is later emphasised in an oblique but powerful manner when she discovers that Iago did tell Othello 'an odious damned lie' (V ii 183). Rapidly fitting together the pieces of the plot, she exclaims : 'I think upon't. I think – I smell't. O villainy!/I thought so then. I'll kill myself for grief' (V ii 194–5). Feelings of guilt and remorse must surely contribute to her audacious determination to trumpet the truth in spite of the threatening swords of Othello (V ii 168) and Iago (V ii 227). Very consciously, she puts truth and loyalty to her mistress above obedience to her husband and indicates that despite appearances to the contrary such behaviour is proper :

Iago.   What, are you mad? I charge you get home.
Emil.   Good gentlemen, let me have leave to speak.
           'Tis proper I obey him, but not now.
           (V ii 197–9; cf. Vii 222–5).

Of course it is not the truth alone which redeems Emilia, but a willingness to die for it; and she knows that : 'So come my soul to bliss, as I speak true;/So speaking as I think, alas, I die' (V ii 253–4).

The manner of Iago's end is antithetical to Emilia's. Although he can spread no more false reports, he seals his damnation by refusing to lighten the darkness in which his motives lie hidden : he bequeathes to his contemporaries, not a lie, but an unanswered question, an everlasting riddle. Othello, on the other hand, is intensely conscious at death of the need for truthful, balanced and appropriate speech. Like Hamlet's, his last wish (V ii 341–58) is that his cause should be reported aright to the unsatisfied and that his wounded name should not be associated with 'a purpos'd evil' (*Hamlet*, V ii 233). But he does not ask for panegyric simplification. If Lodovico and Montano are to report his unlucky deeds in a manner which accords with truth and justice, they must (he indicates) avoid extremes : they must extenuate nothing nor set aught down in malice. They will thus report that he loved, but lacked wisdom in his loving; that he was not jealous by nature, but when wrought to jealousy, jealous in the extreme. They will set it down, too, that he was noble and base, a champion and an enemy of the state, unjust and just: at once a malignant Turk and an upright Venetian who punished him.

But this great speech-act, in which Othello strives heroically to acknowledge and even to resolve the contradictions in his nature, may not be without its imperfections. His claim that he loved 'not wisely but too well' has a touch of paradoxical confusion and is somewhat akin to his description of himself as 'an honourable murderer' (V ii 297); one accepts Timon's apologia much more readily: 'unwisely, not ignobly, have I given' (*Timon of Athens*, II ii 173). And it hardly seems fit that a Christian who righteously slew a circumcised dog of a Turk should slay himself, that a murderer should play the part of judge and executioner; the inturned sword gives a 'bloody period' to the noble speech and must make some feel (with Lodovico and Gratiano) that 'all that's spoke is marr'd' (V ii 360). But despite its possible imperfections (on which, I think, we are expected to ponder and debate), Othello's last marriage of word and deed fits a valiant general and proves that 'he was great of heart' (V ii 364). Seen in relation to the artistic requirements of the play, it is at once inevitable, flawless and superbly imaginative.

III

The tragic end of Othello and Desdemona is caused not just by untruth but by rashness or impatience as well. Emilia's reaction to Othello's charge that Desdemona 'was false as water' points very tersely to the combined operation of these two familiar Shakespearian evils: 'Thou art rash as fire to say/That she was false' (V ii 137–8). Iago's slanderous insinuations are really no more than sparks which derive all their destructive potential from the inflammatory human material on which they descend. Had the principal characters been able to 'sprinkle cool patience' on 'the heat and flame' of their distempers and impulses (*Hamlet*, III iv 123–4), and so allowed their judgements to function properly, their history would have had a happy ending. To say this much might well make one seem to fit the role of what Iago calls 'too severe a moraller' (II iii 288); yet it is an idea which Shakespeare plants in the audience's imagination as early as the third scene of Act I. Just before Brabantio storms into the senate with his band of armed supporters and his accusations of witchcraft, the duke and his colleagues are shown dealing with the news of the Turkish threat in a cool and rational fashion – sifting the evidence, pointing to inconsistencies, and distinguishing facts from exaggerations and fictions before deciding on a plan (I iii 1–19).

Rashness is firmly identified throughout the play with disregard for the circumstance of time and the law of timeliness. Indeed, apart from *Romeo and Juliet* and (perhaps) *The Winter's Tale*, no other play of Shakespeare's devotes so much attention to the fatal consequences of failure to keep time in word and deed. And no other play of Shakespeare's moves to such a hectic tempo. As A. C. Bradley has observed, there is no trace in Act IV of that pause which follows the crisis in the other great tragedies.[3] After Act III, Scene iii, where lies ignite passion beyond all control, the action advances towards its catastrophe with a compulsive movement which is simply the translation into deeds of Othello's desire for instant revenge. Aptly, Othello's movement toward the act of revenge is compared to that strange sea whose current is unaffected by sun and moon – the arbiters of time – and shows 'no retiring ebb' until it is swallowed up in the Propontic and the Hellespont (III iii 457–64).

One is made aware of the problem of timeliness chiefly through the moralisings of Iago, who habitually advises his victims to practise patience and 'keep time in all'.[4] This habit is an aspect of Iago's daring hypocrisy. It also exemplifies a kind of indecorum with which we are now well acquainted : gracious words in an ungracious mouth, wisdom from the coxcomb, morality from the Vice. And it is in keeping with the notion (not peculiar to Shakespeare among the Elizabethans) that the villainous and the vindictive frequently display far more interest in the appropriate and inappropriate moment – in Occasion, Opportunity and Importunity – than do ordinary folk :

> How poor are they that have not patience !
> What wound did ever heal but by degrees ?
> Thou know'st we work by wit and not by witchcraft ;
> And wit depends on dilatory time . . .
> Though other things grow fair against the sun,
> Yet fruits that blossom first will first be ripe.
> Content thyself awhile ! (II iii 358–66)

Iago here shows a regard for timeliness which is impressive but thoroughly perverted and misleading, for his reminder that ripeness is all is really designed to safeguard a plan which will ensure that the fruits of lawful love will very quickly become bitter as coloquintida (I iii 348). Hence the contradiction latent in the sentence 'Though other things . . .', and the accusing evidence of fundamental disharmony with 'proportion'd course of time' (*Lucrece,* l 774) unintentionally introduced by the spontaneous observation which follows immediately in the same speech : 'By the mass, 'tis morning ! /Pleasure and action make the hours seem short' (II iii 366–7). Liar and murderer, demon and supersubtle magician, Iago instinctively plies his business by night and so greets the sunrise exactly as a dedicated workman greets the dusk. All his plots to reduce 'justice, truth,/Domestic awe, night-rest' to their confounding contraries (Timon's curse is most apt here) are hatched and executed in the dark. Brabantio is incensed, Cassio is cashiered, Roderigo is killed, Cassio is wounded, and Desdemona murdered at night.

Iago continually utilises his understanding of the appropriate and inappropriate moment in order to provoke others to ignore time. Knowing that Cassio has no head for drink and that he is 'rash and very sudden in choler' (II ii 265) when intoxicated, he arranges events so that Roderigo easily finds 'occasion' and 'opportunity' to get him into trouble (II i 262, 277).[5] Then by lavishly praising Desdemona's generous nature, he gets Cassio to neglect the elementary rule that a suit to gain or regain favour must on no account be pressed inopportunely.[6] Cassio has scarcely been cashiered when he exhorts him : 'Importune her help to put you in your place again' (II iii 307). Then, having put Othello on the look-out for 'any strong or vehement importunity' (III iii 255) in his wife, he returns to Cassio with the original advice more forcefully urged : 'There is no other way; this she must do't . . . Go and importune her' (III iv 108–9). And Cassio's is certainly a most 'importunate suit' (IV i 26). Reminding Desdemona of 'service past', 'present sorrows', and 'purpos'd merit in futurity', he seems to compress all of time into one unbearable moment : 'I would not be delay'd' (III iv 115–18). Desdemona's sad reply – for Othello has now spoken 'so startlingly and rash' (III iv 79) about the handkerchief – carries an unintended criticism of Cassio's failure to keep time and relates it to the impending destruction of love's harmonies: 'Alas, thrice gentle Cassio!/My advocation is not now in tune' (III iv 123–4). Indirect but even more apt criticism of his behaviour is contained in his own brief conversation with Bianca after Desdemona has left him. He promises the importunate courtezan that he will visit her 'in a more continuate [Q1, 'convenient'] time' and so the scene concludes with Bianca's resigned comment: ' 'Tis very good; I must be circumstanc'd' (III iv 179, 202).

Iago's success in accelerating the natural pace of things is obviously dependent on the sensation, common to those who suffer in mind or body, that time has begun to move with unnatural slowness. Enstranged from Othello's love (III iv 119), Cassio is oppressed with 'leaden thoughts' (III iv 178) and experiences what Bianca complains of: 'lovers' absent hours,/More tedious than the dial eight score times. O weary reckoning' (III iv 175–7). But it is Othello who suffers most keenly from this sensation. And lest by any chance he should acquire the patience necessary to endure it, Iago reminds him of just how intolerable it is: 'But, O, what damned minutes tells he o'er,/Who dotes, yet doubts, suspects, yet strongly loves?' (III iii 173–4). Iago is instantly rewarded by Othello's exclamation, 'O, misery!', and by his assurance that he will never 'follow still the changes of the moon with fresh suspicions' (III iii 175, 181–3). Later, too, Othello abjures patience with the implicit claim that the sufferings of Job are trivial in comparison to the protracted agonies and humiliations of the cuckold – and he likens the cuckold to the figure at which the clock-hand points his slow but seemingly motionless finger (IV ii 48–56). Othello's crucifixion is to a clock-face.

IV

Characteristically, Shakespeare makes use of oaths and vows in this play in order to accentuate the presence of deceit and rashness. Iago's very first words consist of a protesting assurance beginning with an oath: ' 'Sblood ... If ever I did dream of such a matter, abhor me' (I i 4–6). His two speeches to Brabantio in the same scene commence with the oath (I i 87, 109) which Cassio and Othello will use as soon as they succumb to his influence and lose self-control: 'Zounds ['by God's wounds']'.[7] This particular oath marks Iago out as 'a profane wretch' (I i 115) rather than a deceiver, since in his foul way he is telling Brabantio the truth. His oaths 'by the faith of man' (I i 10) and 'by Janus' (I ii 33) – than which few more unreliable could be devised – are much more indicative of the role he is playing.

Perhaps, however, because the power of deceit is shown to derive from the hasty response it induces, the abuse of the solemn word serves almost entirely in *Othello* to heighten the impression of rashness. When Cassio rushes drunkenly into the brawl which precipitates the tragedy, he is 'high in oath' (II iii 227); and most of the fatal acts which succeed this one are similarly introduced.[8] After Desdemona's first petition to Othello on Cassio's behalf, both the suitor and his solicitor are fully aware that further pleading is superfluous: for this is how Emilia describes Othello's reaction:

> ... the Moor replies
> That he you hurt is of great fame in Cyprus
> And great affinity, and that in wholesome wisdom
> He might not but refuse you; but he protests he loves you,
> And needs no other suitor but his likings
> To take the safest occasion by the front
> To bring you in again. (III i 44–50)

But despite this assurance, and this most exact reminder about fitness of time, Cassio deems it 'fit' (III i 51) to importune Desdemona again;[9] and she in turn, showing more bounty than 'wholesome wisdom', solemnly promises that she will plead his cause irrespective of the circumstances of time and place:

> ... before Emilia here
> I give thee warrant of thy place. Assure thee,
> If I do vow a friendship, I'll perform it
> To the last article. My lord shall never rest;
> I'll watch him tame, and talk him out of patience;
> His bed shall seem a school, his board a shrift;
> I'll intermingle everything he does
> With Cassio's suit. Therefore be merry, Cassio;
> For thy solicitor shall rather die
> Than give thy cause away. (III iii 19–28)

Although Shakespeare's audience would not have known the exact outcome of events, it did at least know it was watching a

tragedy; and so, perceiving Desdemona's unthinking determination to marry contraries and ignore time and place, it could not
but have heard the funeral knell behind the charming gaiety of
'I'll perform it to the last article' and 'thy solicitor shall rather
die'.

One sign of the exquisite and meaningful symmetry of this play
is that the last as well as the first indiscretion whereby Desdemona
alienates Othello is enshrined in an oath. In itself this last oath is
irreproachable; but it constitutes one of those miniscule errors of
judgement which often shape destiny. It is prepared for in the
fourth act when Othello derides Desdemona's protestation of innocence in a manner which shows his deep (perhaps superstitious)
regard for the oath : 'Come, swear it, damn thyself . . . be double
damn'd – swear thou art honest' (IV ii 35–8). When he comes
later to kill her, Desdemona unfortunately needs no such prompt-
ing; and as soon as she swears to her innocence ('No, by my life
and soul'), the priest-like calm with which he has striven to speak
begins to crack :

> Sweet soul, take heed,
> Take heed of perjury; thou art on thy death-bed . . .
> Therefore confess thee freely of thy sin;
> For to deny each article with oath . . . (V ii 52–6)

But she goes on to confirm her innocence 'by the general warranty
of heaven' (V ii 63); and with that the calm priest becomes a
furious killer : 'O perjur'd woman! thou dost stone my heart,/
And mak'st me call what I intend to do/A murder, which I
thought a sacrifice' (V ii 66–8). The tide of passion is thus let
loose and Desdemona's life is cut short even more abruptly than
her husband had intended :

> *Oth.* Down strumpet.
> *Des.* Kill me tomorrow; let me live to-night.
> *Oth.* Nay, an you strive –
> *Des.* But half an hour!
> *Oth.* Being done, there is no pause.
> *Des.* But while I say one prayer!
> *Oth.* It is too late. [*Smothers her.*] (V ii 83–9)

– At which instant Emilia knocks on the door. As Chapman said,
'the use of Time is Fate'. And of words too, we might add.

This hideous error is itself the fulfilment of a very solemn vow. When Othello takes that vow he abjures all patience, just as Desdemona does when she promises to sue for Cassio; exactly like her, too, he wants his intention fulfilled 'within these three days' (III iii 476).[10] But there the resemblance ends, for nothing could be more different in quality than the kindly impulsiveness of Desdemona and the malignant, devil-controlled rashness of Othello. He surrenders himself wholly to 'blood' – to passion and violence – as well as to the smooth-tongued demon who stands at his ear. And the demon rewards him by kneeling at his side, mimicking his solemn style, and swearing to support his cause to the uttermost (III iii 455–73).[11]

v

This joint vow provides one of the more obviously ritual moments in a play where the ritual element is relatively inconspicuous, yet at the same time pervasive and very significant. It appears in two distinct but interdependent and interacting forms, the matrimonial and the judicial. For the purpose of clarification and emphasis, one might even say that the tragedy enacts the dissolution of two ritual processes which constitute the basis of social harmony itself and that, interwoven in the design of the whole work, there is a marriage structure and a justice structure. The marriage structure comprises the public announcement and secret performance of the wedding (I i); the tardy consummation of the marriage with epithalamic festivities (II i–iii); and, lastly, the bridal-chamber scenes (IV ii–iii; V ii), where the chamber becomes a brothel, the bride a whore, and the bridal bed destined for a 'tragic loading' (V ii 365) is always before the eye, a silent emblem of rare intensity. The justice structure is founded on three 'causes' (a recurrent word, and one with exact legal significance).[12] There is Brabantio's attempt to arrest Othello and have him punished by the state for practising witchcraft (I ii–iii); there is Othello's inquiry into the brawl, his punishment of Cassio, and the attempts of Cassio's solicitor to have the sentence revoked (II iii–III i; III iv); and, finally, there is the case of 'wronged Othello' against Desdemona and Cassio, in which adultery is first 'proved' and then punished (III iii; IV i–ii; V).

This analysis would be sufficient in itself to remind the reader that in *Othello* – as in *Richard III* and *Hamlet* – 'the form of law' (*Richard III*, III v 42) and the form of marriage are botched, degraded and destroyed. What such an analysis does not show, however, is that in both forms the cause of disorder can be traced to the abuse of the play's two fundamental norms, timeliness and truth. In terms of Elizabethan thought there is, therefore, a remarkable coherence in the play's philosophical structure: for Time, which governs courtship and marriage, was held to be the father of truth and therefore of justice; [13] and, of course, truth conceived as loyalty and candour is manifestly as necessary for harmony in marriage as is the absence of lies and indirection in the pursuit of justice. But even more remarkable than the coherence and clarity of the play's essential ideas is the fact that they are continuously embodied in an imaginative construct of great complexity and symmetry: there is scarcely a turn of the plot or a speech which is not informed by them. The dramatic art which flowers in *Othello* is an astonishing amalgam of cognition and creativity. Such, however, is the respect shown by Shakespeare for the economy and intensity proper to the drama that some of the subtlest aspects of this achievement are in danger of going unnoticed.

The execution of Othello's sentence on Desdemona is marred even at the last moment by haste and misapprehension; Othello may have a 'flaming minister' by his side but, really, the same symbolic phrase applies to this deed as to the attempted execution of Cassio: 'Kill men i' the dark!' (V i 63). What is less likely to catch attention is that at the other end of the play the cause of Desdemona's father against her husband is marred in exactly the same fashion. Brabantio firmly believes that his is 'not an idle cause' (I ii 95) and fully intends to bring 'the justice of the state' against Othello (I i 140). Whether he has a right to expect the state to punish Othello may be open to dispute; but no one can dispute what is of considerable importance in the ironic unfolding of events: that his wrongs compared to Othello's are as substance to mere shadow. And unlike Othello, he does at least submit his case to public consideration and the impartiality of the law.

There are plenty of hints in the text as to how Brabantio should have pleaded and as to what he could reasonably have asked the state to do. He could have begun by reminding the senate in suitably indirect and modest terms that he was not for nothing its most powerful and respected magnifico.[14] He could then have claimed that the foreign general employed by the state of Venice had married his daughter not only without his consent but without even bothering to discuss the matter or indicate his intentions, thus acting with utter contempt for the dues of hospitality and 'the sense of all civility' (I i 134). Iago obviously thought that with some such charge as this Brabantio could – in normal circumstances – have either divorced Othello or put some form of legal 'constraint and grievance' upon him (I ii 14–17). Othello himself, we must remember, attaches paramount importance to the good name and high social standing of the person offended when, as military commander and governor of Cyprus, he punishes Cassio for his part in the brawl. (And, of course, he is profoundly moved by the affront to his own good name when he decides to punish Desdemona and Cassio with death.) But instead of arguing along these lines, Brabantio hotly jumps to conclusions, is overcome by bigotry and superstition, and accuses the black man of practising witchcraft on his daughter. It is no wonder that Othello can almost contemptuously reduce his wife's father to 'this old man' (I iii 78), while at the same time treating the plaintiff's less influential colleagues with the utmost respect : 'Most potent, grave, and reverend signiors,/My very noble and approv'd good masters' (I iii 76–7). Splenetic old age has little hope of winning much sympathy when lodging a complaint of a personal nature against the brave and the dignified : at such times, most people tacitly give way to the proposition that 'age is unnecessary'.

And never was the distraught Brabantio less necessary to the state, or the calm Othello more necessary, than at this very moment. The old man's cause is botched not only because of his own rash judgement and conduct but also because it is a personal matter which becomes confused with 'state affairs' (I iii 72) : and as the rest of the play testifies, that is a confusion which is not conducive to social order and justice. It was far from Brabantio's wish to have Othello tried in the middle of the night. His intention was to have him imprisoned until 'fit time/Of law and course of direct session' called him to 'answer' (I ii 85–7). But while he is trying to effect the arrest he learns to his astonishment that the duke is in council ('In this time of night !' – I ii 94) and that he himself and Othello have both been summoned on state affairs. The time therefore is out of joint, and, as such, it favours Othello (in the short-term view of things). The general's 'haste-post-haste appearance on the instant' has been requested by the senate (I ii 37–8; cf. I ii 40–4), and even before he arrives at the senate Iago can speak of him as being already 'embark'd/With . . . loud reason to the Cyprus wars/Which even now stands in act' (I i 150–2). Moreover, after Brabantio's problem has been disposed of, the senators tell Othello that he 'must away to-night', for 'th' affair cries haste,/And speed must answer it' (I iii 276–7). In such circumstances, it is most unlikely that pertinent questions will be asked or relevant answers given on a private grievance such as Brabantio's.

Brabantio is 'out-tongued', then, not just by the services which Othello has done the signiory, but even more by those which are now expected of him. As Iago remarks (with evident truth), the senators simply cannot discard Othello at this time since they do not have another of his fathom to lead their business (I i 150–4). In responding to Brabantio's charge, Othello grandly considers the possibility of a 'sentence' being passed on him (I iii 119). The duke admittedly does not condone his behaviour and even goes so far as to describe what has happened as *'this mangled matter'* [my italics] (I iii 173). But the only 'sentence' (I iii 199, 212, 214, 216) which he musters consists of sententious consolation offered to Brabantio. It is undoubtedly delivered in a suitably formal style, but its platitudes verge on contradiction and its metronomic couplets recall the brittle elegance of Richard II's judicial pronouncements. Brabantio (who bears a curious resemblance at this point to the aged Gaunt) dismisses it as valueless : it does nothing whatever to shake his conviction that 'what's to come' of his 'despised time is nought but bitterness' (I i 162–3).[15] Once we are aware of the problem of justice, we cannot but recall this scene when Othello is about to pronounce judgement on Cassio for unsoldierly and uncivil behaviour : the witness (Iago), he affirms, 'doth *mince this matter,*/Making it light to Cassio' [my italics] (II iii 239–40). If the 'mangled matter' and the 'minced matter' are studied in conjunction, it will be found (among other things) that the epithets are interchangeable.

Othello's sentence on Cassio might possibly have been different if he had examined the facts when Cassio's head was clearer and his own 'collied' judgement in better order : if he had waited until daylight. At any rate, this nocturnal sentence is 'as a grise or step' (I iii 200) to the sentence of death which he passes in secret on his wife and the degraded lieutenant. In executing the sentence on Desdemona, Othello tries very hard to exclude all suggestion of haste and unreason and to act with ceremonial dignity. His speech at the bedside of the sleeping Desdemona is ravishingly beautiful in the stately, strange and deep-toned manner which is peculiar to him. But like Faustus' enchanted, self-approving praise of Helen (*Doctor Faustus*, II vi 15–17), and like the enchanting songs of Phaedria and Acrasia in *The Faerie Queene* (II xii 74–5), it is language of that special and complex kind at which the great narrative and dramatic poets of the Renaissance excelled : the language of delusion. Utterly different as it is from the style of 'I'll chop her into messes', it serves the important function of restoring pity and even respect and admiration for Othello. But it serves no less to emphasise that his noble mind is the victim of an outrageous lie. The image of himself and of his action which he presents here is no more authentic than the promise of everlasting joy held out by the enchantresses of *The Faerie Queene* and the devil-Helen of *Doctor Faustus* : it is hellishness presented under a 'heavenly show' (see II iii 340–1), savagery 'putting on the mere form of civil and humane seeming' (II ii 236–7). In this speech, Othello insists that his only motive in killing Desdemona is 'the cause . . . the cause . . . the cause' (V ii 1–3). He sees himself as the personification of justice and Desdemona as the type of exquisitely sensuous but adulterate beauty whose sins could not be named in the presence of the chaste. He recognises the seductive power of her beauty, but promises to resist it : he will not allow her to 'persuade Justice to break her sword' ; nor will he allow her to 'betray more men'. The religious overtones of his ceremonial language greatly enhance this pose of incorruptible altruism : the judge is also a high priest who offers a sacrifice to Heaven for the good of mankind, a flaming minister addressing himself to the chaste stars.

The Othello seen by the waking Desdemona, however, is not an impersonal minister of earthly and divine justice but a frightening man who says 'Hum', whose eyes roll fatally, and who gnaws his nether lip as if some bloody passion shook his very frame. And the contrast between the self-possessed judge and the bewildered wife-killer who cries out 'My wife, my wife ! what wife ? I have no wife' is enormous. When Emilia arrives at the door and calls to him, it is as if a spell has been broken : the devil-inspired tra-

vesty of civil and religious ritual – the rhapsody of words – is at
an end; and it remains only for Othello to speak 'in most comely
truth' (*Much Ado*, V ii 7) and to judge and punish himself as best
he can.

The 'execution' of Desdemona marks the completion of a plan
which was conceived on the very night of her wedding : a plan
to destroy 'sanctimony and a frail vow betwix an erring barbarian
and a super-subtle Venetian' (I iii 353–4).[16] In so far as Desdemona's love bears it out even to the edge of doom, Iago's attack
on the marriage rite is a failure. But the rite is made up of two
vows; Othello alters when he alteration finds, and so what seemed
a uniquely beautiful marriage of true minds is shattered. *Othello*,
therefore, is a play in which the great promise of nuptial song or
epithalamion – the promise of grace, harmony and a long, fruitful
life – is violently frustrated.

The cause of this tragedy cannot be located solely in the combination of Iago's malevolence, Othello's jealousy and Desdemona's well-intentioned importunities. Quietly but clearly,
Shakespeare shows that the marriage – as a rite, a formalised
human relationship, and a microcosm of society – was defective
even before Iago's malevolence turned against it : that it was
destroyed by deception and haste because it began in such. There
are several reasons why Shakespeare does not dwell heavily on this
point. One is that he has to get on as quickly as possible with the
complicated business of Iago's intrigue. The original fault has
thus to be treated rather in the same way as Richard II's com-
plicity in the murder of Gloucester, Caesar's killing of Pompey,
or Gertrude's adultery : that is, as a part of the history which
cannot be dramatised but must be considered, an element of the
past which explains the inexorable workings of Nemesis or cosmic
retribution. Another reason is that Shakespeare wishes to make
the strongest possible contrast between the purity and constancy
of Desdemona's love and the corruption and inconstancy ascribed
to it by Iago : strong emphasis on any fault in Desdemona which
was more than 'ignorant sin' (IV ii 73 ; cf. III iii 50) would conflict
with this dramatic purpose. A third and very simple reason is
that the mere facts concerning the courtship and wedding, together with the manifest importance in the play of deceit and
untimeliness, would have been sufficient to encourage a contemporary audience to make the relevant deductions.

We come then to the fact that Desdemona did less than her duty to an affectionate father and Othello less than his to a very distinguished nobleman who 'lov'd' and 'oft invited' him to his home. To suggest that this fact is critically significant is to run the risk of being pigeon-holed for all time with Thomas Rymer – a fate more daunting to the average critic than 'pressing to death, whipping and hanging'. But although it is a viewpoint requiring that we render admiration rather than idolatry to Desdemona (as well as Othello), it is also one which in the present context should serve to enhance rather than to diminish the sophistication of the play's dramatic art. The first piece of evidence in its favour is to be found in the alterations made by Shakespeare to the original story. In Cinthio's novella, Desdemona's parents are both alive and it even seems fair to assume that they have other children; but Shakespeare deliberately makes Desdemona an only child and her father an elderly widower whose affections are wholly bound up in his daughter. In Cinthio, too, the parents suffer no grave emotional shock because of the marriage, even though they were opposed to it; but in Shakespeare the marriage kills Brabantio ('Thy match was mortal to him, and pure grief/ Shore his old thread in twain') – and news of his death is significantly delayed until the very moment when the violent end of the marriage is shown to the world (V ii 208–9). In the original story, moreover, Desdemona's parents know in advance of her intention to marry. There is no hint whatever of the deception practised by Shakespeare's lovers – a deception magnified by Brabantio's hospitable treatment of Othello and by Desdemona's shy and timid disposition. Judging by Brabantio's reaction to the news of the elopement, it is the shock of unexpected betrayal – 'O, thou deceivest me past thought!' (I i 166) – even more than the unsuitable nature of the relationship which causes him to die of grief.

These changes were not made simply in order to give impetus to the play or to heighten its tragic effect. For we are clearly urged to consider whether the original deception is not the first of a series of concatenated deceptions which culminate in the tragic loading of the marriage bed. At the end of the senate meeting, Brabantio bitterly warns Othello: 'Look to her, Moor . . . she has deceiv'd her father and may thee' (I iii 292–3). At that point, the remark means nothing to the happy and confident Othello; and, of course, it is totally erroneous as a prediction of Desdemona's behaviour. But it is an elementary fact of human experience – and one to which Shakespeare often returns – that past disloyalty (to anyone) is often the cause of present distrust. So when Iago later says to Othello, 'She did deceive her father marrying you', Othello accepts this as an undeniable and significant truth ('And so she did'), and thus advances one 'grise or step' nearer to complete acceptance of the great lie (III iii 210, 212).

The rash indifference to time which also puts a blemish on the marriage from its inception is given tragic implications by its connection with the recurrent word 'violence'. *Othello* may 'not be . . . a second tragedy of "violent delights" leading to "violent ends" '; [17] but its affinity with *Romeo and Juliet* is far from trivial. When Iago says to Roderigo concerning the marriage, 'It was a violent commencement in her and thou shalt see an answerable sequestration' (I iii 355–7), and again, 'Mark me with what violence she first lov'd the Moor' (II i 219–20), we are not to dismiss what he says as the cynical geometry of a devilish behaviourist, for up to a point he is echoing Desdemona's own words :

> That I did love the Moor to live with him
> My downright violence and storm of fortune
> May trumpet to the world. (I iii 248–50)

In the scene which follows this remark, moreover, Shakespeare hints that there is a connection between her downright violence in love and her storm of fortune, since we learn there that the ships in which she and Othello sailed were 'parted with a foul and violent tempest' (II i 34). The connection is clear enough when Othello decides to cast her off to a fate much worse than 'beggarly divorcement' (IV ii 159) and promises to do so with the 'violent pace' of that ebbless Pontic sea (III iii 461).

The dangerous impetuosity in love which can be summed up in the explicit Chapman's phrase as 'general marriage-violence' (*Hero and Leander*, VI 103) is dramatised in *Othello* with a most exact but economic attention to significant detail. The wedding takes place not at midday (as in 'Epithalamion') but at 'the odd-even and dull watch o' th' night (I i 124). Worse still, news of it is broken to the bride's father and to the city in the foul language of Iago and to the unmusical accompaniment of what approaches

a civic riot. Iago and Roderigo bellow outside the magnifico's
house,

> ... with timorous accent and dire yell
> As when by night and negligence, the fire
> Is spied in populous cities. (I i 78)

– and when he has responded to their 'terrible summons' (I i 83)
they urge him to 'awake the snorting citizens with the bell' (I i 91).
Brabantio indignantly protests : 'This is Venice. My house is not
a grange' (I i 106–7); but what Iago and Roderigo subsequently
say to him suggests that this distinction is now in doubt. Iago
brutally presents a carter's view of the union of the two lovers
(the old black ram and the white ewe, etc.). By contrast, Roderigo
skilfully appeals to urban and urbane standards of behaviour in
order to insinuate himself into Brabantio's favour, and in this way
(perhaps unintentionally) formulates an indirect criticism of
Othello and Desdemona. Addressing the magnifico as 'most grave
Brabantio' and 'most reverend signior' (I i 94, 107) – a fine anticipation of the way in which Othello treats Brabantio's 'potent,
grave, and reverend' colleagues, but not Brabantio – Roderigo
admits that if Desdemona had not 'made a gross revolt,/Tying her
duty, beauty, wit and fortunes/In an extravagant and wheeling
stranger', and if Brabantio were not ignorant of the fact, then he
himself could rightly be accused of ignoring 'manners' and 'the
sense of all civility', of 'playing' and 'trifling' with Brabantio's
'reverence', and of deluding him in such a manner as to deserve
'the justice of the state' to be let loose on him (I i 130–41).

The consummation of Desdemona's union with Othello is even
more obviously out of tune with time and attended by violence
than is the actual wedding. It is necessarily postponed by the haste-
post-haste of military affairs; which is bad enough. But just where
and when the consummation should take place is a question of
ritual propriety which choice can still determine; and the failure
to deal with this question properly must be construed more as a
tragic error than a consequence of the disjointed times. Othello
tentatively raises this issue when, having accepted his new duties
with what he calls 'a natural and prompt alacrity', he adds a personal request :

Most humbly, therefore, bending to your state,
I crave fit disposition for my wife;
Due reference of place and exhibition;
With such accommodation and besort
As levels with her breeding. (I iii 235–9)

As M. R. Ridley has noted, this pompous speech is 'overloaded with words expressing "suitability" – *fit, due, besort, levels,* and perhaps *accommodation*'.[18] And there are good dramatic reasons for such overloading. Like Othello's subsequent observation to Desdemona, 'We must obey the time' (I iii 300), it serves as an ironical reminder that he has not always been so conscious of decorum. Furthermore, it helps us to appreciate that the duke's response to Othello's request is guided by an impartial estimate of what is proper in the circumstances; and that response is unambiguous and concise: 'If you please,/Be't at her father's' (I iii 239–40). But neither Brabantio, nor Othello, nor Desdemona will have it so. And of the three it is Desdemona who shows most opposition to a proposal which carries in it the germ of reconciliation and salvation: it is as if Perdita were to reject Camillo's plan to save her and Florizel from the perils of that 'wild dedication' of themselves 'to unpath'd waters, undream'd shores' (*Winter's Tale,* IV iv 558–9). Arguing that she would rather not put her father 'in impatient thoughts by being in his eye', Desdemona (the impatient) goes on to speak of her downright violence in loving the Moor and of her unwillingness to be denied 'the rites' of love in the 'heavy interim' of his absence: she would rather go to sea and to war than be left at home as 'a moth of peace' (I iii 248–59). Othello supports this request by reassuring the senators (the irony deepens now) that they need have no worries about him ever allowing matrimonial affairs to corrupt and taint his great business to the state.

But however much the general might protest to the contrary, 'our General's wife is now the General' (II iii 305; cf. II i 74), and he himself will greet her at Cyprus as 'my fair warrior' (II i 180). And when her importunate interferences in a military and civil affair have had the effect desired by Iago, she will miserably and not ineptly describe herself as an 'unhandsome warrior' (III iv 152) – the epithet meaning 'not living up to my character, not proper, not fitting'.[19] Because of the domestic–military confusion

entailed by her decision to leave Venice, she quickly discovers
that she must 'not look for such observances/As fits the bridal'
(III iv 150–1) when at Cyprus. And this sad truth is doubly emphasised by the gracious nature of the welcome extended to her
on arrival and by the consciously formal way in which the epithalamic festivities of her first night with Othello are introduced.
The public proclamation read on Othello's behalf announces that
'sport and revels' are to be enjoyed by the island in celebration of
the general's 'nuptials' as well as of the Turkish fleet's 'perdition':
'All offices are open and there is full liberty from this present hour
of five till the bell hath told eleven' (II ii 7–14). The ethical idea
implicit in this proclamation dominates Othello's subsequent conversation with Cassio and Desdemona. Cassio must 'look . . . to the
guard to-night'; indeed we must all (adds Othello) 'teach ourselves
that honourable stop,/Not to outsport discretion' (II iii 1–3). And
to Desdemona, Othello says: 'Come, my dear love,/The purchase
made, the fruits are to ensue;/That profit's yet to come twixt
me and you' (II iii 8–10). As he goes to consummate his union,
therefore, Othello is conscious that the joys and fruitfulness of this
'good night' (II iii 7, 11) and of marriage itself presuppose respect
for natural order and moral duty as shown particularly in the law
of timeliness. With a becoming blend of gravity and joy, in public
and in private, he evokes the richly decorous and traditional norms
celebrated in epithalamic literature. We are to perceive that his
union with Desdemona properly belongs to a world in which the
civilised gaiety of the marriage evening is succeeded by the sacred
stillness of the night and the ineffable harmony of love's bliss:

> . . . let stil Silence trew night watches keepe
> That sacred peace may in assurance rayne,
> And tymely sleep, when it is tyme to sleepe,
> May poure his limbs forth on your pleasant playne . . .[20]

But although military considerations make respect for silence and
the night watch doubly important in Cyprus, pandemonium is on
the point of breaking loose before eleven o'clock. Working like
the mischievous spirit of darkness that he is, Iago has succeeded
in making the 'night of revels' (II iii 39) thoroughly raucous and
intemperate. Officers of the watch have been 'fluster'd with flowing cups' and turned from 'noble swelling spirits/That hold their

honour in a wary distance' into 'a flock of drunkards' (II iii 49–
55). Iago himself has sung his drab drinking songs to the accompaniment of clinking pewter. The refined Cassio has become a
maudlin and aggressive fool and his good name has been carefully
called in question by Iago's remarks to Montano (II iii 113–36).
After the watch hour has begun, and presumably when Othello
and Desdemona are 'like bride and groom, divesting them to bed'
(II iii 172), the brawl starts, the alarm bell begins its 'dreadful'
clamour, and the affrighted islanders are no doubt convinced that
the Turks have returned. The appearance of Othello and Desdemona in the midst of all this confirms that the precarious balance
between the domestic and the military worlds has broken down.

Although he angrily warns that his best judgement is in danger
of being darkened by passion, Othello displays enormous authority
in dealing with this outbreak of 'violence' (II iii 196): manifestly,
he has in his countenance and manner that which men would 'fain
call master'. But the past is beginning to catch up with him and so
the words of his mighty 'rebuke' (II iii 201) have a much wider application that he is aware of, putting him among those who are at
fault. Taking his cue from Iago's,

> ...gentlemen –
> Have you forgot all sense of place and duty?
> Hold! the General speaks to you; hold, hold for shame!
> (II iii 158–60)

Othello delivers a trenchant lecture on duty and decorum, finely
adjusted to the circumstances of this particular deviation from
the sense of all civility. His general point is that the dreadful bell
and what it signifies 'frights the isle/From her propriety' (II iii
167–8).[21] But he particularises with biting force, telling those who
began 'this barbarous brawl' that they have acted with a complete lack of 'Christian shame', have 'turn'd Turks', and even done
to one another what 'Heaven hath forbid the Ottomites' (II iii
162–4) – a suggestion of the enemy within which looks forward
to murder and suicide and back to Brabantio's warning: 'For if
such actions may have passage free,/Bond-slaves and pagans shall
our statesmen be' (I ii 98–9). Since he can get no explanation from
Cassio as to why he has 'forgot' (II iii 180) himself, Othello turns
to Montano, expressing astonishment that one so 'worthy' and

so 'civil' should exchange his noble reputation 'for the name of a night-brawler'. And then, finding that Montano can give no satisfactory explanation of what has happened, he resumes general condemnation and explains with particular reference to time and place why the barbarous brawl begun by Christian gentlemen and officers is so very improper :

> What ! in a town of war,
> Yet wild, the people's hearts brim full of fear,
> To manage private and domestic quarrel,
> In night, and on the court and guard of safety !
> 'Tis monstrous. (II iii 205–9)

In bringing his 'gentle love' back to bed, Othello resignedly explains to her that it is 'the soldiers' life/To have their balmy slumbers wak'd with strife' (II iii 242, 249–50). But what is customary for him is not for her; and it is 'monstrous' that a gentle bride should be raised by violence on such a night.

After this, the private and public spheres decline to their confounding contraries until the general loses his 'occupation', becomes an eavesdropping cuckold, and finally takes over from those who disturb night-rest with violence. In some way or other, Desdemona had begun to see that it would all lead to the ultimate confusion of loving and killing, of marriage and funeral. 'Prithee, tonight', she says to Emilia, 'Lay on my bed my wedding sheets – remember' (IV ii 105–6); and later, before singing her mournful song, she adds : 'If I do die before thee, prithee,/Shroud me in one of those same sheets' (IV iii 23–4). Perhaps because of Emilia, she belittles her premonition : 'How foolish our minds are !' (IV iii 22). But she seems strangely resigned and calm ; and somewhere in the shadows of the mind she may have arrived at – or come very near to – an intuitive understanding and acceptance of the mysterious paradoxes of her fate. Why should so noble a lord turn so quickly into an erring barbarian, a Barbary horse ? Why should a maiden never bold fall violently in love with what she feared to look on and ignore 'matches/Of her own clime, complexion, and degree,/Whereto we see in all things nature tends?' (III iii 231–3). There may be an answer to such questions in the circumstances of the mournful song which on the night of their deaths insists on being sung : 'That song to-night/Will not go from my

mind' (IV iii 29–30). In singing it, the gentle Desdemona hangs
her head all at one side and becomes for a while 'a maid call'd
Barbary' (IV iii 25).

VI

'What's in a name?' asked Juliet. So far as this play is concerned,
one might begin to answer the question by noting that Desdemona's own name, based on the Greek word δυσδαίμων (ill-
fated') was, as Cinthio remarked, a name of ill-omen ('nome
d'infelice augurio').[22] An 'ill-starred wench' (V ii 275), Desdemona
can speak of 'my wretched fortune' (IV ii 129) as something she
has known all her life. In Cinthio's collection of tales, the characters in the next story blame her parents for giving her such an
unlucky name. In the play, however, it is certainly intended to be
a beautiful name ('Sweet Desdemona, O sweet mistress. . . !'),
one which becomes her in every respect, fitting her nature as well
as her role and destiny. Desdemona's real misfortune is that when
she marries the man she loves and to whom she proves heavenly
true she acquires a name or 'addition' than which none could be
more inappropriate – so inappropriate indeed that she can hardly
bring herself to utter it :

> *Des.* Am I that name, Iago?
> *Iago.* What name, fair lady?
> *Des.* Such as she says my lord did say I was.
> *Emil.* He call'd her whore. A beggar in his drink
>   Could not have laid such terms upon his callat . . .
> *Des.* I cannot say whore.
>   It does abhor me now I speak the word ;
>   To do the act that might the addition earn,
>   Not the world's mass of vanity could make me. (IV ii 119–
>   22, 162–5)

But Desdemona is not the only character in the play whose
name and destiny are closely linked in one way or another. Cassio
acts in a degrading manner, forfeits his reputation, and is stripped
of his military office and title ; and it is his despairing conviction
that what remains of him is bestial after he has lost his good name
(II iii 256) which makes him importune Desdemona. Othello's
regard for reputation, as we have already noted, is intense. 'Her

name', he exclaims, 'that was/As fresh as Dian's visage, is now begrim'd and black as mine own face' (III iii 390–1). That is the Second Quarto reading; in the First Quarto and the First Folio, Othello says 'My name', not 'Her name'. Although both readings are acceptable, the first ('My name') is probably the authentic one, since Othello's impulse to kill is motivated hardly at all by the shame which has fallen on his wife's name and very much by that which has fallen on his own. To be given the name of a cuckold, to be the object of scorn's slow unmoving finger, is something which this proud man cannot endure: 'I'll chop her into messes. Cuckold me!' (IV i 119). It is for good tactical reasons that Iago delivers his homily on the inestimable value of good name just before he introduces the word 'cuckold' and hints that it has now been earned by Othello: 'Good name in man and woman, dear my lord,/Is the immediate jewel of their souls . . .' (III iii 159–65). Othello agrees with this all too earnestly. Even when he discovers that he has killed Desdemona in the wrong, it is in his own name, not hers, that he thinks of; he has defiled his reputation and must die: 'Why should honour outlive honesty?' (V ii 247). His suicide, however, is not only self-punishment but an expression of the belief that an individual who has lost his name is as good as dead anyhow; henceforth, he perceives, he can only be referred to as the man who once had an honourable name:

> *Lod.*   Where is this rash and most unfortunate man?
> *Oth.*   That's he that was Othello – here I am. (V ii 286–7)

That the villain who is chiefly responsible for all this destruction of good name should himself be known to everyone as 'honest Iago' is probably intended to reflect ironically and critically on Othello's and Cassio's very high regard for honour-as-reputation. Like Troilus (though less obviously), the general and his lieutenant tend to assume that the value of a thing lies in the price that is put on it; they tend to forget that 'value lies not in particular will' but 'holds his estimate and his dignity/As well wherein 'tis precious of itself/As in the prizer' (*Troilus*, II ii 54–6). Othello is not automatically ignoble because given the name of cuckold, nor would Cassio automatically regain lost honour by resuming 'the addition whose want kills [him]' (IV i 105). Like most of the play's ethical notions, this one is formulated by Iago himself. 'Honour' he tells Othello, 'is an essence that's not seen; they have it very oft that have it not' (IV i 16); a remark which is as applicable to the seemingly honest Iago as it is to the seemingly dishonest (i.e., unchaste) Desdemona.

The begriming and blackening of noble names is the most palpable and least subtle manifestation of a corrupting influence which is everywhere at work in the way men speak and are spoken of. A slanderer such as Iago is a hypocrite and actor who can ape the stately style of an Othello or the foppish euphuism of a Roderigo; but his spontaneous habit is to speak in base terms of whatever in human nature is covered by the concepts of nobility and beauty: whatever, in short, makes him ugly. Calumny, there- fore, is simply his characteristic mode of speech in its most pro- nounced form. Thus, although he has great verbal skill of a kind, he is presented – like certain other self-absorbed and uncivil Shakespearian characters – as an essentially uneloquent and dis- cordant speaker among generous minds whose instinct is to keep time gracefully in word and deed. But he is not simply an isolated strident voice: he tries successfully to extend his own cacophonies and so debases the speech as well as the names of the noble.

The discordant character of Iago's tongue is felt most strongly in the scene where Desdemona and Othello reunite at Cyprus. In the most fundamental sense, this scene is concerned with unity and harmony: husband and wife, general and lieutenant, gov- ernor, gentlemen, and (by implication) ordinary citizens all come together and confirm in ceremonious words and gestures the fun- damental bonds of human 'fellowship' (II i 93). Moreover, both through their own words and what others say of them, Othello and Desdemona are presented here in all the unsullied splendour of joyous love, virtuous beauty and heroic manhood. Cassio, too, is at his best, leading the chorus of praise which contributes so much to establishing the prelapsarian perfections of hero and heroine. Asked by Montano if the general is married, he replies:

Most fortunately; he hath achiev'd a maid
That paragons description and wild fame;
One that excels the quirks of blazoning pens,
And in th' essential vesture of creation
Does tire the ingener. (II i 61–5)

In tune with epithalamic thought, he stresses the virility of the married lover and sees the union of the pair in mytho-poetic terms as the source of renewed life and energy for society at large:

> Great Jove, Othello guard,
> And swell his sail with thine own powerful breath,
> That he may bless this bay with his tall ship,
> Make love's quick pants in Desdemona's arms,
> Give renewed fire to our extincted spirits,
> And bring all Cyprus comfort! (II i 77–82)

As the literary imagery in the first passage reminds us, Othello and Desdemona are being treated here as a theme of praise. With his fluent and expansive sentences and his daring but well-controlled figures, Cassio handles this theme with impressive decorum. And when Desdemona – the theme of virtuous beauty – steps ashore, he adds gracious gestures to gracious words:

> O, behold,
> The riches of the ship is come ashore!
> Ye men of Cyprus, let her have your knees.
> Hail to thee lady! and the grace of heaven,
> Before, behind thee, and on every hand,
> Enwheel thee round! (II i 82–7)

With good reason, the words 'courtesy' and 'courtship' are made conspicuous in this scene, for Cassio, 'having sense of beauty' (II i 71), and recognising 'worthiness' which does 'challenge much respect' (II i 210), epitomises the courtly ideal of human behaviour. His command of gracious words and gestures is not only an ornament to himself and others but also testifies to his moral and aesthetic discrimination, his magnanimous spirit, and his socially creative intentions.

It is not surprising that Iago should casually refer here to the distinction between 'base men' and 'nobility' (II i 214–15) and to declare in an aside his active opposition to what is 'well tun'd' and musical (II i 198–200). For as soon as he makes his contribution to this scene of union and praise the function of good speech as the touchstone of nobility stands out clearly. The dissonant and destructive character of his tongue is foreshadowed at the beginning of the scene in Montano's comment on the stormy wind : it 'hath spoke aloud at land' and 'if it had ruffian'd so upon the sea' no ship could have survived (II i 5–9). This obviously looks forward to Iago's conversation with Roderigo at the end of the scene, where he recklessly slanders the three most noble persons he knows. But the essentially ruffian-like nature of his speech is also exhibited in the rhetorical exercise which he jovially undertakes at Desdemona's request when she is anxiously awaiting Othello's arrival (II i 100–65). This significant digression is initiated by Emilia's response to his sardonic criticism of her and of wives in general (who have no sense of propriety, being 'players in . . . huswifery, and huswives in . . . bed') : 'You shall not write my praise' (II i 116). Emilia's remark in turn prompts Desdemona to ask Iago to try his wit praising different kinds of women (her own kind included).[23] Although he admits that he has no aptitude for the task ('My invention comes from my pate as birdlime does from frieze . . . my Muse labours'), he does his best, and his Muse is presently delivered of tuneless couplets, obscene innuendo and 'old fond paradoxes to make fools laugh i' th' alehouse'. As Desdemona observes, he 'praises the worst best' and suffers from 'heavy ignorance'; Emilia is not to 'learn of him'. Cassio puts a charitable construction on this ignorance but at the same time confirms that it has shown itself as a linguistic and educational deficiency : 'He speaks home madam, you may relish him more in the soldier than in the scholar'. Speech and manners, however, being a clue to moral character, Desdemona's good-humoured expostulation, 'Fie, slanderer', and Iago's jocular reply, 'Nay, it is true, or else I am a Turk', have a more literal force than the speakers intend.

Iago's plan to make his base vision of human nature fit the facts begins soon after this with an attempt to corrupt Cassio's speech. Quite simply, he attempts to make Cassio speak in the ale-house vein on the very subject which has already spurred him to the heights of courtly eloquence. To put it another way, he would have Cassio finish the epithalamion, which he has already begun so well, with a 'most lame and impotent conclusion' (II i 160). But Cassio clearly wins this encounter (II iii 1–27), his apt diction and nice distinctions showing his wholesome and discriminating mind; no one could be more disposed than he to accept that 'it is meet to auoyd all grosse bourding, and alehouse iesting . . . and Ruffine maners, such as no honest eares can abide, nor yet any wittie man can like well or allowe'.[24] But as Iago is well aware, a few stoups of wine can effect the most extraordinary change in the refined Cassio. Once drunk, his judgement is so completely in abeyance that he enthusiastically praises the ruffian style : 'Fore God, an excellent song!' (II iii 70); 'Fore God, this is a more exquisite song than the other' (II iii 91–2). He declines into prose, nonsense, swearing, bragging and then quarreling ; and so in word and in deed he helps to disgrace the union of two lovers. But it should be noted that when he recovers his senses he seems to feel that he has degraded himself more by his words than by his deeds : 'Drunk! And speak parrot! And squabble, swagger, swear! And discourse fustian with one's shadow !' (II iii 271–3).

Whereas Cassio's characteristic speech is that of a gentleman and a discreet officer (skilled in what Iago dismisses as 'bookish theoric'), Othello's is that of a great warrior and leader who fetches his life and being from men of royal siege. Within the limits defined by his experience of life, it is eloquence of a very potent kind, exciting wonder, admiration and obedience. And nowhere is this eloquence more apparent than when he assures the senators that he is a rough soldier who cannot be expected to speak well in his own behalf : 'Rude am I in speech,/And little blest with the soft phrase of peace . . . little shall I grace my cause in speaking for myself' (I iii 81–2, 88–9). This assurance is only one of several signs from the dramatist that Othello is the artful persuader that a Renaissance audience would expect a great general to be. According to a well-established rhetorical method, he divides his oration to the senate into *exordium* (I iii 75–94) and *narratio* (I iii 128–70) and alerts us to this division when at the end of the exordium he promises to deliver 'a round unvarnish'd tale' (I iii 90). Moreover, he follows Quintilian's recommendation that in pleading causes where the accusation of dishonourable conduct is involved the orator should employ *insinuatio* in the exordium : '. . . should insinuate himself little by little into the minds of the judges'. In the circumstances, nothing could more effectively insinuate the great general into the minds of the most potent, grave and reverend signiors who are his very noble and approved good masters than his blend of flattery, self-depreciation and oblique but sustained allusion to the services he has done – and will do – the signiory in 'broil and battle' (I iii 87). Shakespeare even gives Othello a phrase from the passage in which Quintilian discusses the exordium for causes of a dishonourable nature. The sentence, 'The very head and front of my offending/Hath this extent, no more' (I iii 80–1), is based on Quintilian's 'in turpi . . . ubi frons causae non satis honesta est'.[25]

Othello's disarming of the senators (and of the armed men who come to arrest him) is a dramatically vivid achievement which helps to frame and define the nature of Iago's subsequent victory. That majestic and compelling voice becomes, like Iago's, an instrument which merely wounds and disgusts the ear. The transformation commences in Act III, Scene iii when the animal imagery hitherto confined to Iago's speech begins to invade Othello's: the key line in this process is 'exchange me for a goat' (III iii 184) – the goat being Iago's image for the vice which he ascribes to Desdemona, animal lust. Iago's conquest seems complete when Othello's verse becomes prose, his sentences degenerate into an apoplectic jumble of words (absolute passion), and he finally falls speechless to the ground. Yet this stage of Othello's transformation is less frightening than when he speaks of Desdemona as a whore, of his home as a brothel, and of himself as fornicator and pimp – that is, when the princely general sinks even lower than 'a beggar in his drink'.

Just as Shakespeare shows that Othello's tragic errors commence even before Iago sets to work so, too, he indicates that there were always inherent weaknesses and dangers in his characteristic mode of speech. At times his lofty manner brings to mind the traditional distinction between the grand style and that other style which is closely akin to it, the swollen : with some uneasiness, one recalls the teaching that –

> to those who are inexperienced, turgid and inflated language often seems majestic – when a thought is expressed either in new or archaic words, or in clumsy metaphors, or in diction more impressive than the theme demands.[26]

There is in Othello's speech an element of unhealthy tumidity which helps to make intelligible the ease with which Iago destroys the sonorous 'Othello music'. This tumidity proceeds from an intense self-awareness – a preoccupation with his own life-story, his honour and his reputation – which makes him murderously sensitive to the suggestion of cuckoldry. It is symptomatic, too, of a deep-rooted instinct to magnify trivialities that renders it all too easy for Iago to turn 'trifles light as air' into 'confirmations strong as proofs of holy writ' (III iii 326–8) – to use hints and a handkerchief as a basis for murder. And it may well account for some of Iago's hatred and contempt for the Moor, since the dissatisfied, shrewd mind is generally infuriated by the circuitous and grandiose speech of the complacent.

Iago's contention that Othello won Desdemona by 'prating', 'bragging, and telling her fantastical lies' (II ii 218–19), coheres with his account of the way in which Othello dealt with the 'three great ones of the city' who asked him to make Iago his lieutenant :

> But he, as loving his own pride and purposes,
> Evades them with a bombast circumstance
> Horribly stuff'd with epithets of war. (I i 12–14)

As descriptions of the way in which Othello talks, these remarks are important. They persist in the memory by virtue of their vividness, put our critical faculties on the alert, and are seen to have some foundation. Othello's address to the senate is a moving and skilful apologia ; but if it is viewed strictly from the standpoint of justice and truth, might it not be treated as mere evasion of a private and domestic cause artfully stuffed out with fine talk about warfare and Mandevillian travels? Then, too, one notices that Othello confesses to loving 'the pride, pomp and circumstance of glorious war' (III iii 358); that he speaks of 'my parts, my title and my perfect soul' (I ii 31–2); and that in a self-dramatising fashion he speaks often of 'Othello'.[27] In speaking to Iago, too, about his services to the signiory, his royal ancestry, and his ability to out-tongue Brabantio, he voices and dismisses the possibility that he is boasting (I ii 18–27). Whether he is or is not is a debatable question (there runs through the whole speech a touch of condescension towards the world in general), but he has at least reminded us that bragging is a dramatic issue. Toward the end of the play, when Desdemona and the out-tongued Brabantio are forever silent, Othello again flourishes his heroic past :

>   I have seen the day
> That with this little arm and this good sword
> I have made my way through more impediments
> Than twenty times your stop. (V ii 264–7)

But having been brought face to face with the questionable value of 'this little arm', he checks the incipient bravado : 'But, O vain boast ! /Who can control his fate ?' These words, which greatly increase our respect for him, anticipate the achievement of the final speech where, instead of merely boasting about an heroic exploit of far away and long ago, he enacts it once more – and so marries word and deed.

Such propriety, however, is conspicuously lacking in his last speech at the senate – the speech where he supports Desdemona's request and promises that he will not allow his private life to interfere with military duties. In itself the promise is just what the situation requires; but Othello gets carried away by the contemplation of his own virtue and so delivers an appropriate promise in a quite inappropriate manner. By loftily dissociating himself from all interest in the sexual expression of love, he is less than tactful towards the candid young wife who has just shown her unwillingness to be denied love's rites. And he expands the promise into a grand boast on which his subsequent behaviour makes the most Iagoish comment possible :

> *Oth.*   Let her have your voice.
>   Vouch with me, heaven, I therefore beg it not
>   To please the palate of my appetite ;
>   Nor to comply with heat – the young affects
>   In me defunct – and proper satisfaction ;
>   But to be free and bounteous to her mind.
>   And heaven defend your good souls that you think
>   I will your serious and great business scant
>   For she is with me. No, when light-wing'd toys
>   Of feather'd Cupid seel with wanton dullness
>   My speculative and offic'd instruments,
>   That my disports corrupt and taint my business,
>   Let huswives make a skillet of my helm,
>   And all indign and base adversities
>   Make head against my estimation !
> *Duke.*   Be it as you shall privately determine,
>   Either for her stay or going. Th' affair cries haste,
>   And speed must answer it. You must away to-night.
>   (I iii 260–77)

I have given the duke's terse and business-like reply since it throws the Moor's self-regarding and long-winded manner into relief and indicates that no one but he is interested in all this protestation. But the bombastic quality of Othello's speech here can be explained in fairly precise stylistic terms as well as by reference to its sense and contextual effect. Its diction is rather too Latinate and ostentatious. In its fifteen lines, moreover, it contains eleven instances of the first person pronoun, two oaths, one neologism ('indign' – a word unique in Shakespeare), and eight doublets or near-doublets. There is also an abundance of plosives and fricatives which add greatly (as in Ajax's trumpet speech in *Troilus and Cressida*[28]) to the impression of a wind instrument vigorously used. In another speech of Othello's which somewhat resembles this one, Shakespeare cunningly inserts a phrase which describes exactly, and with onomatopoeic force, the style used here: 'exsufflicate and blown' (III iii 186). The two epithets are, of course, synonymous; but the neologism (unique in the language) has special value: apart from being phonetically suggestive, it is an obvious adaptation of the Latin epithet for the swollen or inflated style – 'sufflatus'.

No other Shakespearian hero – not even Coriolanus – is placed in circumstances for which he is so unsuited by temperament and training as is Othello; in none are the difficulties of adaptation greater. For this reason no other character shows so clearly that the distinction between man's endowments and his limitations is often very fine, indeed, (in a sense) unreal. The decisiveness, the Herculean self-confidence, and the grand manner of Othello can at one moment command intense admiration, at another they can seem either very dangerous or slightly ridiculous: their value depends entirely on the circumstances in which they operate. This duality (or seeming duality) is particularly apparent in what might be called the magical or incantatory speech of Othello. I do not introduce the term impressionistically, for it is posited by Shakespeare himself, who makes brilliant artistic use in this play of the notion that well-tuned speech is a power which irresistibly enchants the hearer. Of course, magic has other symbolic meanings in *Othello*: there is the magic of love and there is the magic of strange regions and peoples beyond the confines of Christian civilisation. But the symbol is not strained, for moving words, romantic love and thrilling regions have something of importance in common: they can be as dangerous as they are delightful.

Since he cannot credit that his quiet and obedient daughter would deceive him, Brabantio concludes that Othello has deceived his daughter, and in the most sinister fashion : he has 'wrought upon her' with 'some mixture powerful o'er the blood', has used 'drugs . . . charms . . . conjuration, and . . . mighty magic' – the 'practices of cunning hell' itself (I iii 91–2, 102–6). In attempting to refute this charge, Othello carefully addresses himself to the 'grave ears' (I iii 124) of the senators. He explains that he won Desdemona simply by talking to her about antres vast and deserts idle, rough quarries, rocks and hills whose heads touch heaven ; about the Cannibals that eat each other, the Anthropophagi and the men whose heads grow upon their shoulders ; about his own disastrous chances and moving accidents by flood and field. 'This only is the witchcraft that I used', concludes Othello ; and he is right to express himself thus, since to talk as he did to a maiden 'never bold' is undoubtedly to use magic of a sort. His narration, in fact, holds Desdemona spellbound and brings about her first dissociation from the world of domestic reality and common duties :

> This to hear
> Would Desdemona seriously incline ;
> But still the house affairs would draw her thence ;
> Which ever as she could with haste dispatch,
> She'd come again, and with a greedy ear
> Devour up my discourse. (I iii 145–50)

'It was my hint to speak [thus] – such was the process', remarks Othello (I iii 142); and the word 'hint' is itself a hint that the whole process – his talk and her response – was not quite so ingenuous and open as he maintains. It is necessary to realise that the word 'hint' had two senses (*N.E.D.* turns to this particular speech for its earliest example of each usage) : it denoted 'opportunity . . . time, occasion (of action)' as well as 'a suggestion or implication in an indirect and covert manner'.[29] Both meanings are involved here. Well aware that his story served as a covert method of wooing Desdemona, Othello waited for the opportunity to hint that at some suitable moment he would, if asked, unfold the whole of that enchanting story which so far had only been told 'by parcels' and not 'dilated' in the best Othello fashion :

> ... Devour up my discourse, Which I observing,
> Took once a pliant hour, and found good means
> To draw from her a prayer of earnest heart
> That I would all my pilgrimage dilate. (I iii 150–3)

Then, when it is all told, Desdemona hints, too, and once more Othello seizes his opportunity : and so Brabantio is deceived past thought and the midnight marriage takes place – such was the process :

> ... she thank'd me,
> And bade me, if I had a friend that lov'd her,
> I should teach him how to tell my story,
> And that would woo her. Upon this hint I spake. (I iii 164–7)

Someone else in Othello's unfinished story will hint, will pliantly wait for the opportunity to practise deception and to inveigle others into neglecting time and duty. Really, witchcraft and devilry are one : and if they can be located at all, they will be found in the tongues of men and women – all other accounts of their origin and nature are mere fable (i.e., witchcraft and devilry).

When Othello's verbal witchcraft calls attention to itself for the second time, the fascinating stranger has begun to assume the frightening contours of the Anthropophagi. Under the spell of his voice and countenance, Desdemona is like Amoretta enchained in the dazzling but claustrophobic House of Busirane, the tyrant lover 'which her hath in ward/By strong enchantments and blacke Magicke leare' (*Faerie Queene*, III xi 16). According to Emilia, Othello 'conjur'd' Desdemona that she would ever keep the handkerchief (III iii 298). The literal sense of the word is most relevant since Othello is upholding a magical view of reality when he implies that the loss of this little handkerchief will mean the end of a world of pure and perfect chrysolite. Like magic, too, the handkerchief connotes not only exaggeration and fantasy but deceit and treachery as well ('fantastical lies' was a very apt phrase). When he questions Desdemona about it, Othello knows that she has lost it; but instead of telling the truth and asking simple and direct questions, he puts on an elaborate pretence of ignorance and then falls into veiled threats and an (unconscious?) effort to trap her. Listening to him now, Desdemona finds – like her father before her – that her credulity is strained to cracking point, her amazement suffused with horror :

> *Oth.* That handkerchief
> Did an Egyptian to my mother give.
> She was a charmer and could almost read
> The thoughts of people ; she told her, while she kept it,
> 'Twould make her amiable, and subdue my father
> Entirely to her love ; but if she lost it,
> Or made a gift of it, my father's eye
> Should hold her loathely, and his spirits should hunt
> After new fancies. She, dying, gave it me,
> And bid me, when my fate would have me wive,
> To give it her. I did so ; and take heed on't ;
> Make it a darling like your previous eye;
> To lose't or give't away were such perdition
> As no thing else could match.
> *Des.* Is't possible?
> *Oth.* 'Tis true. There's magic in the web of it.
> A sibyl that had numb'red in the world
> The sun to course two hundred compasses
> In her prophetic fury sew'd the work ;
> The worms were hallowed that did breed the silk ;
> And it was dy'd in mummy which the skilful
> Conserv'd of maidens' hearts.
> *Des.* I'faith ! Is't true?
> *Oth.* Most veritable ; therefore look to't well. (III iv 55–75)

It would be a complete understatement to say that Othello speaks here about the object in question 'with a solemn earnestness/More . . . than belong'd to such a trifle' (V ii 229–30). It would seem rather that a handkerchief spotted with strawberries – a light-wing'd toy of feather'd Cupid – has been turned into a myth, a myth which embraces all the fraudulence, irrationality and cruelty of witchcraft. Its effect is to paralyse Desdemona's judgement and to drive her into the lie ('I say it is not lost') which damns her in the mind of the enchanter.

Saying far more and far less than it should, Othello's speech on the handkerchief bears a certain resemblance to the primitive habit of poetic riddling. A kind of linguistic atavism, it has great imaginative richness ; but it is completely at variance with the concept of speech as rationality and as a firm bond between words and meanings, speaker and listener. It has a special representative importance in that it combines two basic forms of linguistic disorder which serve in the play both as symptoms and causes of tragic confusion – exaggeration (or excess) and obscurity. The second of these disorders is much the more prevalent of the two; and in dealing with it Shakespeare is more inventive and more truly dramatic than he was in *Hamlet*. He presents it here in three basic forms. Sometimes these are active separately; but quite often, and with the most unobstrusive artistry, he shows two or three of them working in conjunction, steadily eroding the fabric of human relationships with terrible results.

The most obvious sort of dark speech is equivocation, deliberate or otherwise. Brabantio bitterly calls attention to this phenomenon shortly after Othello's quibble on 'hint'. Intentionally making use of the three senses of the word 'sentence' (the judicial, the rhetorical and the grammatical), he dismisses the duke's sententious judgement on his cause as a string of sentences which 'being strong on both sides are equivocal' (I iii 217). Like Polonius, however, Brabantio throws up important ideas without showing much understanding of their relevance to the events in which he is involved, for he adds drily that no one would ever expect words to affect the heart anyhow: whether the duke equivocates or not is of no real consequence to him. The tale of wooing which we have just heard, and, of course, the epileptic fit which will later be induced by an equivocal use of the word 'lie', sharply contradict this attitude.

Equivocation itself comes in different guises. The most striking is to be found in what is customarily treated as dramatic or Sophoclean irony, where a whole sentence or speech has a sinister meaning or a special ineptness of which the speaker is totally unaware. It, too, commences in that crucial third scene of the first act where Othello says of Desdemona, 'My life upon her faith', and of Iago, 'A man he is of honesty and trust./To his conveyance I assign my wife' (I iii 284–5, 294). This unsettling of language flaws even the concord and propriety of the great speeches made after the landing at Cyprus. If Othello were now to die, he probably would be most happy; and although he has married a maid that paragons description and wild fame, he cannot be said to have wived most fortunately.

Another form of equivocation (known to the rhetoricians as 'amphibologia') arises from confusion in grammatical structure, as when Cassio says to the clown, 'Dost hear, my honest friend?', and the clown replies: 'No, I do not hear your honest friend. I hear you' (III i 21–2).[30] But this is artful perversion at its most obvious, and the clown's pun on 'lie' is vastly more characteristic of the semantic uncertainty which infects the speech of the play. Particular words are continually being given, or acquiring, different meanings; and this, far from being presented as evidence of the speaker's wit (or the richness of the English language) is a sign of dishonesty, treachery and error on the one hand, and of change, degeneration and regrettable 'innovation' (II iii 36) on the other. The word shares the fate of the principal characters: it is 'displanted' (II i 272), loses the 'place' for which it is 'fit' and which it 'fills . . . up with great ability' (III iii 250–1 ; cf. II iii 131 ; III i 17–20); it is 'wayward' (III iii 296), 'unfit for' its 'own purposes' (III iii 33), 'erring' – that is, wandering and therefore confused and confusing (I iii 351), 'extravagant and wheeling . . . here and there' (I i 137). The loosening of bonds between words and meanings is cognate with 'the unkind [unnatural] breach' between general and lieutenant (IV i 220), with the 'beggarly divorcement' between husband and wife, and with the yawning 'alteration' (V ii 105) and chaos (III iii 93) in a world which the Word made harmonious and intelligible.

Among the group of recurrent words which account for the strong impression of semantic flux in the play, the word 'move' is of special importance. One obvious reason for its importance is that in its primary sense it denotes changing of place, dislodgement. But the essential reason is that in Elizabethan usage 'moving' was synonymous with speech as persuasion. To be effective, an orator must move the imagination and emotions of his audience;[31] and the act of persuading in itself entails moving the listener from one mental position to another. Aptly, the word first occurs in Othello's address to the senate: he persuades the senators of his innocence by telling them a moving tale – the tale of a young girl who was moved to wonder and pity and then to love by a history of 'moving accidents by flood and field' (I iii 135). One might not reflect at this point that 'moving' could be as dangerous as it is useful and pleasing ; but once Desdemona is 'transported' (I i 125) to Cyprus, the word clearly begins to signify division and violence.

Quelling the brawl, but himself moved to passion, Othello warns that the first man to stir 'dies upon his motion' (II iii 166). Later in the same scene, Iago, supposedly helping but actually frustrating Cassio's attempt to regain his lost place, says : 'My wife must move for Cassio to her mistress' (II iii 371). Thus Othello is no longer the mover : from now on he is moved, and by two persons in particular. The great third scene of Act III constitutes an informal but superlatively cunning piece of persuasion in which the evil genius is continually sensitive to the effect his words are having on his audience : 'Consider what is spoke/Comes from my love; but I do see you are mov'd . . . My lord, I see you are mov'd' (III iii 220–1, 228). These probing words elicit a sadly faint response which indeed shows that the foundations of Othello's trust are beginning to tremble : 'No, not much mov'd./I do not think but Desdemona's honest' (III iii 229–30).

The ultimate success of Iago's exercise in persuasion depends on the fact that Desdemona has already begun to move Othello on Cassio's behalf ('she pleads for him most strongly to the Moor' – II iii 344) and continues to do so after his faith in her has been shaken. In the fourth scene of the third act she sends the clown to Cassio with a message about her efforts : 'Tell him I have mov'd my lord on his behalf, and hope all will be well' (III iv 16–17); and in the same scene, although she has been frightened by the 'strange unquietness' and anger of the handkerchief speech (it reminds Iago that the cannons which blew Othello's ranks into the air left him unmoved), she prepares to renew her efforts : 'If I do find him fit, I'll move your suit,/And seek to effect it to the uttermost' (III iv 168–9). This moving to the uttermost when the time is not fit produces accidents which, in accordance with Iago's plan, 'shake this island' (II iii 122). When Othello awakes her in the night, one of the 'portents' in which Desdemona reads disaster is that 'some bloody passion shakes' his 'very frame' (V ii 47–8). And when he has killed her, his perturbation is such that he thinks there should be an earthquake. But what moves his whole being now is the realisation that the body which might lie by an emperor's side and command him tasks, and the tongue that could sing the savageness out of a bear, will never move again : '*Ha! no more moving?/Still as the grave*' [my italics] (V ii 95–6). Seldom have words so few and so simple expressed so much.

The most iterated word by far in *Othello* is 'honest'.[32] Since in Elizabethan usage it could mean 'chaste' as well as 'morally upright, true in words and deeds', its prominence in a play about marital fidelity, slander and hypocrisy is understandable enough. But it was also used in a loose, latitudinarian fashion to indicate mere approval and so it might easily have significations inconsistent with its two primary meanings : some 'honest' – that is, affable, unassuming, honest-to-God – fellows are not always models of chastity or reliability. Shakespeare was undoubtedly conscious that a word which was fundamental in ethical language – one which derived from a term used on almost every page of the *De Officiis* to designate moral rectitude ('honestas') – was being debased in his own time. He was not, however, making a commentary on semantic changes in contemporary English but using the various meanings of this word (as of other words) for specific dramatic purposes. By showing that 'honest' is attached by general consent to an absolute villain and liar, he proves in the most graphic manner that words are losing all fixity and reliability in the world of Othello and Desdemona. So far as 'honest' is concerned, Iago contributes in word as well as in deed to this process. Othello and Emilia know that 'honesty' is the opposite of 'knavery', 'villainy', 'falsity' and 'disloyalty' (III iii 122–5 ; IV ii 140–5). But Iago completely confounds these obvious contraries by speaking of 'honest knaves' and 'honest fools' (I i 49 ; II iii 342) and protesting with pretended insincerity that 'honesty [is] a vice' (III iii 380 ; cf. III iii 386).

To the very uncertain status of words Othello himself contributes as soon as Iago's words have succeeded in 'shaking' him. He tells Desdemona that she has 'a liberal hand' (III iv 43) : which means that it is 'a good hand, a frank one' – it 'argues fruitfulness and liberal heart'. But 'liberal' also means 'sinful' :

> Hot, hot and moist. This hand of yours requires
> A sequester from liberty, fasting and prayer,
> Much castigation, exercise devout ;
> For here's a young and sweating devil here
> That commonly rebels. (III iv 36–40)

And the word 'obedient' is turned upside-down in the same way. As Lodovico remarks, Desdemona is, 'truly, an obedient lady' (IV i 244), for she will turn back instantly when recalled by the husband who has just ordered her to get out of his sight. But this 'obedience' has a different significance for Othello :

> Ay; you did wish that I would make her turn.
> Sir, she can turn, and turn, and yet go on,
> And turn again ; and she can weep, sir, weep ;
> And she's obedient, as you say, obedient,
> Very obedient. (IV i 249–53)

After he has recovered the appearance of self-possession and succeeded in entertaining Lodovico with 'due ceremony', Othello delivers yet another 'brutal command' to Desdemona :[34] 'Get you to bed on th' instant : I will be return'd forthwith. Dispatch your attendant there. Look't be done' (IV iii 6–7). And Desdemona responds exactly as before : 'I will, my lord'. Although Emilia finds this command very suspicious ('Dismiss me !'), and although she herself senses disaster, Desdemona takes no precautions, does not even think to query her husband's authority. To the edge of doom she is 'subdued', 'inclining' ; and her last words are, 'Commend me to my kind lord' (V ii 128). Sublime but tragically misplaced, this wifely obedience to a kind lord who is not kind is dramatically contrasted with Emilia's subsequent recognition that in certain circumstances it may not be proper to obey one's lord and husband. And it is a very meaningful contrast, since by refusing to obey Othello and Iago, and by speaking 'as liberal as the north' about what they have done, Emilia makes it possible to restore that propriety from which every thing – including Desdemona and the word 'liberal' – has been 'frighted'.

From the beginning of the play to the end, Desdemona's obedience is of profound significance, and in the iteration and 'turning' of the words which express it one can find delicate clues concerning the nature of her tragedy. By far the most important of these words is the one which every respectful Elizabethan and Jacobean lady would frequently use in addressing or referring to her husband – the word 'lord'. But 'lord' is also the term which a lady would use in addressing her father, a social superior and her Creator. Desdemona uses the word in all these senses and seems well aware that the sum total of her duties is comprised within its sphere of reference. She first uses it when she is brought before the senate and asked by her father if she perceives in all the noble company where she most owes obedience. Her short but very dignified reply provides a more concentrated expression of the notion of duty than any other speech in the canon :

> My noble father,
> I do perceive here a divided duty :
> To you I am bound for life and education;
> My life and education both do learn me
> How to respect you ; you are the lord of duty –
> I am hitherto your daughter ; but here's my husband,
> And so much duty as my mother show'd
> To you, preferring you before her father,
> So much I challenge that I may profess
> Due to the Moor, my lord. (I iii 180–9)

As an answer to Brabantio's question this is impeccable. But by its very concentration on the notion of duty it brings home to us the fact that neither Desdemona nor Othello are as faultless as they appear to be and that Brabantio has really asked the wrong question (just as he has lodged the wrong charge against Othello). If Desdemona owes Othello all her obedience now that he is her husband, it follows that she owed the same to her father when he was the lord of her duty : her duty may be divided now (a problem which she has no difficulty in resolving), but it was not divided before she deluded the man to whom she owed life, education and respect. Like Othello's 'plain unvarnish'd tale', therefore, this speech puts a varnish on undutiful behaviour; it is essentially equivocal, and it is in the word 'lord' that the equivocation comes to light. That Desdemona has shorn this word of its true meaning in so far as it applied to Brabantio is emphasised again, and with great delicacy, by the way in which she conducts herself towards the duke – 'most gracious Duke', 'my lord' (I iii 243, 278) – and his colleagues – 'dear lords' (I iii 255). Desdemona recognises that these lords have some authority in the arrangement of her future, and while confessing

> My heart's subdu'd
> Even to the very quality of my lord,

simultaneously pleads most respectfully with them (as does Othello) to allow her to go to Cyprus. Who knows what a similar plea at an

earlier date to the first lord of her duty would have accomplished?
It would, at any rate, have been proper.

In the subsequent mutations of the word 'lord', Nemesis can be
seen at work. It quickly becomes for Desdemona a sign without a
referent: 'My lord is not my lord; nor should I know him/Were
he in favour as in humour alter'd' (III iv 125–6). This breeds confusion and misunderstanding and even helps to frustrate a dialogue
which could have averted tragedy:

> *Emil.*   Good madam, what's the matter with my lord?
> *Des.*   With who?
> *Emil.*   Why, with my lord, madam.
> *Des.*   Who is thy lord?
> *Emil.*   He that is yours, sweet lady.
> *Des.*   I have none. Do not talk to me Emilia;
>   I cannot weep, nor answers have I none
>   But what should go by water. (IV ii 99–105)

Here the abused word is partly a symptom and partly a cause
of the unnatural breach in human relations which leads on to
violence. But in the last moments of Desdemona's life it operates
almost entirely as a cause. When she perceives that Othello is on
the point of killing her, she exclaims: 'O, banish me, my lord, but
kill me not!' (V ii 82). And when that request is rejected, she asks
only for time to say a prayer to her Lord. But he proceeds to
strangle her; and this is what follows in the dialogue:

> *Des.*   O Lord, Lord, Lord!
> *Emil.*   [*Within.*] My lord, my lord! What, ho! my lord, my
>   lord!
> *Oth.*   What voice is this? Not dead? Not yet quite dead?
>   I that am cruel am yet merciful;
>   I would not have thee linger in thy pain.
>   So, so.
> *Emil.*   [*Within.*] What, ho! my lord, my lord!
> *Oth.*   Who's there?
> *Emil.*   [*Within.*] O, good my lord, I'd speak a word with you!
>   (V ii 87–93)

In a state of near-delirium, and hearing only a woman's voice
crying 'lord', Othello presumably imagines that Desdemona speaks

again after the first strangulation and so robs her of her last chance
of survival: the very fact that she can speak a few words after
Emilia has entered proves that she might have lived but for that
second attack. Two other points substantiate this interpretation
of the dramatic significance of the word 'lord' here. First, Othello's
bewildered cry, 'What voice is this?', is echoed by Emilia when
Desdemona utters her last feeble words: 'O Lord, what cry is
that? . . . out and alas, that was my lady's voice' (V ii 120, 122).
For a moment, but only for a moment, Emilia shares Othello's
experience of being unable to identify her lady's voice; if she had
failed to identify it, the truth might never have come to light.
Second, when Emilia is told by Othello that it was Iago who
accused Desdemona she, too, feels that her world has begun to
'reel' and 'totter',[35] and she registers this sensation in her response
to Othello's use of the word 'husband' (her equivalent of 'lord'):
'My husband! . . . My husband! . . . My husband say she was
false!' (V ii 143–54). To which Othello angrily replies (in words
which echo his agonised, 'My wife, my wife, what wife?'):

What needs this iterance woman? I say thy husband . . .
I say thy husband; dost understand the word?
My friend, thy husband – honest, honest Iago. (V ii 153, 156–7)

After this, Emilia addresses her 'good lord' as 'gull' and 'dolt'
(V ii 166) and recognises that she owes no duty either to him or to
the husband who does not deserve that name.

Another word whose semantic inconstancy proves treacherous
is 'commit'. In the brothel scene, Desdemona interrupts Othello's
grandiose but imprecise execrations with the question: 'Alas, what
ignorant sin have I committed?' (IV ii 71). This is an instance of
dramatic art at its most economical, for Desdemona here exemplifies what she defines. Because the word 'commit' could be used
absolutely to mean 'commit adultery', the effect of its use is to
drive Othello into an apoplexy of indignation at what he takes
to be his wife's double-dyed impudence: 'What committed? Committed! . . . What committed! Impudent strumpet!' (IV ii 73–
82). As a result of this fury, of course, the crucial question remains
unanswered and so the exchange contains not one but two kinds
of semantic disorder. The second is what the clown has in mind
when, after much wilful evasion, he answers Desdemona's request

to seek Cassio: 'I will catechise the world for him; that is, make questions and by them answer' (III iv 14–15).[36] In *Othello*, the corruption of the proper relationship between question and answer is even more prevalent, and is certainly of greater import, than in *Hamlet*. Frequently, too, it assumes a form which is peculiar to this play – iteration or echoing: instead of an answer, the questioner gets back his own words two or three times over. Desdemona echoes Emilia ('nor answers have I none'), Emilia echoes Othello, Othello echoes Desdemona, and – which is where it all begins – Iago echoes Othello.

Whereas in others 'echoing' proceeds from great agitation and a feeling that familiar words and the familiar world are about to dissolve, in Iago it is part of the technique of hinting or insinuation employed throughout Act III, Scene iii, in order to undermine Othello's belief in the honesty and constancy of Desdemona and Cassio. Since it rubs against his instinctive desire for absoluteness and fixity, this technique inflames Othello's passions, stimulates his imagination, and renders him incapable of weighing evidence and making judgements:

> *Iago.* Indeed!
> *Oth.* Indeed? Ay, indeed. Discern'st thou aught in that?
>   Is he not honest?
> *Iago.* Honest, my lord?
> *Oth.* Honest? Ay, honest.
> *Iago.* My lord, for aught I know.
> *Oth.* What dost thou think?
> *Iago.* Think, my lord?
> *Oth.* Think, my lord! By heaven, he echoes me,
>   As if there were some monster in his thought
>   Too hideous to be shown. Thou dost mean something. (III iii 102–12).

When Iago says 'Honest, my lord?', there is probably a lingering intonation on the first word which introduces the idea of chastity as well as reliability and so injects the image of Cassio as fornicator into Othello's mind. Iago, therefore, is equivocating as well as echoing and hinting; his words have either no meanings or several and so his listener is forced to try desperately and repeatedly to get him to express clearly what is in his mind: 'I prithee speak to me as to thy thinkings . . . give thy worst of thoughts/The worst of words' (III iii 135–7). As was intended by the 'busy and insinuating rogue' (IV ii 132), the effort exhausts Othello's patience and, as a result, his own heated imagination gives shape to that 'horrible conceit too hideous to be shown'.

When Desdemona appears in this scene, Iago's success in breaking the bonds between thought and word, question and answer, and husband and wife is confirmed by the nature of her conversation with Othello. 'Why do you speak so faintly? Are you not well?', she asks; and he replies: 'I have a pain upon my forehead here' (III iii 286–8). He is not referring, however, to the common headache (as she reasonably supposes) but to the cuckold's horns ('this forked plague' – III iii 280). So when she offers to bind his head with her handkerchief, he roughly brushes it aside ('Your napkin is too small'), it falls, and Emilia enters to pick it up for Iago. Thus, the handkerchief which is soon to be equated with the whole world is lost because of an unanswered question and hinting, equivocal speech. Surely no other tragedy has ever exhibited a pattern of cause and effect so intricate and illuminating as this!

Because speech has become so obscure and indirect, the act of interpretation is all important, and there are many allusions to it in the dialogue. Iago himself – with that mixture of daring and cunning which recalls Richard III – actually moralises on the dangers of faulty interpretation. Putting on a show of candour, he tells Othello that since it is his 'nature's plague/To spy into abuses', he may well 'shape faults that are not' and 'imperfectly conject'; Othello, therefore, should treat what he says with caution and beware of building troubles for himself out of 'scattering and unsure observance' (III iii 150–5; cf. III iii 220–7). But as Iago well knows, words are not the only signs that can be interpreted and misinterpreted. Manners and general behaviour are significant:

> Alas, alas!
> It is not honesty in me to speak
> What I have seen and known. You shall observe him;
> And his own courses will denote him so
> That I may save my speech. (IV i 273–7)

Action – 'the language of the body' – is also significant:

s.d.—5*

Stay you, good gentlemen. Look you pale, mistress? –
Do you perceive the gastness of her eye?
Nay, an you stare, we shall hear more anon. –
Behold her well; I pray you look upon her.
Do you see gentlemen? Nay, guiltiness will speak
Though tongues were out of use. (V i 105–10)

Lastly, even inanimate objects are significant – especially for those
who love, and even more for those who believe in magic. Among
all these signs, both animate and inanimate, there is one which
stands out as having a unifying function. It is that part of the
body with which we manipulate the inanimate – the hand – and
of which so much was made in the arts of eloquence and acting
that it gave rise to a subsidiary art of its own (chironomia).

The problem of interpretation first appears when Cassio kisses
his hand and fingers to Desdemona, takes her 'by the palm' (II i
165–76), and she in turn caresses 'the palm of his hand' (II i 249).[37]
'Didst not mark that?' asks Iago, whereupon Roderigo offers a
gentlemanly interpretation: 'That was but courtesy' (II i 250–1).
But Iago (with an apt oath which will appear again) flatly dis-
agrees: 'Lechery, by this hand; an index [= finger] and obscure
prologue to the history of lust and foul thoughts' (II i 252–3). As
we would now expect, the next person to misinterpret the hand
is Othello, and he does so immediately before he instructs Desdemona on the history and significance of the handkerchief. It is
here that one sees the special role of hand-reading in the semantics
of the play. Etymologically and functionally, the hand is intimately connected with that lifeless object which Desdemona might
use to bind Othello's forehead or Cassio to wipe his beard with.
But Shakespeare exploits the hand not only in order to relate the
handkerchief to all the other signs which are misinterpreted by or
because of Iago, the devilish enchanter of men's minds. By means
of hand-reading, Shakespeare connects the handkerchief with a
specific magical art, an art whose whole purpose is to discover
holy writ in trifles, and one which was associated by Shakespeare's
contemporaries with the Egyptians and the seeming Egyptians
(gypsies) who first arrived in England in the sixteenth century:
palmistry or chiromancia.[38]

Othello's interpretation of the 'heraldry' (III iv 44) in Desdemona's hand is not only ambiguous but so cryptically expressed

that she has no idea of what is really in his mind. Her failure to interpret his words here is part of what she calls her 'wretched fortune', for she says 'I cannot speak of this' (i.e., 'this is all too enigmatic for me to talk about'), and proceeds immediately to importune him about Cassio's reinstatement, thus confirming (it would seem) his interpretation of her frank and liberal hand. Similarly, when he explains to her in equally enigmatic language the significance of what in grandiose fashion he later calls his 'antique token' and 'recognisance and . . . pledge of love' (V ii 217, 219), she promptly takes up the very subject which a correct understanding of his dark speech would have warned her to avoid at all costs : 'This is a trick to put me from my suit :/Pray you let Cassio be receiv'd again' (III iv 98–9).

Othello's claim that the 'Egyptian . . . charmer' who made the handkerchief was filled with 'prophetic fury' and 'could almost read/The thoughts of people' is really a dark hint that he himself can read minds (as well as hands) and that Desdemona had better tread warily. The pathetic ineptness of this claim to clairvoyance is forcibly exposed in the next scene when Iago arranges his dumb-show with Cassio, confident in his belief that the Moor's 'unbookish jealously must construe/Poor Cassio's smiles, gestures, and light behaviours,/Quite in the wrong' (IV i 101–3). Iago hides his spectator at a distance and supplies him with ready-made interpretations of what will follow; he is as good as a prologue :

> . . . mark the fleers, the gibes, and notable scorns
> That dwell in every region of his face ;
> For I will make him tell the tale anew –
> Where, how, how oft, how long ago, and when,
> He hath, and is again to cope your wife.
> I say, but mark his gesture. (IV i 82–7)

Othello can find nothing in what follows to contradict the given interpretation. When Cassio embraces Iago, saying 'by this hand, she falls me thus about my neck', he glosses like a diligent and obedient student : 'Crying "O dear Cassio !" as it were : his gesture imports it' (IV i 133–5). By chance, too, the handkerchief appears in Cassio's hand, since the angry Bianca arrives to return it to him and to repeat her 'vile guesses' that it is 'some minx's token' which accounts for his recent absences (IV i 146–50; III iv 181–5). As soon as he is alone with Othello, Iago quickly seizes the opportunity to show that this unexpected addition to the dumb-show harmonises perfectly with the general sense he has given it:

> *Iago*. And did you see the handkerchief?
> *Oth*. Was that mine?
> *Iago*. Yours, by this hand. And to see how he prizes the foolish woman your wife! She gave it him, and he hath giv'n it his whore. (IV i 169–73)

As interpreted here, Cassio's handling of the handkerchief is a detail which roots itself in Othello's mind. It comes to the surface at the precise moment when Desdemona's final oath of innocence unleashes his murderous passion: 'By heaven, I saw my handkerchief in's hand./O perjur'd woman! . . . I saw the handkerchief' (V ii 65–6, 69). To Othello the judge, it is the one incontrovertible sign of guilt.

So the essential, irreducible meaning of *Othello* probably lies in Desdemona's poignant question:

> Upon my knees, what doth your speech import?
> I understand a fury in your words,
> But not the words. (IV ii 31–3)

Not once during the terrible scene in which it occurs (the brothel scene) does Othello tell Desdemona just why he is torturing her. Twice she asks a specific question designed to elicit the cause and significance of his behaviour, and all she gets in return is exclamation and query (IV ii 41, 72). Later, when he comes to kill her, and warns her vaguely to bethink herself of 'any crime/Unreconcil'd as yet to heaven', she can only ask: 'Alas, my lord, what may you mean by that?'; but again she receives no answer (V ii 27–30). She knows that the rolling eyes and gnawed lips are 'portents' of some bloody passion (V ii 48) and her 'fear interprets' the worst (V ii 77); yet she is aware of no 'guiltiness' in her conduct and so dares to hope that the portents do not 'point' – obscure indexes and fingers that they are – at her (V ii 42, 49). When at long last he names the crime ('That handkerchief which I lov'd and gave thee/Thou gav'st to Cassio'), it is only to tell her in almost the same breath that Cassio's 'mouth is stopp'd' (V ii 51–2, 75). This erroneous statement provokes in Desdemona a cry of dismay ('Alas, he is betray'd, and I undone!') whose significance Othello's jealousy interprets quite wrongly; as a result, he is totally overcome by passion and kills her instantly :

> *Oth.* Out, strumpet! *Weep'st thou for him to my face?* [my italics]
> *Des.* O, banish me, my lord, but kill me not!
> *Oth.* Down strumpet! (V ii 80–3)

'Only connect' : it seems improbable that any play has ever explored this commonplace but enduringly valid truth quite so brilliantly as *Othello*.

5

Macbeth

Macbeth has some obvious and important connections with such plays as *Hamlet, Othello, Richard III* and *Richard II*. Its hero is led on to his doom by 'the equivocation of the fiend that lies like truth'. He is subjected to evil persuasion and becomes himself an evil persuader; and because of his violation of faith – his breaking of the great bond between king and subject – speech becomes corrupted with ambiguous and contradictory meanings.[1] Nevertheless, *Macbeth* is very much closer in its essential preoccupations and characteristics to *King Lear* than to any other play in the canon.

There are probably many ways of defining the nature of this relationship, and my own will not take the reader by surprise. In both *King Lear* and *Macbeth*, I find, Shakespeare was deeply engaged in exploring and confirming the basic principle that propriety is founded on harmony with Nature : that what is fitting is natural and what is natural is fitting.[2] The complex configurations which man's personality, speech and behaviour necessarily assume in the subtle or super-subtle relationships of Court and City are not in evidence in these two tragedies. Here, those who break away from their true selves and their fellow-men do not fail because they are noticeably lacking in wise adaptability or true nobleness of mind. They fail chiefly because they lack or abandon certain 'domestic-door' virtues (*Lear*, V i 30) which any 'homely man' (*Macbeth*, IV ii 67) might share in common with men of royal siege, qualities which have little to do with training in 'arts and arms' or with class distinctions. These qualities are subsumed in what Goneril contemptuously calls 'milky gentleness' and Lady Macbeth (perhaps not so contemptuously) 'the milk of human kindness' : they are benevolence, pity, tenderness, and that kindly feeling which means acknowledging if not reciprocating kindness – gratitude. Such feelings are as proper to man's nature as is the gentle and protective attitude of a mother to the child at her breast, and without them it is impossible to keep 'the sweet milk of concord' (*Macbeth*, IV iii 98) in human society. Throughout his work, but especially in *King Lear* and *Macbeth*, Shakespeare is noticeably conscious that in its primary sense 'kind' or 'kindly' means natural; kindness is naturalness and to say that a man is kind is to say (I follow the indispensable Schmidt) that he is 'not degenerate and corrupt but such as a . . . person ought to be'.

II

The tragedy of Macbeth is that of a kind man who degenerates into a butchering tyrant; but since a tyrant is almost by definition a man who lives in dread of those whom he terrifies,[3] his tragedy is also that of a courageous soldier who becomes cowed by fear. Through this second aspect of Macbeth's transformation, Shakespeare extends his commentary on essential human nature from kindness to manliness; as in *Lear*, he investigates the differentia of man and woman as well as of man, beast of prey and demon.

Although he had never before dealt with the psychologically complex phenomenon of the brave man who becomes a victim of obsessive fears, Shakespeare had already created effeminate and timorous kings (and a cowardly captain). He had also presented (in one and the same play) two women – the Duchess of Gloucester and Queen Margaret – who were both conspicuously more ambitious and aggressive than their husbands, and one of whom carried a 'tiger's heart wrapp'd in a woman's hide'.[4] What makes Lady Macbeth so very much more interesting than those stereotyped viragos is that her mannishness is unnatural in the sense that she manifestly adopts it by an act of will and even, it would seem, with the aid of demonic powers. She, even more than Macbeth, screws nature up to its sticking place – bends up each corporal agent to the terrible deed – and, properly, it is her nature which snaps under the strain. After he has stabbed three men in their beds, Macbeth says to his anxious friends: 'Let's briefly put on manly readiness' (II iii 132). Fiercely inept in its human context, the metaphor is dramatically very apt; but it might be applied even more usefully to Lady Macbeth than to her husband. It is she who formulated the false notion of manliness which now guides him, it is she who 'puts it on' first, and the violence to her womanly nature which it involves is revealed in her terrible vision of dashing out the brains of the babe to which she has tenderly given suck. Had she not been deterred by the resemblance between the sleeping Duncan and the father whom she presumably loved; had she been able to use her knife whether or not the face of the sleeper was covered by blankets and darkness; had she sat on her stolen throne to the bitter end with a brazen face and a stony heart : then she would pass as mere virago and Amazon. Instead, she is a woman : one who should, perhaps, bring forth men-children only, but who really can only assist her husband in the life of violence by chastising him with the valour of her tongue – or by offering him tender words. She lacks the awful hardness and the active ferocity which animates Macbeth when he dismisses the tortures of conscience as 'the initiate fear that wants hard use' (III iv 143). Whilst he wades grimly across his river of blood to join the archetypes of male brutality, she drifts back into a limbo of feminine frailty where the tones of wifely solicitude break through her mad ravings. Her dereliction is inexpressibly moving since, in its way, it is a testament to the womanliness in her nature which she tried so hard to destroy.

But there are creatures in the play who do exhibit an absolute perversion of woman's nature. These are the witches, who 'should be women' but whose beards forbid Banquo to 'interpret' that they are so (I iii 45–7); and Hecate, the demon goddess who enters the action as mistress of Macbeth's fate as soon as his wife is compelled by her nature to relinquish that role : Hecate's words, 'this night I'll spend/Unto a dismal end :/Great business must be wrought ere noon' (III v 20–2), echo Lady Macbeth's, 'this night's great business' (I v 65), just as her determination that Macbeth shall fearlessly spurn fate and scorn death (III v 30–1) recalls Lady Macbeth's exhortations to act courageously and ignore conscience. Devilish females and female devil, these creatures are mythological expressions of the temporary metamorphosis which takes place in Lady Macbeth after she has invoked the spirits that tend on mortal thoughts to take her milk for gall.

Since Lady Macbeth consciously reflects on the act of 'unsexing' herself, it is not surprising that she is the first to raise the question of her husband's manliness. All the world knows him as 'brave Macbeth' and generously admits that he 'well . . . deserves that name' (I i 16). But when he recoils from the thought of killing

Duncan, she tells him sarcastically that he is 'afeard to be the same in . . . act and valour/As in . . . desire' (I vii 37–41); worse still, he is a soldier who is prevented by fear from doing what he swore he would do (I vii 58). On the two subsequent occasions when (as she says) his 'constancy' leaves him 'unattended' (II ii 68–9) – which really means that his true nature is reasserting itself -- she quickly returns to this theme. He is 'infirm of purpose' and un-bends his 'noble strength' to indulge in the brainsickly fears of 'childhood' (II ii 45, 46, 51, 54); he is 'unmann'd' with 'flaws and starts' that 'would well become/A woman's story' (III iv 64–5, 73). The irony, of course, is that her conception of what becomes a man will destroy both his manliness and his humanity, since fear and ferocity become the twin characteristics of his behaviour once Duncan has been killed.

When his wife first appeals to the idea of manliness, Macbeth does indeed perceive that her reasoning is faulty and is quick to protest : 'I dare do all that may become a man;/Who dares do more is none' (I vii 46–7). But so unsteady is his moral position that he is overwhelmed by the sheer vigour of her reply and ignores its sophistry and its reckless misuse of the ideal of fitness :

> What beast was't then
> That made you break this enterprise to me?
> When you durst do it, then you were a man;
> And to be more than what you were, you would
> Be so much more the man. Nor time nor place
> Did then adhere, and yet you would make both;
> They have made themselves, and that their fitness now
> Does unmake you. (I vii 47–54)

The fallacy here that more means better evokes the doctrine of the mean and, in particular, the teaching that courage lies midway between the extremes of timidity and rashness (or fury).[5] This conception of valour has to be kept in mind in order to under-stand both the development of Macbeth's character and the analo-gies and contrasts which are carefully worked into the play in an attempt to establish the difference between daring which is man-like, 'bear-like' (V vii 2) and 'fiend-like' (V viii 69).

Even in his own mind Macbeth is so profoundly identified with valour that as soon as he stops trembling he can exclaim with intense conviction, 'I am a man again' (III iv 108). But he is greatly deceived in this remark since the fears which afflict him so grievously at first are signs of the psychological and social consequences of an attempt to cancel and tear to pieces the great bonds of humankind. It is, rather, when he discovers that he has 'almost forgot the taste of fears' – when night shrieks no longer cool his senses and rouse his fell of hair by striking at his guilty conscience – that Macbeth virtually ceases to be a man (V v 9–12). But although he loses the kind of spiritual and moral fear which is far from unbecoming in a man – 'honest Fear', it is called in *Lucrece* (l 173) – merely physical fear dogs him to the end. When he learns how Macduff was born, and perceives that the witches' 'Fear not' was a trick, his 'better part of man' is instantly '*cow'd*' [my italics] and his refusal to fight Macduff alters only when he is told that he will be put on show as a coward (cow-herd) and a tyrant (V viii 17–27).

One cannot say then of Macbeth, as was said of the first thane of Cawdor (who 'frankly confess'd his treasons,/Implor'd . . . pardon . . . and set forth/A deep repentance'), that 'nothing in his life/Became him like the leaving it' (I iv 5–8). For his display of prowess at the end is involuntary : it is the fierceness of a bear tied to the stake; and it is accompanied not by a contempt of death but by a hatred of life which extends to all living creatures : 'I gin to be aweary of the sun,/And wish th' estate o' th' world were now undone' (V v 49–50). That we should feel deep sympathy and a certain admiration for him at the end is due in part to the grandeur of the language in which, through him, Shakespeare expresses the feelings of world-weariness and despair that are a part of every man. It is due also to the fact that the apparent or perverted manliness of his final stand inevitably reminds us of the valiant and worthy gentleman that once was Macbeth – 'But O ! the pity of it !'

In manipulating the nameless creatures who kill Banquo, Macbeth employs his wife's argument about manly distinction; and they, being reckless what they do to spite the world (III i 109), automatically and laconically accept it : 'We are men, my liege' (III i 90). Neither in Macbeth's view nor in their own do these 'shag-ear'd' (or shag-hair'd) villains (IV ii 82) belong to 'th' worst rank of manhood' (III i 102), much less to the category occupied by 'shoughs, water-rugs and demi-wolves' (II i 93). But there are a number of other characters in the drama who do suffer from fear and who, from the murderers' view-point, might well be entered in the catalogue as cowards. 'Fears and scruples shake us', admits Banquo after the discovery that 'sacrilegious murder hath broke ope/The Lord's anointed temple' (II iii 65–6, 128). This, however, is the wholesome fear of a man who senses the presence of preternatural villainy, and Banquo responds to it properly by girding himself with the armour of God (II iii 128–30). He also fears that Macbeth played most foully for the throne (III i 2–3); but perhaps because he lacks clear evidence of Macbeth's guilt, or because he feels that the time is not ripe for action, he does nothing. Whatever the cause of his inaction, it certainly is not cowardice. As Macbeth regretfully recognises :

> 'Tis much he dares,
> And to that dauntless temper of his mind
> He hath a wisdom that doth guide his valour
> To act in safety. (III i 50–3)

Macbeth's 'fears in Banquo stick deep', then, not only because he has been hailed as father to a line of kings but also because he merits that title : 'in his royalty of nature/Reigns that which would be fear'd' (III i 48–50).

Whereas Banquo cannot suspect that he himself is in physical danger, Malcolm and Donalbain instantly perceive that the fears of the king's unknown murderer will stick deep in them. Their flight, therefore, is quite in accordance with the principle that wisdom is the better part of valour. Banquo himself sees the relevance of this truth immediately an attempt is made on his own life : 'O treachery! Fly good Fleance, fly, fly, fly!/Thou mays't revenge' (III iv 19). Towards the end of the play, the prudent fear which moved Malcolm to fly reappears in more obvious form and is implicitly contrasted with the behaviour of the tyrant, who vacillates between 'valiant fury' (V ii 14) and panic. Malcolm's reaction to the proposal that he should return to Scotland is so cautious and evasive that Macduff is convinced he is a coward (IV iii 34). However, since Macbeth's agents have often sought to trap him with friendly overtures, Malcolm speaks 'not in absolute fear' (IV iii 38) of Macduff. Rather, 'modest wisdom plucks' him 'from overcredulous haste' (IV iii 119–20); and when he sees that the circumstances are propitious he leads his army to the rescue of his country. Therein lies some of the difference between one who is 'fit to govern' (IV iii 101) and one who is not.

Malcolm's consummate prudence distinguishes him not only from Macbeth but also from the very brave man who absents himself from the tyrant's coronation, rejects his invitation to the banquet 'with an absolute "Sir, not I!"' (III vi 40), and eventually kills him in hand-to-hand fighting. After the banquet, Lennox observes that Macduff would be well advised 't' hold what distance/His wisdom can provide' (III vi 45); and Macduff does just that, fleeing to England without wife or children. Various constructions can be put on his flight. There is the view of Lady Macduff herself, who complains that it was madness and not wisdom 'to leave his wife, to leave his babes,/His mansion, and his titles, in a place/From whence himself does fly'; 'as little is the wisdom', she adds, 'where the flight/So runs against all reason' (IV ii 6–14). And according to her, his departure indicates a deficiency in something else :

> He loves us not ;
> He wants the natural touch ; for the poor wren,
> The most diminutive of birds, will fight,
> Her young ones in her nest, against the owl.
> All is the fear, and nothing is the love. (IV ii 8–12)

The curious resemblance here between Lady Macduff and Lady Macbeth, who also accused her husband of being afraid and of not loving her, might perhaps put us on guard against this claim. But one could argue anyhow that Macduff is associated by Lennox with the holy angel who flies to England to bring back a swift blessing to accursed Scotland (III vi 45–9) and that, compelled to choose between the safety of his family and his country, he makes the unselfish choice. Such might be the attitude of Lennox, who assures Lady Macduff that her husband is 'noble, wise, judicious, and best knows/The fits o' th' season' (IV ii 16–17). Unfortunately, however, Lennox leaves us in a state of uncertainty by adding immediately :

> But cruel are the times, when we are traitors
> And do not know ourselves ; when we hold rumour
> From what we fear, yet know not what we fear,

But float upon a wild and violent sea
Each way and none. (IV ii 18–22)

It would seem therefore that in his imprudence Macduff caught
some of the inconstancy – the feverous fits and starts – which
have passed from the tyrant to the nation as a whole, now 'almost
afraid to know itself' (IV iii 165).

There can, however, be no thought of Macduff's shortcomings
after he learns of the murder of his family. He could 'play the
braggart' with his tongue but refuses to do so. He simply promises
that with the help of Heaven he will confront the 'fiend of Scotland' and either kill him or die in the attempt; and as Malcolm
says : 'This tune goes manly' (IV iii 231–5). Manly too, and also
in contrast to the behaviour of the tyrant, is that of young Siward.
Defiantly opposing Macbeth, and needing neither desperate fury
nor promises of everlasting security to bolster up his courage, he
wins even in defeat all that Macbeth has lost :

He only liv'd but till he was a man ;
The which no sooner had his prowess confirm'd
In the unshrinking station where he fought,
But like a man he died. (V viii 40–3)

III

Apart from refusing to play the braggart with his tongue, Macduff
also resists the inclination to 'play the woman' with his eyes (IV
iii 230) ; like Lear, he feels that tears are 'woman's weapons' and
will not let them stain his 'man's cheeks' (*Lear*, II iv 276–7).
But Macduff by no means believes that the softer emotions are
incompatible with manhood. And of course his wife, in accusing
him of wanting the natural touch, obviously takes it for granted
that there can be no essential difference between men and women
in this respect. Her suggestion is that if he had followed his natural
affections for his family – or if they had been strong enough –
he would have been able to act both wisely and courageously.
Throughout the play, the question of valour is continually over-
lapping with or expanding into the larger question of the milk of
human kindness. One is aware that sublime courage can be gener-
ated by simple love (as when the wren attacks the owl, or when

Macduff's boy defies the villain who calls his father a traitor). And one is even more aware that ungoverned prowess negates humanity.

Some remarks made by Holinshed concerning the characters of Macbeth and Duncan had much to do with Shakespeare's concern in this tragedy with hardness and tenderness – or, shall we say, attracted him to the story. According to Holinshed, Macbeth was 'a valiant gentleman, and one that if he had not been somewhat cruell of nature might have beene thought most woorthie the gouernement of a realme'. This side of his nature showed itself even when he was fighting to restore justice and law on Duncan's behalf in the war against the rebel Macdowald. Having taken Macdowald's castle, and having discovered that the defeated rebel had killed himself, his wife and his children rather than be 'executed in most cruell wise', Macbeth nevertheless 'remitted no peece of his cruell nature with that pitiful sight', but 'caused the head to be cut off, and set upon a poles end, and so sent . . . as a present to the king'. By contrast, Duncan was

> so soft and gentle of nature, that the people wished the inclination and maners of these two cousins to haue beene so tempered and interchangeablie bestowed betwixt them, that where the one had too much of clemencie, and the other of crueltie, the meane vertue betwixt these two extremities might haue reigned by indifferent partition in them both, so should Duncane haue prooued a woorthie king, and Makbeth an excellent capteine.[6]

These observations exhibit the typical Tudor mind reflecting on character and morality, and Shakespeare would have deemed them worthy of respect. But he altered and modified the given conceptions of the two men's characters in ways which one might almost say were predictable. Thoroughly gentle, but not excessively so, Duncan is a figure whose early disappearance from the play allows him to be treated as a flawlessly perfect human being by whom the imperfections of the usurper can be measured. And he is the antithesis, not of Macbeth, but of what Macbeth becomes; in fact, he is to the good qualities in Macbeth what Hecate and the witches are to the evil ones in Lady Macbeth – their ultimate expression. The contraries, therefore, which hold antipathy are not (as in Holinshed) between Duncan and Macbeth but between true and treacherous Macbeth. Inside the man who is too full of the milk of human kindness to catch the nearest way, and who sees Pity clamouring throughout the universe against the murder of Duncan, is the pitiless infanticide who 'cannot buckle his distemper'd cause/Within the belt of rule' (V ii 15–16). Fighting for Duncan, and acting as 'justice . . . with valour arm'd' (I i 29), Macbeth is, in potentiality, the very rebels whom he opposes. One by one the hints to this effect accumulate. His contest with 'the merciless Macdowald' (on whom 'the multiplying villainies of nature/Do swarm') is a see-saw affair; 'Doubtful it stood,/As two spent swimmers, that do cling together/And choke their art' (I ii 8–12). Macbeth too 'unseam'd' Macdowald 'from the nave to the chaps,/And fix'd his head' upon the battlements (I ii 23–4). He and Banquo 'doubly redoubled strokes upon the foe' and seemed 'like cannons overcharg'd with double cracks' (I ii 37–8). And, lastly, Bellona's bridegroom confronted the first thane of Cawdor 'with self-comparisons,/Point against point rebellious . . . Curbing his lavish spirit' (I ii 55–8). The ambiguity and the excess – the doubtfulness and doubleness – which pervade the play, and which are so clearly connected, emanate from Macbeth himself, the bright angel who falls, the kindly-cruel captain who for some time has had inclinations to climb into the seat of the king whom he serves so well. As Brabantio noted, it is the peculiarity of equivocation to be 'strong on both sides'.

The nature of that human kindness which Macbeth destroys in himself is -- like the nature of manliness – explored in a series of analogous incidents which exploit contrast and variation. In all of these there is a single implicit question, and one which is not surprising from the author of such plays as *King John*, *Julius Caesar* and *Hamlet*. It is this : how should heart and tongue react to personal bereavement of a violent and untimely nature? Although he is exploring the nature of sorrow and pity in these parallel scenes, Shakespeare is not, of course, dramatising a theme, giving body to a 'topos' or abstraction; rather, he is scrutinising from various angles the exact nature of Macbeth's and Lady Macbeth's departure from the laws of their being and tracing the effect of this on themselves and others. In thus examining men's reactions to the violent cancellation of nature's bond he is continually conscious of what is proper – that is, of what is best suited

to nature – and what is not; and this consciousness extends even
to the characters themselves. It is implied that although there is a
norm it can operate differently from one person and one set of
circumstances to another.

The murder of Duncan is announced by Macduff in words
which establish the leit-motiv of horror and the fundamental problem of feeling-and-expression : 'O horror, horror, horror! Tongue
nor heart/Cannot conceive nor name thee' (II iii 62–3). Everything Macduff says in this scene is noticeably free from self-awareness. Apart from the barbarous and barely credible nature of the
deed, the only thing which seems to engage his thought is the
reaction of Lady Macbeth, whom he treats with great delicacy
on the assumption that she is governed by all the sensitivity of
her sex :

> O gentle lady,
> 'Tis not for you to hear what I can speak !
> The repetition in a woman's ear
> Would murder as it fell. (II iii 82–4)

By contrast, the words of Lady Macbeth and her husband are
distinctly self-regarding, and this, together with the ideas they
harp on, accentuates the necessary divorce between their hearts
and tongues and the general unfitness of their performance. Although Lady Macbeth had argued the incomparable 'fitness' of
time and place for the murder, she now exclaims in a thoroughly
misplaced simulation of what becomes a hostess : 'Woe, alas !/
What, in our house?' (II iii 85–6). And Macbeth, who came to
believe that 'the time' was suited to the murder (II i 59–60), com-
plements her exclamation by claiming that this is a most untimely
deed which will hereafter make time seem meaningless to him :

> Had I but died an hour before this chance,
> I had liv'd a blessed time ; for from this instant,
> There's nothing serious in mortality ... (II iii 89–91)

But Macbeth's display of sorrow does not end with this famous
speech (the essential aptness – or other meaning – of which he can
hardly have been intended to appreciate). Unlike his wife, he
advances into the bombastic style of grief, and does so in deed as

well as word. He announces to Malcolm and Donalbain the death of their father in pompous circumlocutions which merely puzzle the princes and which Macduff has to translate into simple terms: 'Your royal father's murder'd' (II iii 98). And with a spontaneous cunning which even his wife could not have forecast he allows his supposedly violent grief to overflow into violent action by killing the men whose daggers – 'unmannerly breach'd with gore' – outraged him:

> Who can be wise, amaz'd, temp'rate, and furious,
> Loyal and neutral, in a moment? No man...
> Who could refrain,
> That had a heart to love, and in that heart
> Courage to make's love known? (II iii 107–17)

In total contrast to this bragging exhibition of 'an unfelt sorrow' (II iii 135) is the reaction of the dead man's sons, who express no feelings whatever. They are silent, not because they are over-whelmed with grief, much less because they are indifferent, but rather because their wisdom tells them that so far as they are concerned time and place do not 'adhere' for true mourning:

> *Mal.* [*Aside to Donanlbain*] Why do we hold our tongues that may most claim
> This argument for ours?
> *Don.* [*Aside to Malcolm*] What should be spoken
> Here, where our fate, hid in an auger-hole,
> May rush and seize us? Let's away.
> Our tears are not yet brew'd.
> *Mal.* [*Aside to Donalbain*] Nor our strong sorrow
> Upon the foot of motion. (II iii 119–25)

That Malcolm has a heart capable of sorrow and that he is fully aware of the natural necessity to give it due expression becomes very apparent when the murder of Macduff's family is announced by Ross. On learning that his wife and babes have been 'savagely slaughtered' (IV iii 205), Macduff says nothing; and there should, I presume, be a long silence in which his two friends watch him with deep concern – a period when the tongue says nothing but countenance and gesture suggest much. Then

Malcolm's compassion and wisdom come into play. Gently at first, but then firmly, he endeavours to cleanse Macduff's bosom of the perilous stuff that weighs upon the heart ('the poison of deep grief', as it is called in *Hamlet*) and to set him on the path of psychic reintegration. Breaking the silence, he exclaims:

> What, man! Ne'er pull your hat upon your brows;
> Give sorrow words. The grief that does not speak
> Whispers the o'erfraught heart and bids it break. (IV iii 208–10)

But when Macduff's words begin to follow the arid course of self-accusation, Malcolm tactfully implies that there are many Scotsmen who suffer as he does and indicates that the time has come for them to

> Be comforted.
> Let's make us med'cines of our great revenge
> To cure this deadly grief. (IV iii 213–15)

Although Macduff responds to this persuasion, there is no suggestion that his grief is shallow or will easily be dispelled. To Malcolm's, 'Dispute it like a man', he answers:

> I shall do so;
> But I must also feel it as a man.
> *I cannot but remember such things were*
> *That were most precious to me.* [my italics] (IV iii 220–3)

The depths of mortal sorrow that lie behind these restrained and simple words seem fathomless. Macduff here becomes the complete man, full of feeling as well as of valorous determination.

The next announcement of death is made by Seyton to the solitary Macbeth: 'The Queen, my lord, is dead' (V iv 16). The sadness here is not that the bereaved man has no one to comfort him, but that he needs no one. He has already heard the cry of horror raised by the queen's women, and it has reminded him that in the eternity between this moment and the killing of Duncan his heart has died. His lifeless questions – 'What is that noise?' (V iv 8); 'Wherefore was that cry?' (V iv 15) – recall the hysterical, immensely human exclamations which he uttered once upon a time to the woman who has just taken her life: 'Didst thou not

hear a noise? ... Methought I heard a voice cry ...' (II ii 14, 35).
And the answer which Seyton gives to his question here evokes no
surprise, no pity, no sorrow : direness, familiar to his slaughterous
thought, cannot once start him. As the dramatic revelation of a
soul which has come to the conclusion that life is utterly devoid
of value and meaning – as the verbal image of a living corpse –
Macbeth's speech on hearing that the queen is dead is beyond
praise. As the speech of a husband who has lost the wife who
loved and was loved by him, it is profoundly – though sadly – deficient in what one expects. It is, in fact, a variation on the theme of
the speech which he made when Duncan's death was announced :
this, he says, is not a suitable moment for her death or for
such an announcement – indeed, there can never be such a time :

> She should have died hereafter;
> There would have been a time then for such a word.
> To-morrow, and to-morrow, and to-morrow ... (V iv 17–19)

There can be no word of love or sorrow or pity in Macbeth's
lifetime any more, no troops of friends, no consoling rites where
all the living tacitly say to the bereaved concerning his loss : 'No
mind that's honest/But in it shares some woe, though the main
part/Pertains to you alone' (IV iii 197–9). Macbeth has been
beguiled to the very heart of loss.

That the world has neither time nor place for Macbeth is
harshly confirmed when Macduff makes known his death by displaying his head. The only comment is that of old Siward, whose
son Macbeth has killed : 'Here comes newer comfort' (V viii 53).
The point is that the death of a tyrant is not a thing which can be
mourned but is, rather, a source of consolation for those already
bereaved. Before Macduff's arrival in the last scene, attention
has centred on the announcement of young Siward's death, or
rather on the reactions to it. Obviously the juxtaposition of the
two deaths is intended to provide a strong and significant contrast.
But there is a double contrast – not only between reactions to
young Siward's and to Macbeth's death, but also between Old
Siward's reactions to his son's death and Macbeth's to his wife's.
Having died like a man and in a noble cause, young Siward has
become 'God's soldier', and no one could wish him 'a fairer death'
(V vii 46, 48); so his father does not grieve. Malcolm suggests

that he is 'worth more sorrow', but the old soldier quietly dissents : religious faith and a father's pride sustain him in the belief that his son has lived a blessed time and now sleeps well. Old Siward's calmness recalls, but is very different from, Macbeth's : that was the calm of despair, incomprehension, and indifference.

IV

For Macduff, the death of the tyrant signifies above all else that 'the time is free' (V viii 55). By 'the time', Macduff obviously means 'the age', 'the present state of things', 'the world'; but anyone who has been following the play with reasonable care will feel that other meanings are relevant too. In most of his plays, but perhaps especially in this one, Shakespeare refers to the prevailing conditions of life as 'the time' or 'the times' principally in order to insinuate that respect or disrespect for time as a law of natural progression and seasonable behaviour can have the most far-reaching implications. By attempting to make the present conform to hopes, ambitions and prophecies, Macbeth and his wife interfere with the clock and the calendar and there ensues in Scotland a 'woeful time' of terrifying confusion and uncertainty. Few men know either themselves or 'the fits o' th' season'; 'each minute teems a new' grief and 'that of an hour's age doth hiss the speaker' (IV iii 175–6); and 'good men's lives/Expire before the flowers in their caps' (IV iii 171–2). It is a time of nightmare and delirium when 'Nature's germens' and 'the seeds of time' seem to tumble all together even till destruction sicken. 'The time is free', therefore, means that life has resumed its natural distinctions and its 'proportion'd course' : day follows night, season follows season, meals and sleep are undisturbed, and the future has all the predictability that is necessary for human happiness. Temporally speaking, everything is in its proper place and the result will be an abiding sense of fruitfulness and security.

If one compares the opening and concluding speeches of *Macbeth* one can quickly appreciate how important is the notion of time – or time-and-place – in its philosophical structure. The play begins with the First Witch asking two questions – 'When shall we three meet again' (I i 1) and 'Where the place?' (I i 6) – which exhibit the characteristic search of the perverted for the time and place suited to evil deeds :[7] on a foul dark day and on a blasted heath Macbeth will be hailed as 'king hereafter'. At the end of the play, however, Malcolm is telling his friends that he will meet them at Scone where, as everyone knows, he will be crowned king in true succession to his father. In fact, the whole of his concluding speech is dictated by Macduff's announcement that 'the time is free' and by his simultaneous greeting, 'Hail king of Scotland'. As a man who is fit to govern and who takes his place on the throne through 'the natural ordre of enheritauns by lineal dyscent',[8] Malcolm is the mainstay of order and proportion in time and place. Accordingly, he does not spend 'a large expense of time' in reckoning with his friends' love – making himself 'even' with them – but creates them earls on the spot (V viii 60–3). And whatever else 'would be planted newly with the time' – whether it be to call home 'exil'd friends' to their proper abode, or to punish the cruel ministers of the dead butcher and his fiend-like queen (who 'took off her life' untimely) – all this, and whatever else is needful, Malcolm promises to 'perform in measure, time and place' (V vii 65–73).

This concluding speech confirms the impression built up in the last two acts that Malcolm is a prince whose words and deeds are guided by the conviction that ripeness is all. In his first cautious response to Macduff, he promises : 'What I can redress,/As I shall find the time to friend, I will' (IV iii 9–10); unlike Macbeth, he eschews 'overcredulous haste'. Then, having satisfied himself of Macduff's integrity, and having assured him that he is free from that 'boundless intemperance' which 'hath been th' untimely emptying of the happy throne/And fall of many kings', he acknowledges that his 'power is ready' and that Macbeth 'is ripe for shaking' (IV iii 66–9, 236–9). But neither he nor his friends show any signs of complacency about the future. Unlike 'the confident tyrant' (V iv 8), whose military judgement has now deserted him, they calmly regulate their conduct according to the requirements and known realities of the moment :

> The time approaches
> That will with due decision make us know
> What we shall say we have, and what we owe.
> Thoughts speculative their unsure hopes relate,
> But certain issue strokes must arbitrate;
> Towards which advance the war. (V iv 16–21)

The sense of timeliness which animates Malcolm and his supporters is displayed in its spiritual rather than its practical aspect by
two other characters in whom there is an assured royalty of nature.
The famous speeches made by Duncan and Banquo on their
arrival at Inverness castle (the second of which is a sensitive and
fruitful amplification of the first) are essentially affirmations that
all choices which are to bear fruit – winning the approval of Nature
and of Heaven – must be in perfect harmony with time and
place (I vi 1–10). The temple-haunting martlet builds his loved
mansionry when and where the air sweetly and nimbly commends
itself to the gentle senses; as a result, his pendent bed becomes a
procreant cradle over which the love of Heaven breathes wooingly.
Duncan and Banquo are in harmony with the martlet (as with
each other) for they, like him, are guests of summer who value the
beauty of the moment and the place. And if they are deceived
about the other inhabitants of the castle, if their almost mystical
joy in the harmonies of creature-filled time and space is seen to be
as fleeting as the breath of summer and as vulnerable as the pendent bed poised on jutty, frieze, buttress, or coign of vantage,
that in no sense invalidates either their experience or the assumptions on which it rests. It simply shows (and with intense poig-
nancy) that we live in a world whose times of radiant contentment
can be savagely terminated by men and women who misunder-
stand or seek to escape from the ineluctable laws of Nature. While
Banquo is rejoicing in his proximity to the temple-haunting martlet and the Lord's anointed temple, the Macbeths have all but
decided that on this cheerful summer's day, and in this pleasant
seat, time and place 'adhere' and 'suit with' a crime against love,
loyalty, gratitude, pity, kinship and hospitality. Theirs is a Satanic
view of fitness which will soon unmake many a procreant cradle.
And it will unmake them, too; for they, more than anyone else,
are dupes.[9]

To say that the cause of Macbeth's undoing is ambition does
not illuminate his character or the play on even the most elementary level of understanding. We come much nearer to Shakespeare's intentions, and begin to perceive the universality of
Macbeth's experience, if we think of ambition as a form of the
intemperate desire which threatens in every man to nullify the
riches of the moment by making other times and places unduly
attractive: men are tempted (as we are told in *Lucrece*, ll 142–

54) to gamble the present for the future, what they have for what they have not, and are in danger of losing all. The witches' prophecy that Macbeth will be king hereafter is simply the exteriorisation of Macbeth's ingrained tendency to dwell on possibilities and a gilded future. As soon as he hears their 'great prediction/ Of noble having and of royal hope' (I iii 55–6) his mind is 'rapt' from his body and carried to where 'nothing is but what is not' – to a time where the satisfactions that are impatiently longed for are bought at the price of the self he knows. The whole of Macbeth's subsequent development is telescoped into this moment. He suffers from a process of psychic disintegration in which his true self looks amazedly at another self in action; he becomes spiritually disengaged from society, ceases to be a 'noble partner' (I iii 54, 143) to his friends and fellow-soldiers; and when he returns to the present it is not to renew the bond of speech ('let us speak our free hearts each to other' – I iii 154) but to lie and play the hypocrite – his 'dull brain', he apologises, was lost *in the past*, 'wrought with things forgotten' (I iii 145–50).

It is in keeping with this obsessional intensity that he should write immediately to his 'dearest partner in greatness' about the witches' promise concerning 'the coming on of time' (I v 7, 9). He will not have her remain 'ignorant of what greatness is promis'd' and thus 'lose the dues of rejoicing' – as if rejoicing were due for what we have not rather than what we have (I v 11–12). And when they meet, it is apparent that the witches' 'more than mortal knowledge' (I v 2) has given them a mutual infatuation with the future which makes them at once contemptuous and ignorant of the present: 'Thy letters have transported me beyond/This ignorant present, and I feel now/The future in the instant' (I v 53–5). Macbeth even 'burn'd in desire' to acquire 'more' of the witches' 'more than mortal knowledge' (I v 5; I iii 70). In every way, 'more' is his defect.

It is possible that the witches' prediction was true only in the sense that they foresaw the effect it would have on Macbeth and his wife. More likely, it was true in the sense that, for reasons hidden in the providential design of history, he would have attained to the crown in a lawful manner, much as Banquo's descendants did. His mistake was to ignore the promptings of his wiser nature to allow 'time and the hour' to run through its ordained course (I iii 144).[10] Automatically, his rejection of ripeness involves him

in a sustained attempt to 'hoodwink', 'beguile' or 'mock the time'
(I v 60; I vii 81). And this means not only that he has to play a
part, wear robes and speak words that do not fit him, but that
he actually interferes with the clock and calendar, destroying their
natural and proper relationship with the movement of the heavenly bodies, much as he seeks to make 'the eye wink at the hand'
(I iv 52; cf. I v 49). On the morning after Duncan's untimely
death, 'dark night strangles the travelling lamp' when 'by the clock
'tis day' (II iv 6–7). This disorder is a continuation of the confusion which Macbeth and his wife caused by mistiming the
midnight bell to suit their own purpose on the previous night :
then, the distinction between one day and another was lost. After
the banquet, and before retiring to bed, Banquo and Fleance are
perplexed about time, for they 'have not heard the clock' which,
they know, should have struck twelve when the moon went down
(II i 1–4). The reason for their failing to hear the midnight bell
is that the Macbeths have decided to use it not as a public 'summons' (II i 6) to 'repose' (II i 9, 29) but as a private signal for
murder – a premature 'summons . . . to heaven or to hell' (II i
64). The knell which is rung by Lady Macbeth and which 'invites'
her husband to kill Duncan, telling him that 'the present horror'
suits with the time (II i 59), ushers in a universal, reposeless dark,
when the drowsy chimes of midnight are replaced by the howl of
the wolf (II i 53–4), the cry of that 'fatal bellman', the owl (II ii 3),
and the yawning peal of the shard-borne beetle – rung 'to black
Hecate's summons' (III ii 41–3) – all of which serve as 'the murderer's way of knowing the passage of the night'.[11] This is the time
of clockless nightmare in which Lady Macbeth – the first fatal
bellman – moves before taking her own life : 'One, two ; why then
'tis time to do it' (V i 33–4); it is a time in which temporal sequence is totally destroyed and the moment of horror is never-
ending.

One of the more remarkable signs of the way in which the subject of time pervades and shapes the language of the play is that,
once the thought of murdering Duncan has entered Macbeth's
mind, all his communications with his second victim become dominated by the notion of opportunity or occasion. In these con-
versations, Macbeth pretends allegiance to that sense of fruitful
timeliness which Banquo himself exhibits in his reply to Duncan's
promise to 'plant' him in his heart – 'There if I grow,/The harvest

is your own' (I iv 28–33). Macbeth's pretence is not surprising since he, too, is eager to plant Banquo in his heart and to promise mutually beneficial results. Banquo himself first introduces the idea of opportunity when he gently retrieves Macbeth from futurity with the polite words: 'Worthy Macbeth, we stay upon your leisure' (I iii 148). 'Leisure' here is a term of courtesy signifying 'pleasure'; but the word could also mean 'convenient time, a time fit for something' (as well as 'free time'),[12] and it is this sense that Macbeth has in mind in his response to Banquo:

> *Macb.* Think upon what hath chanc'd; and, at more time,
> The interim having weigh'd it, let us speak
> Our free hearts each to other.
> *Ban.* [*Aside to Macbeth*] Very gladly.
> *Macb.* [*Aside to Banquo*] Till then, enough. – Come friends.
> [*Exeunt.* (I iii 153–7)

Their next conversation concludes with a similar probe. But Macbeth, unable to obey the rule of 'till then, enough', feels the future in the instant and slips now into the royal 'we':

> I think not of them [the Weird Sisters];
> Yet, when we can entreat an hour to serve,
> We would spend it in some words upon that business,
> If you would grant the time. (II i 21–4)

Banquo's courteous reply – 'At your kind'st leisure' – seems to suggest to Macbeth that he has found the appropriate moment for his persuasion, so he proceeds further in 'this business' – and is, of course, rebuffed: Banquo recalls that to 'augment' might mean to 'lose' and simultaneously distinguishes between inner and outward honour (II i 26–8). The two men meet again after the discovery of Duncan's body, and that meeting concludes with Macbeth taking up the manly and loyal words of Banquo (II iii 125–8) and varying them in a manner which carries the faintest echo of the First Witch's 'When shall we three meet again?' and 'Where the place?' Says Macbeth: 'Let's briefly put on manly readiness/And meet i' th' hall together' (II iv 132–3). It sounds admirable: readiness and ripeness is all. But it is a premonition of what is to be all too obvious in Macbeth's next and final encounter

s.d.—6

with Banquo : that Macbeth has taken control of destiny and is from now on the sole appointer of time and place.

As Banquo prepares with a sense of controlled urgency for the journey which he little imagines will be his last, he and Macbeth exchange ceremonious parting words, most of which turn on the question of time (III i 18–39). Banquo rides 'this afternoon' and his journey 'will fill up the time/Twixt this and supper'; but if this horse does not go well he will perforce 'become a borrower of the night/For a dark hour or twain'. He and his son therefore must 'Hie ... to horse' for, as he says (and these are his last words to Macbeth), 'our time does call upon's'. Macbeth politely regrets that he will not have Banquo's good advice 'in this day's council', but he will 'take to-morrow' instead ; and in the meantime he wishes Banquo's 'horses swift and sure of foot'.

The irony of Banquo's eagerness to keep time becomes obvious when, immediately after his departure, the new king sends for his shag-ear'd villains. 'Every minute' of Banquo's being, he tells them, is a threat to his own life. And the moment he perceives that they will have no qualms whatever in making Banquo and Fleance 'embrace the fate/Of that dark hour' (III i 136–7), he cuts short the First Murderer's protestations, briefly acknowledges his manliness, and hurries on to the business of time and place :

> *1 Mur.*   Though our lives –
> *Macb.*   Your spirits shine through you. Within this hour at
>   most
> I will advise you where to plant yourselves,
> Acquaint you with the perfect spy o' th' time,
> The moment on't ; for't must be done to-night,
> And something from the palace ; always thought
> That I require a clearness. (III i 126–31)

This is the tyrant's parody of royal wisdom. The true king plants 'deservers' (I iv 42) in measure, time and place, and reaps a plenteous harvest of honour, love and obedience; Macbeth plants murderers by night and will become a withered tree in a barren land. Even his dearest partner in greatness will soon have to petition him for a little of his stolen time : 'Say to the King, I would attend his leisure/For a few words' (III ii 3–4). And shortly after those few sad words he will have no time left for her either : 'There would have been a time for such a word ...'

Because Macbeth's actions are calculated rather than impetuous, the plot of the play, unlike that of *Othello*, does not incorporate ideas about time. It is not propelled to any notable degree by coincidence, accident or the ill-timed word; we never feel that the delay of a minute or a day would have averted tragedy. But Shakespeare has to induce the feeling that Macbeth's murder of Duncan and seizure of the crown is a violent acceleration of time's 'proportion'd course'; and he does this more by poetic than by specifically dramatic means – by allusion, figurative expression and symbolism. There is, for example, an obvious and important group of equestrian images which combine notions of running and leaping, of controlled or uncontrolled speed or force; closely related to it is the imagery of winged creatures – flying with ferocity or fleeing in fear. Posts bringing news of the rebels' defeat and Macbeth's triumph come towards Duncan as 'thick as hail' and with 'haste looking through their eyes' (I ii 47; I iii 97).[13] This hints at the sweep of events which will soon engulf the gracious king; and that Macbeth will be the leading spirit in it is implied by the second sentence which Duncan speaks to him: 'Thou art so far before/That swiftests wing of recompense is slow/To overtake thee'. This metaphor becomes symbolic action when Macbeth gallops ahead of the king and Banquo to talk to his wife about the coming on of time:

> We cours'd him at the heels and had a purpose
> To be his purveyor; but he rides well,
> And his great love, sharp as his spur, hath holp him
> To his home before us. (I vii 21–4)

Like Lady Macbeth's equivocal use of the word 'dispatch' (I v 65) (which could signify murder and speed as well as care),[14] the phrase 'sharp as his spur' firmly identifies haste (disguised as hospitality in action) with cruelty and violence.

After Duncan's death, the horse remains for a while the symbol of swift and uncurbed violence. 'Beauteous and swift, the minions of their race', the royal horses break out from their stalls (their appointed place), eat each other and threaten to make war on humankind (II iv 14–18). And the thudding hooves which tell of Banquo's approach – 'Hark, I hear horses' (III iii 7) – are not a sign of his timely arrival to take his place at the banquet table, but an uncannily expressive symbol of the untimely death that is about to descend upon him in the dark. However, when the murderer's 'Hark' is repeated by Macbeth on the blasted heath (after he has cursed the infected air whereon the witches 'ride') – 'I did hear/The galloping of horse. Who was't came by?' (IV i 139–40) – the auditory symbol indicates that time and force are now turning against the tyrant himself; for what Macbeth has heard are the messengers who bring news that Macduff (almost bird-like) has fled to England for help. Macbeth can still descend like a 'hell-kite' and with 'one fell swoop' upon Macduff's 'pretty chickens and their dam' (IV iii 217–18); but it is too late: Macduff's 'flighty purpose' cannot be 'o'ertook' (IV i 145). The witches' promise that 'our *high-plac'd* Macbeth/Shall live the lease of nature, pay his breath/To *time* and mortal custom' [my italics] (IV i 98–100) will soon prove false: time has anticipated his dread exploits (IV i 144).

The process of retribution – the 'even-handed justice' – which begins to operate in the third act, can be construed in its entirety as time's revenge. It was not difficult for Shakespeare to introduce this conception to the play, since of its very nature Nemesis affirms that there is an indestructible relationship between past, present and future which man will ignore to his cost: it is impossible to 'o'erleap' today and 'take to-morrow', just as it is impossible to trammel up the consequence of what was done yesterday or today; the gilded future simply becomes a problematical or boring succession of todays and yesterdays, and the past persistently intrudes upon the present until the moment arrives when life on this bank and shoal of time seems unbearable or pointless – nothing remains then but the life to come, which, being timeless, cannot be 'jumped'.

The turning of the tide is marked with great nicety in the middle of the third act when Macbeth, echoing Banquo's 'How goes the night boy?' (II i 1), asks his wife, 'What is the night?', and she replies, 'Almost at odds with the morning, which is which' (III iv 126–7). Just as the question revives the guilty past, so the answer anticipates the retributive future when Malcolm's power is 'ready' and he tells his friends that 'the night is long that never finds the day' (IV iii 240). But the whole of the third act is retributive by nature, since it shows that what Macbeth has sought eludes him and what he would elude seeks him. The consequence of his attempt to order the future has been to put rancours in the vessel of his peace and to 'spoil the pleasure of the time' (III i 65; III iv 98). Apart from his fears by day, there is his insomnia by night. This may be taken as an elementary sign of the past asserting itself; but it is to be seen as a part of time's revenge for another reason. Sleep is 'great nature's second course' (II ii 39), in the sense that it refreshes and delights the body as the second or main course in a meal does. But it is also a course in Nature in the sense that it marks a division between one day's labour and the next: it is an integral part of time's 'proportion'd course' and of what the Book of Homilies called the 'comely course and order' of the universe. By destroying repose and identifying themselves for a while with those black agents who rouse by night, the Macbeths violate the order of time and are punished accordingly. In Lady Macbeth's sad remark, 'You lack the season of all natures, sleep' (III iv 141), there is a quibble on season which suggests that sleep is time's gift and without it life loses all its savour.

But the past asserts itself in another and much more disturbing fashion. When Lady Macbeth gently accuses her husband of keeping too much to himself and 'making companions of sorriest fancies' which 'should have died with them they think on' (III ii 8–11), she is really describing herself as well as him. Moreover, her figurative expression tells us that the two 'dearest partners' are now less familiar with each other than they are with the dead, whose repose they envy (III ii 6, 19) and – worse – whose wrongs accuse them. To his horror, Macbeth finds that 'the rebellious dead' will not keep their places and their secrets or allow him to sit at ease in the place for which he has given everything:

> The time has been
> That when the brains were out the man would die,
> And there an end; but now they rise again,
> With twenty mortal murders on their crowns,
> And push us from our stools. (III iv 78–82)

Macbeth is tormented, too, by the very future which he thought he could 'take'. As soon as he gets the crown he becomes obsessed with the hereafter in which no son of his will reign: whereas Banquo has been hailed as 'the root and father/Of many kings', he himself has simply won 'a barren sceptre' and 'a fruitless crown'

(III i 5–6, 60–1). It is ironical that he should speak so bitterly of that sceptre being 'wrench'd' from him 'with an unlineal hand' (II i 62), since no one makes more determined efforts than he to destroy the natural process of lineal succession – withholding from Malcolm 'the due of birth' (III vi 25), murdering Macduff's wife and children 'and all unfortunate souls/That trace him in his line' (IV i 152–3), and, of course, attempting to ensure that 'the seeds of Banquo' (III i 69) will never grow to royalty. In Shakespearian thought, lineal succession – symbolized by the family tree and its 'earthbound root' (IV i 96) – is as much a function of time's procreant order as the succession of the seasons; and it is because he sets out to 'unfix' it (IV i 96) that Macbeth himself declines suddenly into the sere and yellow leaf. The escape of Malcolm, Donalbain and Fleance is Nature's guarantee that he cannot continue to do as he pleases with 'the seeds of time' (I iii 58): the father of kings may be destroyed as if he were a serpent, but 'the worm that's fled', although it has 'no teeth for the present', 'hath nature that in time will venom breed' (III iv 29–31). Earnestly gazing at that future which his 'heart throbs to know', Macbeth beholds a line of kings stretching out from Banquo to the end of time – and it is a vision of the future which makes the present utterly unendurable : 'Let this pernicious hour/Stand aye accursed in the calendar' (IV i 101, 133–4).

We need not examine in detail the process of time's revenge beyond this; but a few points should be mentioned in order to show how thorough that process is. Macbeth's attempt to unfix the lineal tree is punished not only by his own sterility but by the moving of Birnam wood to Dunsinane. His premature wrenching of the sceptre is matched by his death at the hands of a man 'untimely ripp'd' from his mother's womb. And if he does not become 'the show and gaze o' th' time' in life, he does so in death : 'Behold where stands/Th' usurper's cursed head. The time is free' (V viii 24, 54–5). 'And so his knell is knoll'd' (V viii 49). There are no gentle words and no noble rites for this dead king : just ignominy, and then oblivion.

v

So, in a sense, Macbeth is merely a poor player who struts and frets his *hour* upon the stage and then is heard *no more*. He has secured the principal part in a swelling drama on the imperial theme, has adorned himself with 'the gorgeous garment majesty' (*II Henry IV* V ii 44), has carried the sceptre, worn the crown, and done his best to speak like a gracious king. He has thus beguiled and mocked the time with fairest show. But in the end, time and 'the time' mock him.

The subject of usurpation inevitably brings into *Macbeth* the notion of life as a play, pageant or rite in which men should accept the role 'appropered unto them by God their creator' and perform it with the maximum of propriety.[15] But as critics have long recognised, much more extensive use is made of the kindred notion of proper and improper costume.[16] This is an obvious adaptation of the Tudor conception of honour, good name or title as a glittering and precious robe which will bring contempt rather than admiration to the wearer unless he deserves and becomes it – a conception which would have had special force in an Elizabethan or Jacobean play since it was known that the players were often attired in 'a Lords cast suit'.[17] The description of Macbeth as a man whose title hangs loose upon him like a giant's robe upon a dwarfish thief (V iii 20–2) is an obvious and vigorous version of the traditional figure. But just as the whole play is distinguished by its unpolitical and humane interest in what it actually *feels like* to be a usurper, so the dress imagery becomes a vehicle not for external impressions of social and aesthetic unfitness but for those feelings of unease, strain or constriction which beset a man who undertakes a part for which he is not naturally suited. If we look more closely at Angus' description of Macbeth as a dwarfish thief in giant's attire, we shall see that it is not society's view of Macbeth which is being presented, but Macbeth's : 'Now does he feel . . . now does he feel' (V iii 16, 20). Like the blood that seems to stick to his hands, like the dreams and ghosts of the past and the vision of the future, the very clothes on his back make him feel 'cabin'd, cribb'd, confin'd' – envious of the naked innocence that strides the blast and inhabits the broad and casing air.

The traditional symbolism is also transformed by its association with ideas of time, change and lost identity. Banquo explains Macbeth's 'raptness' by referring to his 'new honours' and likening them to 'strange garments' which 'cleave not to their mould/ But with the aid of use' (I iii 144–6). Although Macbeth's wonder is caused here by the 'horrid image' of himself as a murdering usurper (an image which certainly takes time getting used to : 'We are but young in deed'), he later develops the figure in the sense intended by Banquo, telling his wife that the right thing to do is to go on wearing the golden opinions he has just won, and not to cast them aside so soon : we must 'grow' into our honours as into our clothes. When it is made known that he will be 'nam'd' and 'invested' at Scone, Macduff predicts that (for everyone) an easy and comfortable present will give way to an uncomfortable future – 'our old robes' will 'sit easier than our new' (II iv 31–2, 38). This is graphically borne out during Macbeth's conversation with his wife's doctor. Talking all the while about mental and national sickness, he furiously dons his armour (before it is needed) and then just as furiously tears it off again (V iii 31–6, 46–50, 54). But here unease has developed into the mad 'flaws and starts' of personal disintegration; on the Elizabethan stage, nothing could show more clearly that Macbeth is ripe for shaking – 'action is eloquence' (*Coriolanus*, III ii 76).

More obviously, the clothes symbolism is used to indicate the conscious deceit in which Macbeth's theft of the crown involves him. We might say, therefore, that it is an essential part of Shakespeare's concern in the play for the question of appearance and reality. But as the reader might guess from what I have written so far in this book, the notion of a discrepancy between appearance and reality is, in my view, rather too vague and general to be of much use in identifying and understanding the phenomena to which it is referred. What Shakespeare is really concerned with whenever this notion seems relevant is a breakdown in natural and appropriate relationships, and the semantic disorders and social confusion which are necessarily attendant upon such a breakdown. *Macbeth* tells us that it is natural for king and subject, kinsman and kinsman, host and guest, parent and child to 'infold' (I iii 31) each other with 'strong knots of love' (IV iii 27), to be with 'a most indissoluble tie/For ever knit' (III i 17–18) in duty as well as love, and to seek, out of gratitude for kindnesses done, to 'bind' themselves even more lastingly one to the other (I iv 43). But Macbeth and his wife are prepared to cancel and tear to pieces these bonds (III ii 49), and as a result all the signs – verbal and otherwise – which express, sustain and confirm such bonds become confused and confusing. The bond between name and man disappears : 'signs of nobleness' (I iv 41) are attached to those who act most ignobly. The bond between thought and expression is broken too : eye, hand and tongue express welcome but there is poison in the heart (I v 61-3; III ii 31; IV iii 118); the mouth speaks honour but deep curses form in the timid heart (V iii 27); minds are 'infected' by thoughts of unnatural deeds but have to discharge their secrets 'to their deaf pillows' (V i 69-71); men 'think but dare not speak' (V i 77); and everywhere unconscious equivocation eats insidiously into the bond between words and matter to swell the number of 'imperfect speakers' (I iii 70) and to make language as changeable and two-faced as the times.

That all the deceit and falsity in Macbeth's Scotland is to be apprehended as semantic disorder might be inferred from Lady Macbeth's comment on her husband's face: it is, she tells him, a book where men may read the strange matters that are forming in his heart; and she advises him to make it in that sense illegible (I v 59-60). It is not true then that 'there's no art/To find the mind's construction in the face' but rather that people like Lady Macbeth and the first and second thane of Cawdor have all but destroyed that art. Duncan himself, one must suppose, is a perfect refutation of his own maxim. 'The order of God's creatures in themselves is not only admirable and glorious, but eloquent',[18] and Scotland's anointed king is an active part of that eloquent order. Cast in the right role, and playing it with perfect grace, he will suit the word to the action and modulate his voice and countenance in such a way that his kindly and gracious heart will be manifest to all men. His whole manner will be like a garment that cleaves to its mould by the aid of use : it will fit.

But Macbeth and his wife, being committed to a permanent 'faith-breach' (V ii 18), are compelled to make their faces 'vizards' to their hearts, disguising what they are (III ii 34-5). Macbeth himself has to 'put on' the semblance of manly readiness because his 'naked frailties suffer in exposure' (II iii 125-6, 132) or because he cannot endure his wife's taunts that she would 'shame to wear a heart so white' as his (II ii 64). He has to 'mask' his 'bare-fac'd' savagery from 'the common eye', wailing at the fall of the men he himself strikes down (III i 118-24). And among his guests, he must try hard to 'sleek o'er' his 'rugged looks', since 'the rugged Russian bear' and the shag-haired villain or demi-wolf that he is beginning to resemble does not become the royal banquet table (III ii 27; III iv 100). The sleeking of Macbeth's rugged looks is perhaps the most potent of all the dress-disguise images. By the

lightest of associative means, it calls up the terrible spiritual transformation which has taken place in him and at the same time defines the conflict between civility and barbarity which is implicit in
the banquet scene. The likening of Macbeth's uneasy looks to
bristling or shaggy hair puts him in the catalogue with the 'rough,
rug-headed [Irish] kerns,/Which live like venom where no venom
else' (*Richard II*, II i 156–7); with the mad rebel Cade who
seemed 'like a wild Morisco' or 'a shag-hair'd craft kern' (*II Henry
VI*, III ii 356–7); with 'the rugged Pyrrhus' and 'Hyrcanian beast'
(*Hamlet*, II ii 444); in short, with the hirsute, cave-keeping
creature which man becomes once again when he defies humane
statutes that purged the gentle weal.

There is one other passage in which dress imagery indicates an
attempt to deck out barbarism in the guise of humanity and gentleness. It occurs when Macbeth follows much too literally his wife's
suggestion that they should 'roar' their 'griefs and clamour' when
Duncan's death is announced (I vii 78). What gives this passage
particular interest here is that the rhetoricians' habitual analogy
between dress and speech-style is implicit in it and is subtly employed for dramatic effect. At the end of his first sorrowing speech,
Macbeth claims that there is nothing left for him in life to 'brag' of
– a remark which prepares us for his next speech, where he protests that love, grief and 'courage' made him kill the sleepy grooms.
The style of this speech (which I have already quoted in part)
matches Macbeth's posture; and, by a familiar Shakespearian
stratagem, the indignant speaker specifies and condemns impropriety while in the act of displaying it :

> Here lay Duncan,
> His silver skin lac'd with his golden blood;
> And his gash'd stabs look'd like a breach in nature
> For ruin's wasteful entrance : there, the murderers,
> Steep'd in the colours of their trade, their daggers
> Unmannerly breech'd with gore. Who could refrain . . .
> (II iii 110–15)

It was so unnatural and improper that daggers should be covered
with gore instead of sheaths, and that a king's body be dressed in
blood rather than in lace, silver and gold : so Macbeth suggests
and, of course, he is right. But it is also improper that anyone should

speak in this manner, least of all the man who bore the knife himself. The figure of imperfectly trousered daggers (reinforced by the
inept 'unmannerly') is really grotesque and, together with the
rhetorical questions with which the speech begins and ends, confirms the impression of rhetorical extravagance. It is not surprising
that Lady Macbeth chooses this moment to put on womanly gentleness and faint, for any moderately perceptive listener would have
sensed that her husband's speech was simply 'bombast and . . .
lining for the time' (*Love's Labour's Lost*, V ii 769). In penning
the dress metaphor, too, Shakespeare must have been reflecting
that the literal term for material used to pad out garments and the
figurative term for overblown language was 'bombast'.

VI

When the Macbeths make their entry as king and queen – heralded
by a sennet and accompanied by lords and attendants – one's first
thought should probably be that Macbeth is now wearing the
clothes of the man he murdered : the neutrality of the Elizabethan
stage and the costliness of the costumes used would dictate such a
response. Our next conscious perception, induced by oral rather
than visual language, should be that Macbeth and his wife are
playing in a grand manner the very role which was theirs when
they were preparing to kill Duncan : for these are their first words
(on stage) as king and queen of Scotland :

Macbeth.   Here's our chief guest.
Lady M.   If he had been forgotten,
   It had been as a gap in our great feast,
   And all-thing unbecoming.
Macbeth.   Tonight we hold a solemn supper, sir,
   And I'll request your presence. (III i 11–15)

This solemn feast, during or before which the host has his chief
guest murdered, and where everything else is in some sense unbecoming, synthesises all that is said or implied elsewhere in the
play concerning the divorce between what Macbeth should be (or
was) and what he is. Within the sphere of behaviour defined by the

key word 'welcome', he and his wife endeavour to beguile the time with the fairest show of order and propriety. But the show very obviously does not fit the facts, and the facts keep intruding in the most strident fashion.

The meeting begins with Macbeth and his wife attending rather stiffly to the niceties of time and place, explaining them to the guests, and using gracious words which we are meant to see do not come from the heart :

> *Macbeth.*　You know your own degrees, sit down.
> 　　At first and last the hearty welcome.
> *Lords.*　Thanks to your Majesty.
> *Macbeth.*　Our self will mingle with society
> 　And play the humble host.
> 　Our hostess keeps [to] her [chair of] state ;
> 　　but in best time
> 　We will require her welcome.
> *Lady M.*　Pronounce it for me, sir, to all our friends ;
> 　For my heart speaks they are welcome. (III iv 1–8)

The rest of the performance is structured on Macbeth's triple and abortive effort to get beyond the formula which urges the company to 'prepare for mirth, for mirth becomes a feast' (*Pericles*, II ii 7). His wife has reminded him to be 'bright and jovial' among his guests (III ii 28) and, accordingly, he now says : 'Be large in mirth ; anon, we'll drink a measure/The table round' (III iv 11–12). The delay signalled by 'anon' is caused by the appearance of the First Murderer at the door, with whom he goes to confer. On returning, he is suavely rebuked by his wife for neglecting 'ceremony', drinks a cup to 'good digestion' and 'health', and this time is prevented from taking his seat by the appearance of Banquo's ghost. When the ghost vanishes and he has recovered his composure, he drinks a full cup pledging love, health, and joy to all the table (III iv 87–9), but again is unable to sit down. By now, his terrified monologues have completely spoiled 'the pleasure of *the time*', have '*displac'd* the mirth', and 'broke the good meeting/With most admir'd *disorder*' [my italics] (III iv 97, 100–11). And the last words heard by the guests are very different to the first ; 'Stand not upon the order of your going,/But go at once' (III iv 118–19). They are forced to leave in much the same manner as the Macbeths have come to their seat of state – with a scrambling disregard for the order of time and place.

Macbeth's inability to get beyond the formula which starts the solemn supper is a kind of spiritual impediment that recalls the moment when he had most need of blessing but found 'Amen' stuck in his throat (II ii 31–3); it is as if he were being punished for trying to say grace. To wish joy, love and health at the beginning of a meal may not be in a strict sense to say grace; but it is very close to it and we are, I think, meant to take it as an equivalent. Certainly the word 'grace', on whose multiple meanings (including that now in question) Shakespeare was wont to capitalise, is put in our minds when Macbeth is in the act of starting the meal; for to his second formula he adds a wish that 'the grac'd person of Banquo' were present (III iv 41), and Ross responds by urging him to 'grace' the table with his royal company (III iv 45).[19] Before the banquet, too, Macbeth admitted in his soliloquy that by killing 'the gracious Duncan' (III i 65) he had damned his soul – just as immediately after the banquet Hecate refers to him as a 'wayward son' who will put himself beyond 'grace' (III v 11, 31). What I am suggesting here, and wish to develop by way of conclusion, is that within the range of manners and conduct specified by the notion of hospitality – of welcoming and feasting – Shakespeare concentrates attention on that quality or complex of qualities which is most proper to a king and which Macbeth, the 'untitled tyrant' (IV iii 104), is necessarily most deficient in: the quality of grace. As we have seen, 'grace' is the humanist term for the beauty which inheres in whatever is said or done with propriety and so is virtually a synonym for decorum: 'and everything that hee doth or speaketh', observes Castiglione, 'let him doe it with a grace'.[20] But in royal contexts Shakespeare uses the word to designate that which is proper from the divine as well as the human point of view: the natural graces of the ideal king are simply confirmations that he rules by the grace of God and divine right, and that he is God's substitute on earth. Duncan, therefore, is nothing if not gracious: that epithet is almost part of his name. When, however, the man who takes his place is addressed as 'your Grace', the title is deliberately made to sound grotesquely unbecoming in the context (IV i 135; V iii 30; V v 30). King Macbeth can dignify no noble presence with his company; he is devoid of mercy and favour; he is untouched by the regenerative influence of Heaven;

and everything he does lacks becomingness. All of which means that he is without grace, for all of these meanings are embraced by that word.[21]

In the play which I have cited above on the fitness of mirth to feasting, there is a structurally prominent contrast between the improper and the proper kind of royal welcome (*Pericles* I i; II iii). In *Macbeth*, the only ritual action which follows the abortive banquet is that of the secret, black and midnight hags to whose evil brew and company Macbeth compulsively gravitates: his presence once more on the blasted heath, above all his desperate conjurations there (filled with blasphemous and misanthropic venom), show what a masquerade his ritual of love has been. But although Shakespeare does not dramatise the festal norm, he does manage to communicate in the latter part of the play a strong impression of a court where the social and religious virtues associated with grace and ceremony are expressed through welcome and hospitality. In the conversation between Lennox and another lord which closes Act III, we learn that Macduff 'lives in disgrace' because he 'failed/His presence at the tyrant's feast' (III vi 22–3). But the tyrant's grace and favour is like the tyrant's feast, and so Macduff is linked here with grace itself – with the holy angel which, sped by Scottish prayers, flies to the court of England to bring back a swift blessing for a land suffering and accursed (V vi 45–9). In that court there rules a 'holy king' (III vi 30) who possesses all the attributes seen in the 'most sainted king' (IV iii 109) who once ruled Scotland. And Macduff will 'pray' to him for help so that (says Lennox),

> (with Him above
> To ratify the work) we may again
> Give to our tables meat, sleep to our nights,
> Free from our feasts and banquets bloody knives,
> Do faithful homage and receive free honours. (III vi 32–6)

Already Malcolm lives in that court and 'is receiv'd ... with such grace/That the malevolence of fortune nothing/Takes from his high respect' (III vi 26–9).

Malcolm is at home in Edward's court in more than one sense, for he understands and lives its ethos. It is he who speaks the praise in which the royal saint is represented as the antithesis of those malignant creatures which seduced Macbeth : Edward's powers, Malcolm emphasises, are given him by Heaven and are used only to cure 'the evil' ; he has a gift of prophecy which is 'a heavenly gift' ; and all the blessings which hang about his throne 'speak him full of grace' (IV iii 146–59). Malcolm implicitly contrasts the bounty of 'gracious England' (from whom he has received offer of 'goodly thousands') with 'the tyrant's grasp' (IV iii 36, 43–4). And despite his experience of the goodly exterior of the malevolent he can still, because of Edward, hold on to his faith that the good will inevitably be seen as good – will 'wear' its proper graces :

> That which you are, my thoughts cannot transpose.
> Angels are bright still, though the brightest fell ;
> Though all things foul would wear the brow of grace,
> Yet grace must still look so. (IV iii 21–24)

Yet Malcolm temporarily undermines this truth by painting a picture of his moral character which is as improper as the humane exterior of brutal Macbeth (or, to go back to the beginning, the brutal aspect of kindly Macbeth). According to himself, he possesses none of 'the king-becoming graces' and so is not 'fit to govern' (IV iii 91, 101). But he unspeaks his own detraction as soon as he has 'reconcil'd' his thoughts to Macduff's 'good truth and honour' (IV iii 116–17); and the suggestion, I think, is that with this reconciliation and the mutual trust and solid friendship which follows, the warring contrarieties that 'confound/All unity on earth' (IV iii 99–100) begin to disappear. 'Such welcome and unwelcome things at once/'Tis hard to reconcile', says Macduff (IV iii 138–9); he is explaining the silence with which he greets Malcolm's retraction, but, in fact, is summarising the essential experience of the play.

Malcolm is obviously equipped to effect the wonderful harmony at which Macduff stops short. When Ross enters, Malcolm fails to recognise him ; but when Macduff says, 'My ever-gentle cousin, welcome hither', Malcolm exclaims : 'I know him now. Good God betimes remove/The means that makes us strangers !' (IV iii 161–3). This is only one of many signs that Malcolm is destined to bring back 'the sweet milk of concord' (IV iii 98) ; that, like Richmond at the end of Richard III's reign, he will restore meaning to the 'ceremonious vows' and 'rites of love'.[22] And so his last speech, to which we have already referred, can now be viewed as a whole : it is a promise that, 'by the grace of Grace' (V viii 72), love, friend-ship and gratitude will be renewed, and all other duties fulfilled, 'in measure, time, and place'.

6
Antony and Cleopatra

I

Between the first divorce of Henry VIII and the rise of Oliver Cromwell, one art which was taken very seriously was the art of dying. Flourishing in times of despotism, reckless ambition and religious persecution, this art enables men to face sudden death with a steadfast countenance and so snatch a kind of victory in the moment of total defeat. Those who attain to it – be they stoical aristocrats or devout martyrs – often secure the admiration if not the affection of their enemies. They appear to redeem whatever faults may have blemished their lives, complicate all tendencies to judge them unfavourably, and demand an honourable place in the roll of history. Indeed, they have the strange effect of making one wonder whether the art of wise winning is not less admirable than that of gracious losing.

Shakespeare's keen interest in the ability of princes and queens to prove themselves most royal just when Fortune has stripped them of all prosperity can be traced back from *Henry VIII* and *The Winter's Tale* to *Henry VI*, that early work in which hindsight can see so much that is prophetic. There, both Henry and the pretender York are nowhere more royal than at the point of death; York's crowned son commands most admiration when he is uncrowned by Warwick; and Margaret, the wrangling queen whom nothing becomes, impresses herself as queen on the audience's imagination for the first and only time when she appears at the French court as an uncrowned suppliant:

> *K. Lewis.* Fair Queen of England, worthy Margaret,
>   Sit down with us. It ill befits thy state
>   And birth that thou shouldst stand while Lewis doth sit.
> *Q. Mar.* No, mighty King of France. Now Margaret
>   Must strike her sail and learn a while to serve
>   Where kings command. I was, I must confess,

Great Albion's Queen in former golden days;
But now mischance hath trod my title down
And with dishonour laid me on the ground,
Where I must take like seat unto my fortune,
And to my humble seat conform myself.
K. Lewis. Why, say, fair Queen, whence springs this deep
despair?
Q. Mar. From such a cause as fills mine eyes with tears,
And stops my tongue, while heart is drown'd in cares.
K. Lewis. What'er it be, be thou still like thy self,
And sit thee by our side. [Seats her by him]
Yield not thy neck
To fortune's yoke, but let thy dauntless mind
Still ride in triumph over all mischance
                              (*III Henry VI*, III iii 1–18)

The difference between this scene and that where the captured
Cleopatra negotiates with Proculeius and then Caesar (V ii) pre-
dicates a miracle of artistic achievement which seems to render
comparison absurd. But the miracle is rooted in nature and the
early scene is beyond doubt a fairly well developed foetal image
of the late one. Cleopatra presents herself as 'fortune's vassal',
kneels to Caesar, and seems resigned – almost happy – to accept
the role of 'sweet dependency'. But this abject bowing to Fortune
(and 'Fortune's knave') is apparent rather than real, for Cleopatra's conduct, like Margaret's, combines political astuteness
with a proud awareness that servility does not become her. Moreover, her performance glitters with an irridescent, elusive irony
which allows her to commune with herself and the audience on
the grotesqueness of the role which she is being asked to play and
the asininity of those who think she will play it in earnest :

If your master
Would have a queen his beggar, you must tell him
That majesty, to keep decorum, must
No less beg than a kingdom. (V ii 15–18)

I do not wish to suggest, however, that Queen Margaret was in
any real sense a preliminary sketch for Cleopatra. The truth is that
before Shakespeare turned his attention to her Cleopatra was already well defined in literary tradition as a character who com-

pletely transcended whatever was unqueenly in her life by the rare queenliness of her death. This conception of her character was first expressed by Horace (*Odes*, I xxvii); it was reaffirmed by Plutarch in his 'Life of Marcus Antonius'; and it was very conspicuous in two neo-classical tragedies of the Renaissance – Garnier's *Marc Antonie* (translated, in 1592, by Sir Philip Sidney's sister) and Daniel's *Cleopatra* (1594). It is necessary also to record that in *The False One* (*c.* 1619–22), which treats of Pompey's fall and Cleopatra's affair with Julius Caesar, Fletcher invents a threat to Cleopatra's life simply in order to introduce her sublime display of self-respect and courage in the face of death.[1]

But it was as an admiring student of Shakespeare that Fletcher was prompted to do this. A few years after the composition of *Antony and Cleopatra*, he himself had probably cooperated with Shakespeare in dramatising the fall of England's dignified Queen Katherine ('nothing but death/Shall e'er divorce my dignities' – *Henry VIII*, III i 141–2). And the whole of *The False One* shows how closely he had studied and how completely he understood *Antony and Cleopatra* : in a sense, his own play on Cleopatra is the first interpretation of Shakespeare's, and in some respects it is still the best. By making Cleopatra's gesture of marble constancy an integral part of a sustained study of loyalty and disloyalty, Fletcher showed his awareness that the magnificent finale of *Antony and Cleopatra*, far from being an artful evasion of the moral issues raised by the rest of the action, clarifies the intention of the whole play and derives all its significance and most of its splendour therefrom. In death, and by a deliberate act, Shakespeare's lovers achieve a starry fixity; dolphin-like, they rise above the vast ocean of flux, uncertainty, suspicion, envy and treachery which has been eroding the whole of civilisation : 'Egypt and Greece, goodbye, and goodbye Rome!'

II

Of all Shakespeare's tragedies, none dwells on the process of fall and change quite so continuously as this one. Antony's bitter complaint about the youthful partner who holds him in contempt –

    ... he seems
Proud and disdainful, harping on what I am,
Not what he knew I was. (III xiii 141–3)

– typifies the play's pervasive vision of a magnificent but dissolving spectacle in which the individual painfully or regretfully perceives that he and others are no longer what they once were. There is an abundant flow of criticism, self-criticism and taunting which does not cease until the First Guard's angry question : 'Is this well done?' (V ii 323), is everlastingly answered by the dead queen's dying attendant. And the language of the play is full of constructions turning on the reflexive pronoun ('If I lose mine honour, I lose myself') and the preposition 'like' ('Show me, my women, like a queen'), all of which – like the resonant iteration of proper names – is symptomatic of a ceaseless preoccupation with identity. This preoccupation is established at the outset in the dialogues of Philo and Demetrius which frame the first appearance of the protagonists. The two officers – unequivocal spokesmen of Roman morality – are analogous to the plaintive and moralising choruses in Garnier-Pembroke and Daniel. But they also exemplify a peculiarly Shakespearian technique, being even more akin to those stage spectators who comment on the improprieties in some performance within the play ('This is not Cressida!'); for they agree that the disciplined and all-powerful general who once glowed like plated Mars has been transformed into a strumpet's fool. It is true that the man whom they and we are watching happens to deny this charge in his first speech; but the impressive denial (or protestation) has been wrung from him by a cunning comedienne who knows full well that women can make him bend and turn this way or that just as they wish.

There is, however, a link between Antony's words and Philo's which must be observed : Philo urges his companion to 'take but good note' of the general's behaviour (I i 11), while the general expresses his eagerness to 'wander through the streets and note/ The qualities of people' (I ii 53–4). This echo is, I suspect, a delicate reminder of the kind transmitted to us through the disingenuous words addressed by Claudius to the spectators of *his* play : 'And you the judges bear a wary eye'. But although Philo's judgement of Antony probably does not accommodate an understanding of all his qualities, we can let it stand for the moment and note how extensively it is supported by Antony's subsequent behaviour, by the judgement of others, and by the harshly candid self-criticism in which he himself engages from time to time.

Antony is shown to 'degenerate from kind' as a Roman, as a

soldier or military leader, and even as a man. The comic strain in
the tragedy, embodied principally in the mocking and playful side
of Cleopatra's character, stands for an Eastern levity to which
Antony's Roman *gravitas* continually succumbs. The dismissal of
Caesar's ambassadors unheard – which the sober Philo and Demetrius note so well – constitutes a triumph for sensuous levity the
effect of which overflows abundantly into the frivolous and bawdy
first half of the scene which follows. There the mocking defeat of
gravity (represented, not by a Roman, but by the soothsayer and
his enigmatically profound : 'In nature's infinite book of secrecy/
A little I can read' – I ii 9–10) is obliquely but firmly related to the
general sense of indecorum which has prevailed since the start of
the tragedy. Charmian's flippant request, 'Good Isis, hear me this
prayer, though thou deny me a matter of more weight' (I ii 63), is
backed up by Iras with mock fervour : 'Amen. Dear goddess . . .
keep decorum, and fortune him accordingly !' But so rapid is the
oscillation between contraries in the play that even in this scene
Antony's gravity reasserts itself and he is found dealing with matters of weight in the appropriate fashion : 'He was dispos'd to
mirth; but on the sudden/A Roman thought hath struck him',
observes Cleopatra – and immediately despatches Enobarbus to
'bring him hither' (I ii 79–82). As her spokesman, Enobarbus
mocks Antony's decision to leave his chosen 'space'; indeed, Enobarbus is levity itself, all his jesting being about death ('death's the
word' – I ii 132) – Cleopatra's feigned and sexual deaths, and
Fulvia's real one. But Antony rebukes him in the manner of a preoccupied leader ('No more light answers' – I ii 170), proceeds to
explain the business of state which requires his quick departure,
and so the scene ends. Yet this is an incomplete victory for *gravitas*, since Enobarbus is a poor substitute for the wily Cleopatra.
Her little exhibition in the next scene of celeritous dying and cunning 'folly' (I iii 57, 98) may not prevent Antony's departure but
it enables her to extract from him the sworn assurance that he will
return and that he goes hence making peace or war just as she
affects. She is 'quickly ill and well' (I iii 71) because he is quickly
grave and foolish.

  There could be no more striking evidence that he is so than the
carousals which follow so hard on the negotiations with Caesar and
Pompey. Leading the Egyptian Bacchanals, he seems much more
like the Lord of Misrule than the triple pillar of the world : he even

succeeds in drawing Caesar into a drunken spree from which they are both lucky to escape alive. Caesar, however, soon dissociates himself from the performance in disgust : 'Our graver business/ Frowns at this levity . . . The wild disguise hath almost/Antick'd us all' (II vii 118–19, 122–3). These words recall not only the frowns of Philo and Demetrius but the conversation with Lepidus which forms our introduction to Caesar. Except for the fact that his words do not recoil sharply on himself, Caesar's detailed and acid commentary there on the impropriety of Antony's Egyptian escapade (I iv 1–33) is a rebuke of the kind delivered by Othello to his drunken officers : Antony may be absent, yet the effect of the speech is essentially the same as that of a direct rebuke and, in fact, Caesar concludes with a direct exhortation to the absent offender ('Antony, leave thy lascivious wassails . . .'). Viewing all the faults, Caesar finds Antony's conduct inexcusable chiefly because he has shown an adolescent inability to distinguish between a time for gravity and a time for gaiety :

> . . . yet must Antony
> No way excuse his foils when we do bear
> So great weight in his lightness. If he fill'd
> His vacancy with his voluptuousness,
> Full surfeits and the dryness of his bones
> Call on him for't ! But to confound such time
> That drums him from his sport and speaks as loud
> As his own state and ours – 'tis to be chid
> As we rate boys . . . (I iv 23–31)

Even more opposed to the Roman ideal of conduct than this unseasonable levity is the vice denoted by 'voluptuousness' and 'full surfeits' – intemperance. Though we must acknowledge that Caesar himself is incapable of perceiving that Antony's intemperance is partly the excess of a noble virtue in which he himself is signally deficient, yet intemperance it is, and of an extravagant kind : 'Some wine,/Within there, and our viands !' (III xi 73–4) is Antony's characteristic cry when he would mock the midnight bell and escape the heavy responsibilities of the moment. Not that one could say to him, as he says to Cleopatra,

> I am sure
> Though you can guess what temperance should be,
> You know not what it is. (III xiii 120–2)

For heroic disciplining of the appetites has been – as Caesar recalls – an integral part of the achievement which has made him pre-eminent among soldiers; and it 'wounds his honour' now to recall this fact (I iv 58–71).

The idea of Antony as a 'noble ruin' (III x 19) dominates Act III and much of Act IV. And it is given satiric edge by the suggestion that he is clinging stubbornly to a superannuated renown. Even as early as the negotiations with Caesar, 'the greatest soldier of the world' (I iii 38) shows some of the touchiness of a man who suspects that his laurels have begun to fade. Just how he should conduct himself in parleying with the youthful colleague who disapproves of his behaviour is a point raised by others :

> *Lep.* Good Enobarbus, 'tis a worthy deed,
> And shall become you well, to entreat your captain
> To soft and gentle speech.
> *Eno.* I shall entreat him
> To answer like himself. If Caesar move him,
> Let Antony look over Caesar's head
> And speak as loud as Mars. (II ii 1–6)

Antony succeeds in following a middle course between these two extreme views of what becomes him; yet his performance is not entirely without blemish. There is a trace of petulance in his complaint that Caesar spoke 'derogately' of him, and of prickly stiffness in the remark that he will 'so far ask pardon as befits' his 'honour to stoop in such a case' (II ii 39, 101–2). One's feeling here that Antony may have become 'the name and not the thing' (*All's Well*, V iii 302) is certainly confirmed at the start of Act III when the prudent Ventidius – his sword still red with Parthian blood – ironically remarks : 'I'll humbly signify what in his name,/ That magical word of war, we have effected' (III i 30–1). The 'fame' and 'renown' accrue to Antony, the 'great act' and 'soldier's virtue' (III i 13, 15, 19, 23) belong to his lieutenant. This is an incident which gives a hollow ring to Antony's subsequent complaint that at Philippi Octavius 'dealt on lieutenantry' and 'kept/ His sword e'en like a dancer' while he himself struck the enemy with Philippan, that sword of which we hear so much (III xi 35–40). After the Ventidius episode, it is natural that Antony should seem least admirable whenever he insists on his admirable reputation. Indeed, he is almost contemptible when he despatches Octavia back to Rome (like 'a market-maid', 'not like Caesar's sister' or 'the wife of Antony' – III vi 42–3, 51) largely because her brother did not give him unqualified praise in public (III iv 6–10).

According to the admiring Silius, Ventidius had that 'without the which a soldier and his sword/Grants scarce distinction' – wisdom; and the wisdom consisted in perceiving that it is fatal for a soldier to let himself become 'his captain's captain' (III i 22, 28–9). But a far more serious form of this type of disorder takes place; for when Antony eventually makes the abject admission, 'I have lost command' (III xi 23), it is not because he has been supplanted by Ventidius, Enobarbus or Scarus, but by Cleopatra, whose full supremacy over his spirit has enabled her at will to beck forth his wars and call them home again (one thinks of 'Captain Margaret' in *Henry VI* and of Othello's 'fair warrior'). And the unfitness of this subjection is magnified by frequent reminders that it entails a loss of manliness as well as of leadership. Cleopatra's speech (II v 18–23) recalling how she once dressed him up in her attires and wore his sword Philippan is softened by an exquisite lyric blend of affection, gaiety and nostalgia ('That time? O times . . .') But the naming of the sword accusingly recalls that other time when someone else and not Antony behaved like a dancer; and it is not accidental that in the previous brief scene Lepidus parted from Maecenas and Agrippa saying: 'Till I shall see you in your soldier's dress,/Which shall become you both, farewell' (II iv 4–5).

It is at the battle of Actium that this intoxicated confusion of roles and sexes becomes conspicuous. Enobarbus insists that Cleopatra's 'being in these wars . . . is not fit' and carefully explains why:

> Your presence needs must puzzle Antony;
> Take from his heart, take from his brain, from's time,
> What should not then be spar'd. He is already
> Traduc'd for levity; and 'tis said in Rome
> That Photinus an eunuch and your maids
> Manage this war. (III vii 10–15)

But Rome can sink and tongues rot that speak against her: she 'will not stay behind', she bears a charge in the war, and is determined to 'appear there for a man' (III vii 15–19).[2] In keeping with this new role, she rebukes 'the emperor' as soon as he arrives for his negligent attitude towards time; and the extent of her supremacy over his manly spirit is to be measured by his admiring response :

> A good rebuke,
> Which might have well becom'd the best of men
> To taunt at slackness. (III vii 25–7)

This prepares us for his willingness to fight by sea in obedience to her unthinking and obstinate decision and in opposition to the considered advice of Enobarbus and Canidius. When Caesar told Lepidus that Antony was 'not more manlike/Than Cleopatra, nor the queen of Ptolemy/More womanly than he' (I iv 5–7), his words rang like satire for its own sake, but now they seem unpleasantly true: 'So our leader's led,/And we are women's men', says Canidius in tones of bitter shame (III vii 69–70).

'Shame' is one of Shakespeare's favourite words for designating impropriety and disgrace and the sensation which they excite in any right-thinking person. It is very prominent in this play, and distinctly so when Antony deserts his men to follow Cleopatra as she scurries from battle like a flea-bitten cow in June: there one sees how very literally the great leader is led and how much of himself he loses in the process. 'I never saw an action of such shame', says Scarus; 'experience, manhood, honour, ne'er before/Did so violate itself' (III x 22–4). But in no one's imagination does the thought of this disgraceful act burn so intensely as in Antony's :

> O, whither has thou led me, Egypt? See
> How I convey my shame out of thine eyes
> By looking back what I have left behind
> 'Stroy'd in dishonour. (III xi 51–4)

Now he must send to the young man humble entreaties, 'dodge and palter in the shifts of lowness' (III xi 61–3): he is 'pluck'd' (III xii 3), as spiritually naked as Shame itself. Yet such are the strange mutations of the human heart that those who visibly suffer from an acute sense of disgust at their own aberrations can excite in us the utmost compassion, even win back much of the respect they have lost. And that is what Antony begins to do when he bows his head and hides it from the world.

III

Since Cleopatra is the temptress who exploits Antony's weakness, and since her individuality as a character is so absolute, it might well seem artificial to view her, too, as someone who deviates from her better self. One might argue that the only sensitive way to respond to her is to adopt the attitude of the poet in the sonnets who says: 'You alone are you' (LXXXIV) – to go as far as but no further than his deeply admiring acceptance of infinite variety:

> What is your substance, whereof are you made,
> That millions of strange shadows on you tend? (LIII)

But the Friend and the Mistress of the sonnets are alike shown to be subject to 'time's million'd accidents'; and the confusing constitution and impact of both is held up to analytic scrutiny. As for Cleopatra, her integrity (or psychic coherence, or whatever one may choose to call it) does not become a manifest fact until Antony's death; up until then she is a startlingly volatile confusion of opposites: a cursing drab and a grand lady – a 'wrangling queen'. In her first appearance she accuses Antony of shameful subordination to either a boy or a shrew:

> *As I am Egypt's Queen,*
> Thou blushest, Antony, and that blood of thine
> Is Caesar's homager. Else so thy cheek pays shame
> When shrill-tongu'd Fulvia scolds. The messengers! [my italics]
>   (I i 29–32)

Whatever the irony of the situation here (Cleopatra herself is scolding him into obedience), one must take the regal flourish seriously and view her on her own terms as a monarch who fully knows where homage is due and where it is not. Seen thus, her behaviour for most of the play is like one extended catachresis: it was intended to effect a degree of surprise and shock – to provide a special artistic *frisson* – which a modern audience can hardly savour to the full. To respond correctly to a queen and tragic heroine who is capable of hopping forty paces through the public street, it is not simply necessary to have in mind the assumption that 'in a prince it is decent to goe slowly . . . and with a certain granditie'.[3] One should be familiar with certain literary conventions based on social assumptions of this kind; in fact, one must even realize that Cleopatra derives some of her capacity to shock from two other tragic heroines of the same name – Garnier-Pembroke's and Daniel's. The Countess of Pembroke's translation, published twice in the 'nineties, is of historical importance in that it initiated a courtly Senecan movement in England which produced tragedies on mainly Roman themes and was conceived as a continuation of Sir Philip Sidney's endeavour to – in Daniel's words – 'chase away this tyrant of the North; Grosse Barbarisme'.[4] So absolute is literary decorum in the two plays on Cleopatra (as in the other works) that in spite of her sexual misdemeanors she is never exhibited as anything but a proud, sorrowful and thoroughly dignified queen; nothing seems more remote from the authors' minds than the notion of dramatising her seductive arts or acknowledging that these are rich in comic potential. It must be added, however, that Shakespeare does not simply play his Cleopatra off against stately paradigms for merely 'catachretic' effect; as always, he makes it quite clear that his own breach of decorum is more apparent than real and that it is part of a conscious and sustained approach to human behaviour in the light of that principle. Moreover, it is arguable that in no other play does he probe quite so deeply or provocatively into our thinking about what is proper and graceful as he does in this one.

Whereas in the first scene of the tragedy Cleopatra is an artful comedienne who makes Antony cut a rather ridiculous figure, in the two scenes with the messenger who brings news of his second marriage it is she who appears in a ludicrous light; and not only is she the grotesque victim of her own vixenish temper and feminine inconsistency, she is even mocked by Charmian in essentially the same way as she mocked Antony. What I would stress is that throughout this two-part farce Shakespeare heightens the ludicrous and equates it with indecorum by oblique but continuous allusion to the queenly paradigm which is being abused. As soon as the messenger begins to speak he is interrupted and told that if he brings good news about Antony he will be given gold and the 'bluest veins to kiss – a hand that kings/Have lipp'd and trembl'd kissing' (II v 29–30). Whether an empress should be so liberal with her hand to a common messenger would undoubtedly have seemed a serious question of decorum to the Countess of Pembroke – it does to Antony later in the play; but the principal effect of Cleopatra's words in the given context is simply to establish her majesty before she flies from extreme liberality to its opposite – grabbing the messenger by the hair and haling him up and down with screaming promises that he will be whipped with wire and stewed in brine for reporting the unpalatable truth. And lest we miss the effect intended by that proud allusion to blue veins and all the homage they have received, there is the queen's own admission after her passion has subsided : 'These hands do lack nobility, that they strike/A meaner than myself' (II v 82–3).

Comic incongruity in the scene of the messenger's next visit is of a finer kind since it is caused by mental rather than bodily antics. In fact, one must assume that Cleopatra's whole mien as she listens to the word-picture of Octavia is loftily calm and dignified – but self-consciously so, as in a middle-aged lady who is intent on establishing her charming superiority over a youthful rival. Much of the humour of this scene then depends on how well we remember its noisy predecessor, for the whole purpose of Cleopatra's cool interrogation of the messenger is to establish that Octavia is quite devoid of that which the queen possesses : 'majesty' – in voice and movement, as in appearance. Having been first addressed – she obviously expects this in her present mood – as 'Good Majesty!', 'Most gracious Majesty!', and 'dread Queen' (III iii 2, 7–8), she asks the messenger about Octavia's size ('Is she as tall as me?') and voice ('Is she shrill-tongu'd or low?'). Ignoring the possibility that a voice which is soft, gentle and low might be an excellent thing in woman, Cleopatra construes the simple answers to both questions to her own advantage : 'Dull of tongue and dwarfish!' Then comes the next question : 'What majesty is in her gait? Remember,/If e'er thou look'dst on majesty'. To this there can be no mere factual answer free from aesthetic judgement, so the messenger prudently forgets all about Octavia's April beauty and quiet dignity, tells Cleopatra the kind of emphatic untruths she wants to hear, and is sagely commended for his diplomatic skill (the irony is delightful) : 'I will employ thee back again ; I find thee/Most fit for business' (II v 35–6). Charmian concurs with this assessment of the messenger : 'A proper man' (I v 37) – and her words are not simply the chime of courtly complaisance but the beginning of a mockery which knows itself invisible : Cleopatra is now as blind to her own fatuity as is Orsino or the cross-gartered Malvolio to his :

Char. A proper man.
Cleo. Indeed he is so. I repent me much
   That I so harried him. Why, methinks, by him,
   This creature's no such thing.
Char.   Nothing, madam.
Cleo. The man hath seen some majesty, and should know.
Char. Hath he seen majesty? Isis else defend,
   And serving you so long! (II v 37–43)

This is Shakespearian art of the very finest vintage. Those with good memories will recall here not only the shrieks and leaps of Cleopatra during the messenger's last visit but her conversation with Charmian at the end of the scene in which the first message about Antony was brought to her (by Alexas) from Rome:

Cleo. Who's born that day
   When I forget to send to Antony
   Shall die a beggar. Ink and paper, Charmian.
   Welcome, my good Alexas. Did I, Charmian,
   Ever love Caesar so?
Char. O that brave Caesar!
Cleo. By Isis, I will give thee bloody teeth
   If thou with Caesar paragon again
   My man of men.
Char. By your most gracious pardon,
   I sing but after you.
Cleo. My salad days,
   When I was green in judgement, cold in blood,
   To say as I said then. (I v 63–75)

If one hopes to 'sing after' this gracious madam one has obviously to forget old songs and change one's tune very often. It is to be supposed that discords and bloody teeth are a perpetual hazard at her court.

IV

Brave Caesar – brave Antony. One is always aware that kings have kissed more than Cleopatra's blue-veined hands and that even the smallest problems of decorum are related in one way or another to constancy. When Antony comes upon her extending her

hand to Thyreus he is completely overcome with feelings in which
an aristocratic disgust at the improper is prominent (III xiii 96–9,
123–6). It is not, however, the social discrepancy between the
messenger and the queen which primarily accounts for his disgust
and rage, but the suspected discrepancy between her 'kingly seal'
of love and her actual behaviour. The possibility that she is shifting her allegiance to Octavius Caesar fills him with a nauseous
awareness of her successive liaisons with Julius Caesar, Pompey
and now himself : who is she, this left-over scrap from other men's
orgies? how can one possibly identify a triple-turned whore who
has surrendered herself to every tourist of note, in whom each man
has been temporarily lost 'as water is in water'?

Yet, if the queen has given herself indiscriminately to this one
and that, it is the emperor – 'the firm Roman' (I v 43), as he styles
himself – who is seen to break the kingly seals of high hearts.
Philo's phrase 'now bend, now turn' sums up the restless mobility
and changefulness of a man who is passion's slave. Antony is a
tragic Proteus, caught from the start of the action in the unseemly
and mutually destructive contraries of 'plural faith' (*Two Gentlemen*, V iv 52). Cleopatra has no good reason to believe that his
heady protestation of infinite and undying love is anything but
'excellent falsehood' since he has said the same thing to another
woman : this is what lies behind all her taunts and accusations :

> Why should I think you can be mine and true,
> Though you in swearing shake the throned gods,
> Who have been false to Fulvia? Riotous madness,
> To be entangled with those mouth-made vows,
> Which break themselves in swearing! (I iii 26–31)

Not even Fulvia's death can make him credible in her eyes : if he
mourns his wife, he does not really love his mistress; if he does not
mourn, the same conclusion follows (I iii 62–5).

Moreover, his conduct after he leaves Egypt hardly refutes her
suggestion that 'the greatest soldier in the world' has 'turn'd the
greatest liar' (I iii 38–9). He wants her to regard his visit to Rome
as a period of absence which will provide an 'honourable trial' and
'true evidence' of his love for her (I iii 74–5). And indeed it is made
clear from the moment he arrives in Rome that his constancy is
on trial in every way. 'You have broken/The article of your oath',

says Caesar, beginning the parley; to which Antony answers (looking over Caesar's head at the others): 'The honour is sacred which
he talks on now' – this is the scene where he shows himself haughtily
exact about what 'befits' his 'honour' (II ii 85–6, 89). Nevertheless, Antony welcomes the opportunity offered by Maecenas to
erase, by yet another bond, whatever negligence he may have
shown in regard to the last:

> To hold you in perpetual amity,
> To make you brothers, and to knit your hearts
> With an unslipping knot, take Antony
> Octavia to his wife. (II ii 129–32)

And there is no hesitation or consciousness of duplicity in the way
he solemnises 'this act of grace' and unslipping knot, either when
he assures his brother of his constancy (II ii 148–53) or promises
his gentle wife that his future conduct 'shall all be done by th'
rule' (II iii 4–6). Yet within seconds of these last words he is saying: 'I will to Egypt . . . I' th' East my pleasure lies' (II iii 39–41);
and at the moment of departure he reacts with obvious irritation
to Caesar's earnest and by no means untactful plea not to let the
fortress of new-made love fall into disrepair (III iii 33–6). No
honour of any kind attaches then to Antony's return, as promised,
to his Egyptian dish: it is inspired partly by fear of Caesar's luck,
partly by the old impulse towards pleasure (there is no mention of
love); if it is oath-keeping, it is of a kind founded on total indifference to the sacredness of oaths.

Of its very nature, then, the relationship between Antony and
Cleopatra is no more durable or unmoving than those fortressed
cities which the emperor in his hey-day built upon green Nep-
tune's back: it seems destined to melt or sink in the waters of the
Nile, Tiber or Mediterranean. In his view she has been 'a boggler
ever' (III iii 110); and she knows perfectly well that he is the equal
of any Egyptian in the gipsy knot-trick of 'fast and loose' (IV xii
28).[5] Their relationship ties, unties and ties itself again continually
('Let him for ever go – let him not' – II v 115). Their feelings for
each other (and especially his for her) swing back and forward
with astonishing swiftness between admiration and scorn, idolatry
and loathing, magnanimous trust and schizophrenic suspicious-
ness: she is 'this great fairy' one moment (IV viii 12), 'this foul

Egyptian' the next (IV xii 10); he is 'painted one way like a Gorgon,/The other way a Mars' (II v 116–17). And as his abandoned second wife would say, there's 'no mid way/'Twixt these extremes at all' (III iv 19–20).

But the blemishes of change, distrust and betrayal are by no means confined to Antony and Cleopatra. Everywhere relationships and identities seem to rest on 'quicksands' (II vii 58), and time and history teach the melancholy lesson that each thing 'does become/The opposite of itself' (I ii 121–2). Rome is no longer what it was when great Pompey lived and the republican ideal of 'beauteous freedom' ensured that 'one man [was] but one man' (II vi 17, 19).[6] Coming as he does 'to scourge th' ingratitude that despiteful Rome/Cast on' his 'noble father' (II vi 22–3), Pompey the younger appears in the name of that ideal; but he is quickly bought off and persuaded to leave the triumvirate as it is – declining towards dictatorship. In the course of the negotiations he taunts Antony for having – cuckoo-like (II vi 28) – seized and inhabited his father's house in Rome; but his father's name and dignities, which have been thrown on him for the time being (I ii 183–9), suit him no better than his father's house suits the imperial cuckoo. 'Thy father, Pompey, would ne'er have made this treaty', says Menas in an aside (II vi 82); and Menas' plan to make him 'lord of the whole world' (II vii 61) is angrily rejected simply because Menas did not do the killing before discussing dictatorship: such is Sextus Pompeius' idea of Roman 'honour' (II vii 75). There is more then than an unvigilant ear will catch in the relaxed and agreeable words which Pompey, Caesar and Lepidus exchange as allies after the hard bargaining is over :

> *Caes.* Since I saw you last
>   There is a change upon you.
> *Pom.* Well, I know not
>   What harsh fortune casts upon my face;
>   But in my bosom shall she never come
>   To make my heart her vassal.
> *Lep.* Well met here.
> *Pom.* I hope so, Lepidus. Thus we are agreed.
>   I crave our composition may be written,
>   And seal'd between us.
> *Caes.* That's next to do. (II vi 52–60)

– 'Fair words', indeed, but one can hardly say they have 'fair meanings' (II vi 65–6). We soon hear that Caesar has waged new wars against Pompey (III iv 3–4). And we hear, too, that Lepidus – whom Caesar in his most Roman and moral mood assured of his loyalty : 'Doubt not sir;/I know it for my bond' (I iv 83–4) – has been deposed from the triumvirate and deprived of all his revenue : according to Caesar, the mild fellow 'was grown too cruel' and 'so did deserve his change' (III vi 28–34).[7]

Inevitably, the 'slippery people' (I ii 179) mirror the defects of their masters. It is they who 'begin to throw/Pompey the Great and all his dignities/Upon his son' (I ii 181–3). Having 'grown sick of rest', they 'would purge/By any desperate change' (I iii 53–4), and the son of the forgotten hero appears in time to assume the shape of their hearts' desire. They find him, as Nature would have it, where 'the anger'd ocean foams' (II vi 21); another Proteus for the Proteans, he emerges from that element in which Antony will one day turn from himself and his men and be metamorphosed into a doting mallard. Caesar's messenger reports : 'Pompey is strong at sea/And . . . To the ports/The discontents repair' (I iv 36–9). And Proteus himself, remembering the waxing but not the waning of his mistress the moon, confidently proclaims :

> I shall do well.
> The people love me, and the sea is mine ;
> My powers are crescent, and my auguring hope
> Says it will come to th' full. (II i 8–11)

Lastly, Caesar identifies the shifting loyalties of those who give Pompey his present shape with the ocean that perpetually embraces and deserts the varying shores of the world (I iv 41–7).

Does this superbly sustained evocation of universal change (and I have touched upon only a fraction of it) mean that Mutability rules over all? that Octavia should give intellectual assent to the deterministic philosophy with which Caesar politely smothers her attempt to reconcile warring opposites – 'let determin'd things to destiny/Hold unbewail'd their way' (III vi 84–5)? As always in Shakespeare (and as in Spenser's 'The Legend of Constancy'), the answer to this question is 'no'. Pompey himself, though his conduct scarcely confirms it, is well aware of the limits of Mutability's claim when he tells Caesar that however much Fortune has changed his face she will never enter his bosom. Though the price may be life itself, men can choose to be true to themselves and to others and so make the essential orderliness of Nature plain for all to see. But everything – and in this play everything is the end, the last 'act' which earns or loses us a place in the story – depends on that decision to be true or revolt, knit or untie, seal or melt. 'Alexas did revolt and . . . did dissuade/Great Herod to incline himself to Caesar/And leave his master Antony'; but the gods keep decorum and fortune him accordingly, since 'for this pains/Caesar . . . hang'd him' (IV vi 12–16). 'Canidius and the rest/That fell away' find 'entertainment, but/No honourable trust' (IV vi 16–18). And Enobarbus, forever ranked 'in register a master-leaver and a fugitive', dies by his own judgement in a ditch : 'the foul'st best fits/ My latter part of life' (IV vi 38–9). So the near-universality of change, then, and the fact that their own natures and relationship seem almost as subdued to it as the dyer's hand is to what it works in, turns the suicide of the lovers into a triumphantly decorous act wherein they become what they should be.

v

But such an interpretation needs extensive comment; and besides, the phenomenon of change impinges on the question of decorum in quite another way. Given the fact that men and the world they inhabit are constituted of contraries which are not always in harmony, that the observer and the observed are subject to alteration and forever adjusting to new circumstances, it follows that what is deemed graceful at one moment may seem graceless or disgraceful the next, or even that two minds can simultaneously ascribe contrary attributes to the same person or action. Consciousness of this epistemological problem is essential to the vision of reality embodied in *Antony and Cleopatra*. Indeed, if one were to extract and synthesise all those passages which touch on it, one might put forward a good case showing that in Shakespeare's view decorum – whether as an ethical or aesthetic phenomenon – has ultimately no objective status whatever :

> . . . Men's judgements are
> A parcel of their fortunes, and things outward
> Do draw the inward quality after them,
> To suffer all alike. (III xiii 31–4)

Although I do not believe that Shakespeare did, in fact, hold to this view, I would not say that he rules out the possibility of its being valid; certainly one cannot dismiss it on the evidence of the play with complacent certitude. For example, even the didactic young Caesar is made to comment on the impropriety of Antony's conduct in a dialectical rather than a dogmatic fashion :

> *Let's grant it is not*
> *Amiss* to tumble on the bed of Ptolemy,
> To give a kingdom for a mirth, to sit
> And keep the turn of tippling with a slave,
> To reel the streets at noon, and stand the buffet
> With knaves that smell of sweat. *Say this becomes him –*
> As his composure must be rare indeed
> Whom these things cannot blemish – yet must Antony
> No way excuse his foils when we do bear
> So great weight in his lightness. [my italics] (I iv 16–25)

However disapproving his whole tone, and however emphatic his final verdict on Antony's indifference to time, *gravitas* and duty, Caesar does introduce the possibility that Antony might be the kind of person who can gracefully carry off what in the majority and as a rule is reprehensible and disgusting. This certainly is how Cleopatra views him at the end of that exultant speech prompted by Alexas' favourable message from Rome :

> O well-divided disposition ! Note him,
> Note him, good Charmian; 'tis the man ; but note him !
> He was not sad, for he would shine on those
> That make their looks by his ; he was not merry,
> Which seem'd to tell them his remembrance lay
> In Egypt with his joy ; but between both.
> O heavenly mingle ! Be'st thou sad or merry,
> The violence of either thee becomes,
> So does it not man else. (I v 60–9)

Attempting to note her lover well, Cleopatra passes suddenly and unconsciously here from praising what is commonly praised (the avoidance of extremes and harmonising of opposites) to praising what is usually reprehended. It would appear from the whole speech that Antony is a uniquely harmonious blend of grace and blemish.

The last sentence of Cleopatra's speech is, of course, an echo of Antony's affectionately bewildered praise of her in the opening scene ('Fie, wrangling queen! Whom everything becomes', etc.). And that in turn is amplified into the great panegyric which is Enobarbus' attempt to explain why Antony can never leave her. The mode of expression now, however, is such as to bring clearly into focus the paradoxical union of contraries implicitly praised in the other two speeches:

> I saw her once
> Hop forty paces through the public street;
> And, having lost her breath, she spoke, and panted,
> That she did make defect perfection,
> And, breathless, pow'r breathe forth ...
> Age cannot wither her, nor custom stale
> Her infinite variety. Other women cloy
> The appetites they feed, but she makes hungry,
> Where most she satisfies; for vilest things
> Become themselves in her, that the holy priests
> Bless her when she is riggish. (II ii 231–44)

The transformation of defect into perfection which is peculiar to Antony and Cleopatra – and finely localised in a kind of continuous quibble on the verb 'become' (each thing 'becomes the opposite of itself')[8] – can be explained in two ways; but they are somewhat contradictory explanations whose disagreement will only be resolved in a consideration of what the lovers themselves (in Plutarch) called 'Synapothanumenon (signifying the order and agreement of those that will dye together)'. One of these explanations I would call the mythological. It is latent in the argument employed by Lepidus when he forces Caesar to discuss Antony's blemishes in a partly dialectical manner: Antony's faults are hereditary rather than acquired, and besides, there are not enough evils to darken all his goodness (I iv 1–15). Agrippa is thinking in similar terms when, on hearing of Antony's death, he remarks:

> A rarer spirit never
> Did steer humanity. But you gods will give us
> Some faults to make us men. (V i 31–3)

But Agrippa has advanced the argument, for he has (I think) suggested that Antony is one of those superhuman mortals who so approach the divine as to incur the envious hostility of the gods. And that is the view vigorously expressed by Cleopatra when she tells 'the injurious gods ... that this world did equal theirs/Till they had stol'n our jewel' (IV xv 75–8).

This grandiose blend of mythology and hyperbole is an outstanding characteristic of the language of *Antony and Cleopatra*. It seems perfectly intelligible if, on the one hand, we consider the classical subject and if, on the other, we recall that in Donne's poetry hyperbole of essentially the same kind is very common – the lover transvalues the macrocosm and the microcosm and looks on the world at large as an inferior imitation of himself, his mistress and their little room that is an everywhere : 'She is all States, and all Princes I,/Nothing else is : Princes do but play us'. Such considerations, however, do not account for the deeper meanings which dictate the use of mythological hyperbole in *Antony and Cleopatra*; and the resemblance in technique to Donne is a mere accident. The real reason for the predominance of hyperbole and mythological allusion in the tragedy is that both are inherent in Plutarch's fascinating *Life* of Antony. A quick look, therefore, at Shakespeare's principal source in the light of this fact will not be out of place.

Plutarch was a Greek who admired the Roman empire, a Platonic transcendentalist with a Ciceronian devotion to morals and the golden mean, an historian who believed in the existence of demi-gods and held that the essentials of Western philosophy are to be found in Greek and Egyptian mythology. As such, he treated the lives of the Roman triumvir and the Egyptian queen with a rare comprehensiveness of vision in which imagination and reason, sympathy and judicial detachment, often seem at odds. Again and again he speaks in censorious tones of the arrogance, feasting and sumptuousness of the lovers as 'exceeding all measure and reason'.[9] And he adduces vivid evidence of their extravagance in the habit of publicly apparelling themselves and their children as well-known divinities. Yet his manner of narration tends at least in part to support the claims implicit in such behaviour and to suggest that he himself thought the pair might have belonged to that rare class of beings discussed by him in the long essay on Isis and Osiris in his *Moralia*. Demi-gods (who include

Isis, Osiris, Hercules, Dionysus and Bacchus) are 'stronger than men, and, in their might, greatly surpassing our nature, yet not possessing the divine quality unmixed and uncontaminated'. They must, moreover, 'pay the penalty for the sins they commit and the duties they neglect ... until when they have thus been chastened and purified, they recover the place and position to which they belong in accordance with Nature'.[10]

If Plutarch did not see some kinship between Antony and Cleopatra and these beings, then there is a good deal of purportedly historical detail and of rhetorical amplification in his *Life* of Antony which is imperfectly harmonised with his sincere regard for 'temperaunce, modestie, and civill life'.[11] He records that the banquet hall in which Cleopatra entertained Antony was 'the rarest thing to behold that eye could discerne, or that euer books could mencion'. He not only acknowledges 'the charmes and inchauntment' of Cleopatra's 'passing beawtie and grace', but adds that 'her voyce and words were maruelous pleasant ..., her tongue ... an instrument of musicke to divers sports and pastimes, the which she easely turned to any language that pleased her'. Moreover, Antony was 'so ravished with the love' of this creature, and she with love for him, that they both 'made an order betwene them, which they called Amimetobion (as much as to say, no life comparable and matcheable with it) ...'[12] The famous description of Cleopatra sailing to meet Antony on the river Cydnus certainly corroborates the lovers' conception of their own unparagoned selves.[13] If Plutarch had wished to expose mere pride and decadent artificiality in Cleopatra's apparelling herself 'like the goddesse Venus', her attendant boys like the god Cupid, and her fairest ladies 'like the nymphes Nereides (which are mermaides of the waters) and like the Graces', he would not have penned the passage with such enthusiasm nor proceeded to admit by implication that the honey-tongued and infinitely graceful queen who ravished Antony was another Mermaid or Venus; nor would he have recorded the rumour which ran through the people that 'the goddesse Venus was come to play with the god Bacchus, for the generall good of all Asia'.[14] Likewise, if he had seen mere arrogance in Antony's habit of copying in his dress the Hercules of pictorial tradition he would not have recorded as historical facts that Antony was directly descended from Hercules and bore a physical resemblance to him.[15] Whereas, then, one part of Plutarch sees disastrous folly and hubris in the lovers' conscious and unconscious imitation of the immortals, another part of him finds in their characters and lives a dazzling incarnation of what is ascribed in legend and art to the demi-gods.

It is not difficult to detect in Shakespeare's tragedy the possibility that Antony and Cleopatra might belong to an order of beings, and are capable of living a life, with which nothing else in this world is 'comparable and matcheable'; that what in others would be extravagant pretence or gross immoderation is no blemish to their 'rare composure' at all since ordinary laws do not always apply to them. This possibility is epitomised in the use of that word 'rare' (borrowed with interest from North's Plutarch) – 'O, rare for Antony! ... Rare Egyptian!' (II ii 209, 222). It probably lies, too, at the root of Lepidus' characterisation of Antony's faults as 'hereditary rather than purchased': Antony's virtues can never be darkened because they, like his faults, are inherited from his divine ancestor and because in that mythological type of humanity at its very greatest ('a rarer spirit never did steer humanity') faults are unseen or quickly forgiven and in no way impede apotheosis. If it is true that Antony and Cleopatra are often not 'like' themselves, it is equally true that no one is ever quite like them and that they have in their possession some secret alchemy which transforms and ennobles everything mean or base associated with them:

> How much unlike art thou Mark Antony!
> Yet, coming from him, that great med'cine hath
> With his tinct gilded thee. (I v 35–7)

But the play also allows for the possibility that those who see the lovers thus – and it is primarily they themselves who do so – may be the victims of some kind of temporary delusion (and with this point I must necessarily turn back a little in my tracks). Cleopatra is furious with Charmian for attempting to paragon her man of men with Julius Caesar and ascribes her own previous opinion of Caesar as a youthful aberration from good judgement. But her mature attitude to Antony, and his to her, and ours to both, is just as likely to suffer a complete reversal as that early view of Caesar. Like the Elizabethan toy known as a perspective (which Shakespeare deliberately alludes to in II v 116–17), they can, in a twinkling, present quite distinct images to the eye – Mars or Gorgon, hero or ass, Venus or whore, Egyptian sovereign or vulgar gipsy; each is 'a natural perspective that is and is not' (*Twelfth Night*, V i 209). Cleopatra herself consciously reflects on the subjective and changing character of her own and Antony's graces at that point where he is about to 'break off' from her and she perceives that eternity is no longer in their lips and eyes. Urging him to pretend sorrow at parting by weeping for the dead Fulvia, she provokes a show of his hereditary wrath :

> *Ant.* You'll heat my blood ; no more.
> *Cleo.* You can do better yet; but this is meetly.
> Ant. Now, by my sword –
> *Cleo.* And target. Still he mends ;
>   But this is not the best. Look, prithee, Charmian,
>   How this Herculean Roman does become
>   The carriage of his chafe. (I iii 80–5)

Cleopatra loves and admires the Herculean Roman, but not this one, I think ; the wrath is only superficially attractive since (as her mockery seems to suggest) it is largely a pretence designed to exclude the softer feelings and facilitate a quick departure. Within moments, too, she perceives that he feels the same about the enchanting effusion of self-pity ('O, my oblivion is a very Antony') which she suddenly turns on in order to weaken his resistance ; and perceiving this, she cuts short the attempt : 'But sir, forgive me ;/ Since my becomings kill me when they do not/Eye well with you' (I iii 95–7). At another time she will only have to say with a large and liquid eye, 'Pardon, pardon !', all will be forgiven, and Rome rather than Egypt will seem as clay to his mind.

That the lover's vision of the beloved can have the insubstantiality as well as the brilliant intensity of a midsummer night's dream ('Think you there was or might be such a man/As this I dreamt of ?'), and that love induces a 'liver vein' which can turn a green goose into a goddess, are notions which Shakespeare made much of in his early and middle comedies. But if a backward glance is helpful here it must be in the direction of the sonnets. For the poet there seriously reflects on the perversions done to his judgement by affection and lust, and knows, too, the disillusion of waking lucidity, the stench of festered lilies. Love, he recognises, is an alchemy which can turn monsters to cherubins, 'creating every bad a perfect best' (CXIV). The transformation may be of a merely aesthetic kind (CXLIV), or it may be both aesthetic and ethical :

O, from what pow'r hast thou this pow'rful might
With insufficiency my heart to sway?
To make me give the lie to my true sight,
And swear that brightness doth not grace the day?
Whence has thou this becoming of things ill,
That in the very refuse of thy deeds
There is such strength and warrantise of skill
That in my mind thy worst all best exceeds? (CL)

And this incomprehensible paradox is evidenced by the Friend as well as by the Dark Lady : physically graceful but (in time) morally corrupt, he is the embodiment of 'lascivious grace in whom all ill shows well' (XL). Enslaved to the Friend's charm, the poet ruefully watches himself spinning sophistries in order to authorise trespass (XXXV) and harmonise discord (XLI). And just as Enobarbus and the holy priests could share with Antony a feeling that the vilest things become themselves in the rare Egyptian, so even the world at large is capable of reacting to the Friend in the same way as the poet :

That tongue that tells the story of thy days,
Making lascivious comments on thy sport,
Cannot dispraise but in a kind of praise :
Naming thy name blesses an ill report. (XCV)

The poet however does not stop short at stupefied wonder and idolatry but goes beyond this response in a manner which corresponds with and clarifies the dramatist's solution to the moral-aesthetic problem raised by the characters of Antony and Cleopatra. Despite his admiration for those rare ones who can combine grace with inconstancy or untruth (for that is what all the vice is reducible to), he recognises that this is a union of contraries which cannot endure for long : 'Take heed dear heart of this large privilege,/The hardest knife ill-used doth lose his edge'

(XCV). He differentiates between 'external grace' and inner grace, physical attractiveness and truth, and recalls that one is a beauty which decays, the other a kind which lasts for ever (LIII, LXIX, XCIII). The great and simple moral which the Friend is offered – and even the Dark Lady is privileged to hear some of it – is that beauty is perfect, admiration undying, and Time defeated when the two graces are one :

> O how much more doth beauty beauteous seem
> By that sweet ornament which truth doth give !
> The rose looks fair, but fairer we it deem
> For that sweet odour which doth in it live.
> The canker-blooms have full as deep a dye
> As the perfumed tincture of the roses,
> Hang on such thorns, and play as wantonly
> When summer's breath their masked buds discloses;
> But for their virtue only is their show,
> They live unwoo'd, and unrespected fade ;
> Die to themselves. Sweet roses do not so :
> Of their sweet deaths are sweetest odours made.
> And so of you, beauteous and lovely youth,
> When that shall vade, by verse distills your truth. (LIV)

VI

The rare but uncertain splendours of Antony and Cleopatra are distilled by the truth which they attain to in defeat, death and grief. After the catastrophe at Actium they begin to associate Octavius with the bud of youth and themselves with the blown rose in whose presence the unceremonious world stops its nose (III xiii 20, 38–40). Yet the truth is almost the reverse of this : it is they who begin to burgeon in glory and Caesar whose odour turns offensive. What makes him so distasteful is that from Actium until the discovery of Cleopatra's death he is coldly conscious of his conquering superiority and wholly preoccupied with adding the final touches to his triumph by 'indirect crook'd ways'.

Being a 'politician' who relies greatly for success on psychological insight into other men's weaknesses, Caesar exhibits a clinical interest in the process of Antony's disintegration :

Observe how Antony becomes his flaw,
And what thou think'st his very action speaks
In every power that moves. (III xii 34–6)

Following R. H. Case, we can say that Caesar's intended meaning
here is: 'Observe how Antony bears himself as a broken (*or* dis-
graced ...) man and what may be augured of his state of mind
from a close observation of his behaviour'.[16] But for those who
have been educated by the play to note all the qualities of people,
the first line introduces another meaning of which the single-
minded Octavius is unaware; and it is the magic potentiality
referred to in the secondary meaning which enables the lovers to
come from the world's great snare uncaught and steal from Caesar
the triumph that he confidently assumed to be his. Because of his
smooth tongue, Thyreus will be able to report that Antony displayed all the self-destructive rage of an old lion dying (III xiii 93)
and Caesar will have something irritably contemptuous to say
about the old ruffian. But there are two ways of looking at Antony's explosion of wrath when he beholds Caesar's Jack kissing
Cleopatra's hand. One can view it as evidence of that diminution
in the captain's brain (III xiii 198) which will allow him to be
tricked into fighting by sea after he has won a victory on land. Al-
ternatively, one might see it as a kind of epiphany, a genuine revelation of 'the god Hercules whom Antony lov'd' (IV iii 16) and
who alone could 'teach' him such rage (IV xii 43–4): Thyreus,
the unfortunate victim of deceit and misconstruction, being to
Antony what Lichas was to his divine ancestor. This response
would find support in the feeling that the last ferocious outbursts
of the dying king of beasts (whose skin was the Herculean garb)
are proof of his indestructible nobility (see *Richard II*, V i 29–35),
and in the possibility that when Cleopatra praises the emperor
whose 'voice was as the rattling thunder' she may have been thinking of the explosion which begins with, 'Favours, by Jove that
thunders!' (III xiii 85). At any rate, this outburst serves as a pre-
lude to the only incident in the play where Antony exhibits the
authentic virtue of a superhuman warrior. Whereas in Plutarch
the battle outside Alexandria is a mere skirmish, in Shakespeare
it is a dazzling victory for true soldiership which shows Antony at
one with his ancestor, a Herculean Roman in deed as well as in
name. It is not until after this battle – when Antony is led seaward

by policy – that the god leaves him. For this and other reasons the episode is of immense importance in the total pattern of the play.

Although Thyreus's mission to divide the lovers meets with some immediate success, the moment of intense discord merely enhances and indeed prepares for the mood of deep harmony which takes possession of them immediately afterwards – a harmony which persists until the last suspicion and the last fit of Herculean rage become the instrument of their death-union. Like the Egyptian navy, the lovers are 'sever'd' and 'knit again' (III xiii 170–1) and Antony, in the flush of renewed love, is inspired with the belief that he can bathe his 'dying honour in the blood/Shall make it live again' (III xiii 174–5; IV ii 6–7). Shakespeare's art works in almost every line to create the impression that loving concord is at once the cause and the chief effect of this hoped-for victory in which Antony is sublimely true to himself. This concord is evident in the words exchanged between him and Cleopatra when – in his mood of sudden exhilaration – he decides to feast all his sad captains and so to celebrate (unwittingly) her birthday :

> *Cleo.* It is my birthday.
>   I had thought t' have held it poor ; but since my lord
>   Is Antony again, I will be Cleopatra.
> *Ant.* We will yet do well.
> *Cleo.* Call all his noble captains to my lord. (III xiii 185–9)

Antony has not remembered nor does he now reflect on Cleopatra's birthday : he continues to dwell only on the battle ahead and the morale of his men. That Cleopatra does not resent this shows how completely at one with herself and her lover she is at this point. She has no desire to compete with his noble captains and seems well aware that his 'doing well' depends on his being at one with them. And yet she – who has just subdued his terrible wrath with the simple 'Not know me yet?' (III xiii 157), and who stands for the feminine principle in his nature – is responsible for the outpouring of affection towards captains and household servants which Enobarbus fears will transform them all to women. Antony's union with his men at the feast (as at the battle) is an ideal one; they do and have done much for him and he desires to do the same for them :

Mine honest friends,
I turn you not away; but, like a master
Married to your good service, stay till death. (IV iii 29–31)

As we have seen, the transformation of which Enobarbus is
afraid took place when Cleopatra changed clothes with the
drunken, sleeping Antony, and when she became the general's
general at Actium. The transvestite incident (which is really only
a symbolic anticipation of Actium) has its origins in the 'base and
unseemly service' done by Hercules 'in maides attire' at Om-
phale's distaff – an event recalled by Plutarch and Garnier.[17] But
it is also an echo of 'what Venus did with Mars' (I v 18), since
Venus put the god to sleep while Eros (Cupid) playfully donned
his armour. This myth – immortalised in Botticelli's serenely beautiful painting – is very pertinent here, since the ludicrous and
unseemly aspect of man's subjection to woman, or of Valour to
Pleasure, was not the only meaning traditionally found in it. As
Plutarch explained in 'De Iside et Osiride', and as Renaissance
mythographers and emblematists were well aware, the myth was
for the Greeks a symbol of the peace and concord which prevail
when the conflicting opposites in Nature are reconciled: out of
the union of Venus (Aphrodite) and Mars (Ares) is born the goddess Harmony.[18] The myth of Venus and Mars then – like that of
Isis and Osiris, as interpreted by Plutarch – was a vehicle for the
philosophy of cosmic order which passed from classical antiquity
into the moral, psychological and aesthetic outlook of the Renaissance.

Almost inevitably, therefore, a principal clue to the nature of
the relationship perfected by Antony and Cleopatra in death and
at the battle of Alexandria (their 'lightning before death') is
Shakespeare's use of the name of Eros – the emancipated slave in
whom are symbolically united bondage and freedom, love and
war, Antony and Cleopatra.[19] The symbolism of his role is casually but precisely indicated in the sentences which open the scene
where Antony arms for battle after his night of feasting:

Ant. Eros! mine armour, Eros!
Cleo. Sleep a little.
Ant. No, my chuck. Eros! Come, mine armour, Eros!
   (IV iv 1–2)

Antony is Antony again, the chivalrous warrior who 'goes forth gallantly' (IV iv 35) knowing that love should assist rather than frustrate valour. And Cleopatra instantly responds to his mood. Whereas Helen (in *Troilus and Cressida*) disarms Paris and Hector with her 'soft enchanting fingers', Cleopatra does the opposite, enthusiastically entering into the royal occupation. Although (as Antony says) she is the armourer of his heart (IV iv 7), there is nothing awry in her successful attempt to do Eros' job of arming his body as well. Apart from the obvious fact that this allows Eros to hasten with his own defences (IV iv 9), the vocative use of Eros' name in the midst of Antony's speeches to and about Cleopatra has the effect of intimating that Eros and Cleopatra are interchangeable, one : she will be temporarily absent when her warrior's long task is finally done, yet she will, as Eros, unarm him for his everlasting sleep – a metympsychosis which we can prophesy even here if we read carefully in Nature's infinite book of secrecy :

> *Cleo*. Is not this buckled well ?
> *Ant*. Rarely, rarely !
>   He that unbuckles this, till we do please
>   To daff't for our repose, shall hear a storm.
>   Thou fumblest, Eros, and my queen's a squire
>   More tight at this than thou. (IV iv 11–15)

The arming ritual (sufficiently extended to allow Antony to converse with newly arrived soldiers) merges into the briefer ritual of farewell ; and the second ceremony is as remote from shame and rebuke as the first, for in it Antony begins to behave like the man of steel that Cleopatra has helped him to become :

> Fare thee well, dame, whate'er become of me.
> This is a soldier's kiss. Rebukeable,
> And worthy shameful check it were, to stand
> On more mechanic compliment ; I'll leave thee
> Now like a man of steel. You that will fight,
> Follow me close ; I'll bring you to't. Adieu. (IV iv 29–34)

The disjunction clarified by the 'leave–follow' antithesis is as important as the conjunction enshrined in 'a soldier's kiss' ; the

harmonious mingling of opposites postulated by that kiss rests on
the recognition that opposites *are* opposites. Cleopatra will not
bear a charge in the war or 'appear there for a man', nor will
Antony turn tail 'like a cow in June'. In consequence, the emperor
and his men achieve heroic unity on the battle-field, victory is
theirs, and when they return to tell their women-folk of their
'gests' (the slightly archaic word evokes an ideal chivalry in which
knights and ladies ceremoniously act out their differences and inter-
dependence). Male and female, pain and pleasure, sorrow and
joy, war and love, wounds and kisses are all fused in a deeply
satisfying wholeness :

> I thank you all ;
> For doughty-handed are you, and have fought
> Not as you serv'd the cause, but as't had been
> Each man's like mine; you have shown all Hectors.
> Enter the city, clip your wives, your friends,
> Tell them your feats ; whilst they with joyful tears
> Wash the congealment from your wounds and kiss
> The honour'd gashes whole.[20] (IV viii 4–11)

Thus the triumph of manhood and valour and of womanhood and
love become indistinguishable – are visibly as well as metaphorically united – and a rare moment of infinite virtue is recorded for
the god-like hero, his divine mistress, and all those who have followed them close :

> *Ant.* [*To Scarus*] Give me thy hand. –
> To this great fairy I'll commend thy acts,
> Make her thanks bless thee. O thou day o' th' world,
> Chain mine arm'd neck. Leap thou, attire and all,
> Through proof of harness to my heart, and there
> Ride on the pants triumphing. (IV viii 12–17)

It might be said that whereas love is ennobled here by its union
with valour, the process is reversed in Antony's last triumph : for
that triumph is really a defeat which love's alchemy translates into
what ought to be. This truth is ironically emphasised by Antony's
decision that his navy was defeated because Cleopatra decided to

leave him for Caesar. Such is his rage that he is prepared to 'subdue' his 'worthiest self' (IV xii 47) by killing her (just as Hercules in his fury intended to kill Deianira).[21] The contraries of love and strength have thus declined once more into 'confounding' or destructive opposition – a momentous drama which the repeated, vocative use of Eros' name (he does not even appear) helps to define (IV xii 24–49). In the brief scene which follows this, the dazed Cleopatra accepts the stratagem devised by Charmian to leap through proof of harness to Antony's heart by a piteously worded message of her death. She is absent from the next scene, yet her spiritual presence is intensely felt : in the opening words : 'Eros, thou yet behold'st me?'; in the bitter complaint which precedes the renewed intention to kill her : 'She, Eros, has/Pack'd cards with Caesar, and false-play'd my glory/Unto an enemy's triumph' (IV xiv 18–20); in the softening pity of : 'Nay, weep not, gentle Eros; there is left us/Ourselves to end ourselves' (IV xiv 21–2); and in Mardian's piteously worded, prophetically truthful fiction : 'My mistress lov'd thee, and her fortunes mingled/With thine entirely . . . The last she spake was "Antony! most noble Antony!" . . . She render'd life/Thy name so buried in her.' (IV xiv 24–34). With Mardian's tale, love triumphs and violent Mars instantly obeys the call to sleep and peace :

> *Unarm, Eros;* the long day's task is done,
> And we must sleep . . .
>   . . . Apace, *Eros*, apace. –
> No more a soldier. Bruised pieces, go ;
> You have been nobly borne. – From we awhile. [*Exit Eros.*]
> I will o'ertake thee *Cleopatra*, and
> Weep for pardon. So it must be, for now
> All length is torture. Since the torch is out,
> Lie down, and stray no farther. Now all labour
> *Mars* what it does ; yea very force entangles
> Itself with strength. Seal then, and all is done.
> *Eros* ! – I come, *my queen* – *Eros* ! – Stay for me ;
> Where souls do couch on flowers, we'll hand in hand,
> And with our sprightly port make the ghosts gaze.
> Dido and her Aeneas shall want troops,
> And all the haunt be ours. – Come, *Eros, Eros* ! [my italics]
>   (IV xiv 35–54)

'Mars' – the beloved queen – Eros: a quibble on the verb was surely intended (without love, strength mars itself); at any rate, Antony is now speaking exactly as Cleopatra would speak in her Venus-role ('Sleep a little') and as the goddess herself spoke to her mythological lovers: 'Lie quietly . . . do not struggle, for thou shalt not rise'.[22] In dramatising the concord achieved by Antony and his 'serpent of old Nile', Shakespeare must have been acutely conscious of the fact that the most famous use of the phrase and concept *discors concordia* occurs in that passage at the beginning of Ovid's *Metamorphoses* (I 416–37), where the fruitful harmonising of earth's warring elements is illustrated by reference to the action of the sun on the mud of the Nile basin.

As I have already intimated, the distinctive feature in Shakespeare's presentation of the mingling of love with strength is that Antony's identity is by no means lost or blurred in the process: indeed, quite the contrary. Just when his whole being has been overwhelmed with the conviction that he is about to become as indistinct as water is in water (IV xiv 1–14), he finds in love the inspiration to re-define his noble self with calm confidence. The truthful fiction of Cleopatra's suicide (what is a mere detail of time in the death-act of timeless lovers?) serves in this moment of despair and self-pity as 'a good rebuke/Which might have well becom'd the best of men'; and he sees it as such:

> Since Cleopatra died
> I have liv'd in such dishonour that the gods
> Detest my baseness. I, that with my sword
> Quarter'd the world, and o'er green Neptune's back
> With ships made cities, condemn myself to lack
> The courage of a woman; less noble mind
> Than she which by her death our Caesar tells
> 'I am conqueror of myself'. (IV xiv 55–62)

But this is not quite enough to teach blemished valour to be itself again; he who a short time ago asked Hercules to 'teach' him how to kill a woman is now given yet another lesson in courage by love:

> Thrice nobler than myself!
> Thou teachest me, o valiant Eros, what
> I should, and thou couldst not. My queen and Eros

S.D.—8

Have, by their brave instruction, got upon me
A nobleness in record. But I will be
A bridegroom in my death, and run into't
As to a lover's bed. Come, then; and Eros,
Thy master dies thy scholar. To do thus [*Falling on his sword.*
I learn'd of thee. (IV xiv 95–103)

Just how we are to interpret the fact that Antony does not die instantly is an interesting question. He himself says: 'I have done my work ill, friends' (IV xiv 105). It is possible that up to a point we should ascribe more than medical significance to these words. That might help us to be more responsive to the unique harmonising of opposites which is achieved in death by Antony's friend-and-beloved: valiant Eros, martial Venus. Moreover, it is artistically right that if there is to be repetition in this triumph of Love over Policy it should constitute a progression from better to best, and that the question provoked by Cleopatra's suicide ('What work is here? . . . is this well done?') should be answered with a triumphantly unqualified 'yes'. But to say that Antony bungled his suicide is, I am sure, very wrong indeed. For one thing, there is not the slightest suggestion in either Plutarch or Garnier-Pembroke that the suicide was deficient in Roman nobility because it was not immediately effective. Apart from that, the delay allows Shakespeare to turn Antony's bridal death into a theatrically striking reality: he dies where he has lived, bestowing the last of many thousand kisses on the woman who is determined to become his wife in death, and in a tomb which will unite them eternally ('No grave upon the earth shall clip in it a pair so famous'). In this way the drama visually confirms the 'heavenly mingle' of what in Shakespeare are usually presented as irreconcilable opposites – marriage and funeral. But above all, it would be an extraordinary aberration on Shakespeare's part if he sought to have us look on Antony's suicide as a botched affair when he was so obviously intent on showing us that the firm Roman died exactly as he ought: 'So should it be, that none but Antony/Should conquer Antony' (IV xv 16–17). *So should it be*: what else does that specify but decorum, *id quod decet*? And for visual as well as verbal confirmation of that restored decorum – that sense of balance, of proportion, of like answering like – we can look to the scene where Dercetas hands to Caesar the bloody sword taken from Antony's

body, the sword of which Antony was once 'robb'd' by a 'vile lady'
(IV xii 22):

> He is dead, Caesar,
> Not by a public minister of justice,
> Nor by a hired knife; but that self hand
> Which writ his honour in the acts it did
> Hath, with the courage which the heart did lend it,
> Splitted the heart. This is his sword;
> I robb'd his wound of it; behold it stain'd
> With his most noble blood. (V i 19–26)

Suicide has changed 'scars upon . . . honour' (III xiii 58) into
'honour'd gashes' (IV viii 11), stained nobility into noble stains.[23]

Cleopatra's 'so should it be' is not inserted by Shakespeare
solely as an evaluation of Antony's end; it serves also to mark the
emergence in Cleopatra of a conscious and total dedication to
what is fitting. As she and Eros have instructed Antony, so he has
taught her: with his death, their spirits mingle entirely, and for
what remains of her life she will be intent on acting in 'the high
Roman fashion' and frustrating Caesar's attempt to secure at least
a posthumous moral triumph over him by degrading her. In this
struggle to keep decorum she has to exercise all her perceptiveness
and histrionic skill, for Caesar greatly intensifies his cunning endeavour – begun after Actium – to present himself as a man who
is replete with all the virtues proper to a conqueror. In order to
secure time, she has to act in a manner which he in his heart expects of the defeated (consider the crude and scornful 'Bid him
yield' – V i 1) but which, in his magnanimous persona, he depre-
cates. As he represents the situation, the queen's yielding to him,
and his response to her compliance, will constitute nothing less
than a noble union of princely hearts; it will be exactly what the
union of Antony and Octavia was supposed to be and assuredly
was not – an 'act of grace'.

Before scrutinising this last tussle between grace and disgrace
I must pause to comment once more on a word whose independent
value and richness of meaning added greatly to the status
of decorum as an all-embracing ethical and aesthetic philosophy.
We know that grace is the attractiveness of whatever is presented,
said or done with propriety. We know also from Shakespeare's
royal contexts that grace – in its theological senses – is something

which should adorn a monarch, since he rules by divine right and is God's substitute on earth. The same contexts, however, have emphasised the importance of grace in the sense of favour and liberality (a sense which survives in the collocation 'grace and favour') : to bestow favours graciously, to be bountiful, is a pre-eminently royal attribute. In dramatising Caesar's effort to secure Cleopatra's submission, Shakespeare was greatly concerned with grace in this last sense – and concerned also to have it understood that the last sense is, in the circumstances, a logical extension of the first one. And he would have been quite confident that the educated would respond to his intentions in this matter without any sort of lexicographical harassment, since the motif of the Three Graces – so popular in the visual arts, iconography and poetry – had rendered grace-bounty almost as familiar as grace-comeliness and had, in fact, served to associate the two. Here for example is 'E.K.'s' gloss on a line in the April eclogue of *The Shepheardes Calender* (1579):

> The Graces be three sisters, the daughters of Jupiter, whose names are Aglaia, Thalia, Euphrosyne . . . otherwise called Charites, that is thanks. Whom the Poetes feyned to be the Goddesses of al bountie and comelines, which therefore (as sayth Theodontius) they make three, to wete, that men first ought to be gracious and bountiful to other freely, then to receiue benefits at other mens hands curteously, and thirdly to requite them thankfully : which are three sundry Actions in liberalitye.[24]

Although prominent in the last act of *Antony and Cleopatra*, the issue of royal grace and favour does not arise abruptly but inheres in the total structure of the play. It is introduced at the end of the first act when Alexas, gilded with Antony's tinct, brings to a delighted Cleopatra the gift of an 'orient pearl' – a gift enriched with the promise that when the giver returns he will 'mend the petty present' by piecing her opulent throne with kingdoms (I v 38–47). The theme is characteristically varied in the scene where the anonymous messenger is manhandled by his 'gracious madam' : the interview began with that promise of gold and the bluest veins to kiss (a hand that kings had lipped). The royal hand – and the concomitant bended knee – becomes thereafter an important image in the dramatist's exploration of grace and favour. In his interview with the queen, Thyreus asks : 'Give me grace to lay/My duty on your hand'; and while she performs this act of grace, the queen musingly recalls that Julius Caesar bestowed his lips on that same hand after he had 'mused of taking kingdoms in' (III xiii 81–5). Seeing all this, Antony thunders his disgust: 'Favours . . . ?' In his view, a whipping is what Thyreus merits for his sauciness; a view which is supported by the ironical servant who reports Thyreus' reaction to the whipping: 'He did ask favour' (III xiii 133).

Antony's treatment of Thyreus is, in part, a natural reaction to the brutal message which his schoolmaster-turned-ambassador brought back from Caesar. Through this humble mouthpiece, Antony and Cleopatra had greeted Caesar as lord of their fortunes, admitted that their future was hazarded to his 'grace', and made modest petitions (III xii 11–20). To this, Caesar's answer was that he had no ears for Antony's request but that the queen would not 'sue unheard' if she should 'From Egypt drive her all-disgraced friend/Or take his life there' (III xii 22–3). Or as Antony puts it bitterly, 'The Queen shall then have courtesy, so she/Will yield us up' (III xiii 14–15). The cunning of Caesar's ambassador then lies in the application of his invention and eloquence (III xii 26–31) to his master's theme that in turning from Antony, Cleopatra will simply be turning from disgrace and emptiness to the very fount of courtesy and bounty. Caesar, says Thyreus, 'entreats' her to be allowed to exercise his liberality; he will thus meet her half-way in playing the beggar; and he even recognises – courteous lord that he is – that her connection with Antony was due to fear rather than love and that the blemishes on her honour were thus 'constrained' rather than 'deserved' (III xiii 52–72).

To suppose with Enobarbus and Antony that Cleopatra is in the least beguiled by this fiction is to ignore her insistence that Thyreus address her in the presence of her women and Enobarbus (who jumps to conclusions and goes off to tell Antony). It is to ignore the fine film of irony which encases her replies to Thyreus. Above all, it is to overlook the fact that Cleopatra is playing exactly the same flattering and servile part that she will play (after Antony's death) in response to the embassage of Proculeius and the personal appearance of Caesar: Thyreus, the 'most kind messenger', is to tell Caesar that she will kiss his conquering hand, lay her crown at his feet, and kneel there to hear the doom of Egypt (III xiii 73–8).

The difference between Proculeius' mission and Thyreus' is that the truth breaks through the second scene of excellent dissembling. Without committing his master to any particular promise, Proculeius indicates that the queen's wish (V ii 15–21) to keep decorum in playing the beggar will be respected. She is 'fall'n into a princely hand', the hand of a 'lord/Who is so full of grace that it flows over/On all that need'; and if he is assured of her 'sweet dependency' she will find 'A conqueror that will pray in aid for kindness/Where he for grace is kneel'd to' (V ii 21–8). In reply to this, Cleopatra plays the suppliant as before : she is 'fortune's vassal' and would like to look her new lord in the face and 'kneel to him with thanks' (V ii 21, 28–32) – like Antony on an earlier such occasion, she is 'studied for a liberal thanks' (II vi 45–9), a true act of grace requiring that liberal giving be matched by courteous, unstinting gratitude.

It is the sudden entry of Gallus and his soldiers to seize the queen, and her immediate attempt to commit suicide, which temporarily disarranges Caesar's play and discloses the unsuitability of the actors for the allotted parts. Cleopatra makes it perfectly clear to Proculeius that she considers herself to be 'a queen worth many babes [i.e., fools] and beggars' (V ii 47), and, moreover, that she knows exactly what Caesar has in store for her at Rome. Proculeius' attempt to placate and reassure her has the simultaneous effect of confirming the falsity of Caesar and resurrecting the ghost of that noble master on whose godlike bounty Cleopatra will presently rhapsodise :

> Cleopatra,
> Do not abuse my master's bounty by
> Th' undoing of yourself. Let the world see
> His nobleness well acted, which your death
> Will never let come forth. (V ii 42–6)

Despite having seen these two rehearsals, we cannot find the performance with Caesar disappointing, for Cleopatra brings her own invention to bear on it by the introduction of Seleucus. Not only is Caesar led into 'supposing he had deceiued her' when 'in deede he was deceiued him selfe'.[25] The spectacle of Cleopatra squirming with rage and 'wounding shame' (V ii 158) at the thought of a mere servant letting a royal visitor know all about her thieving preoccupation with 'lady trifles' and 'immoment toys',

thus increasing 'the sum' of her 'disgraces' (V ii 162–5) – this piece
of incomparable dissembling gives him the immense satisfaction
of producing, at minimal cost, concrete evidence of his own
liberality. Grandly, he refuses to frown on such lady-like weaknesses – 'Caesar's no merchant'; and as for the future, she is as
free to do with it as she is to keep her trinkets – he merely asks her
'counsel' in the matter (V ii 179–86). Her reaction is exactly what
he would expect for such a display of royal bounty – a show of
amazed and humble gratitude, graced no doubt with a 'court'sy':
'My master and my lord!' (V ii 189). But immediately he leaves,
Cleopatra throws off the garment of humility which she knows to
be rarely base: 'He words me, girls, he words me, that I should
not/Be noble to myself' (V ii 190–1).

One reason why Cleopatra is not fooled by Caesar is that she
has had the most intimate acquaintance with, and felt the deepest
admiration for, Bounty itself. As I have hinted, there is a contrast,
more or less sustained throughout the last two acts, between the
grand, spontaneous bounty which makes Antony an emperor in
nature as well as in name, and the bounty which hangs on Octavius
like a giant's robe upon a dwarfish thief. We have seen signs of
Antony's bounty in the 'orient pearl' and in the 'liberal thanks'
for kindness done to his mother by Pompey. But it is at the battle
of Alexandria that this great virtue shines forth in all its captivating
splendour. 'I will reward thee/Once for thy sprightly comfort, and
tenfold/For thy good valour', he tells Eros and Scarus in the heat
of battle (IV vii 14). And he takes the wounded Scarus by the
hand to be honoured by the queen: 'To this great fairy I'll commend thy acts,/Make her thanks bless thee' (IV viii 13–14). Thus,
when he and Cleopatra have embraced, and their exultant spirits
mingled entirely, they mutually perform – as emperor and empress
– that perfect act of grace and favour of which there are so many
spurious copies:

Ant. Behold this man;
   Commend unto his lips thy favouring hand –
   Kiss it my warrior – he hath fought to-day
   As if a god in hate of mankind had
   Destroyed in such a shape.
Cleo. I'll give thee, friend,
   An armour all of gold; it was a king's. (IV viii 23–8)

The supping together which follows (IV viii 33) is no less important than the words and tokens of royal gratitude. Caesar is not
present at the one feast which he orders for his soldiers; and that
feast is an economist's afterthought prompted largely by the need
to tidy up an over-stocked larder :

> ... Within our files there are
> Of those that serv'd Mark Antony but late
> Enough to fetch him in. See it done ;
> And feast the army; we have store to do't,
> And they have earn'd the waste. Poor Antony ! [*Exeunt.*
>   (IV i 12–16)

'Poor Antony' : ambiguous and ironic, this phrase sums up with
fine dramatic ease the essential differences between Caesar and his
fallen rival. Antony is certainly 'pluck'd' and Caesar greatly enriched at his expense; yet Antony (like Cordelia) is most rich
being poor, most choice forsaken, and Caesar never seems more
impoverished than now, when Fortune smiles upon him. In the
scene which follows immediately upon Caesar's contemptuous
remark, Antony is calling forth his household servants, shaking
hands with them one by one, thanking them with deep sincerity
for having served him well, and saying to Cleopatra : 'Let's to-
night/Be bounteous at our meal' (IV ii 9–13). And the unexpected
glory of his last battle on land is enhanced by Enobarbus' dying
tributes to his 'bounty overplus' (IV vi 22), a bounty which evokes
thoughts of kingship and of faithful service lavishly rewarded
(IV vi 31–4).

All of which, of course, culminates in Cleopatra's rhapsody on
an emperor whose voice was propertied as all the tuned spheres,
and that to his friends; whose bounty was an autumn without
winter and grew the more by reaping; a universal monarch in
whose livery walked crowns and crownets and from whose careless possession fell realms and islands. Dolabella, who is privileged
to hear this lament, acknowledges that Antony was indeed great
and that Cleopatra's grief is justified : the sheer grace and proportion and gravity of her grief – 'Your loss is, as yourself, great ; and
you bear it/As answering to the weight' (V ii 101–2) – strikes his
Roman heart at root and prompts him to warn her of Caesar's
deceit. Yet he gently denies that there ever was or could be such a

man as this she dreams on. Her angry rejection of his scepticism ties in with the immediate distinction between dissembling (or acting) and reality (Caesar will arrive in a moment), and with the pervasive but related distinction – so often encountered in the philosophy of grace and decorum – between art and nature. Cleopatra asserts emphatically that fancy or imagination could never invent an Antony; he is a rarity whom Nature alone could create:

> Nature wants stuff
> To vie strange forms with fancy; yet t' imagine
> An Antony were nature's piece 'gainst fancy,
> Condemning shadows quite. (V ii 96–9)

To gloss on this statement in the manner of Spenser's 'E.K.', we would have to remark that although much grace can be acquired by art or self-discipline, perfect grace – the grace which is seen in Antony and Cleopatra and which works on the beholder 'like enchauntment' – is an art which is 'planted naturall':

> Thereto great helpe dame Nature selfe doth lend
> For some so goodly gratious are by kind,
> That every action doth them much commend,
> And in the eyes of men great liking find,
> Which others that have greater skill in mind,
> Though they enforce themselues, cannot attaine;
> For euerie thing to which one is inclin'd
> Doth best become, and greatest grace doth gaine.[26]

In the supreme grace of bounty then – supreme because plenitude was felt to be Nature's most characteristic attribute – Antony is Nature's child. And Octavius is not simply a diligent student who strives to polish his limited gifts; he is a mere shadow exposed and condemned by contrast with the true substance, a common player (the other meaning of 'shadow' is relevant) acting in the borrowed robes of royalty.

As for Cleopatra's graces, that amorous dying of hers, which makes one suspect on occasions that 'she is cunning past man's thought' (I ii 141), is as natural to her as was (to him) the cunning

of the fertility god who turned himself into a shower of golden
rain in order to ravish Danae (I ii 142–6).[27] And the seductive art
displayed by her at Cydnus is natural too, for the winds themselves
were 'lovesick' and the quickened waters 'amorous' as she took
her way; while her person 'beggar'd all description' (exposed the
poverty of verbal art) and 'o'erpictured' (i.e., surpassed) 'that
Venus where we see/The fancy out-work nature' (II ii 198–205).[28]
Her last cunning death is another characteristic triumph, and it
is one which has no end :

> . . . she looks like sleep,
> As she would catch another Antony
> In her strong toil of grace. (V ii 343–5)

Antony ('Nature's piece') and Cleopatra ('a wonderful piece of
work') are Shakespeare's most generous and subtle tribute, in
terms of human personality, to the art of Nature : to creative
Nature itself as distinct from the conscious art with which man
orders and perfects his natural endowments. That, no doubt, is
one reason why the arts of language and adjustment on which
social good depends figure so very little in the tragedy and find no
more dignified expression than in the cunning persuasions of
Caesar's Jack.

VII

Yet one must not lose sight of the art with which Cleopatra seeks
to ensure that her fortune and Antony's mingle entirely and that
his name will be buried in hers. Her constancy is studied and involves a determination to acquire Antony's Roman and masculine
virtues. Dolabella's praise of the way in which her mourning
'answers' her loss is even more justified than he imagines since there
is as much resolution as pain in her sublime show of grief : she will
not 'be comforted' since 'our size of sorrow,/Proportion'd to our
cause, must be as great/As that which makes it' (IV xv 2–6). And
her confession to Caesar that she has been 'laden with like frailties
which before/Have often sham'd' her 'sex' (V ii 122–3), although
part of an artful deception, expresses a new and genuine consciousness that irresolution and fear are qualities which can make

queens indistinguishable from milkmaids and prevent them from being nobly constant to the memory of the dead ('Frailty, thy name is woman'). She is utterly sincere when she tells her dying lord that her honour and safety do not go together and that she will trust only her resolution and her hands (IV xv 46–9).[29] But her fainting fit after his death makes her realise that her claim to the title with which Iras arouses her ('Royal Egypt: Empress!') is an insecure one. She looks at her frightened women, is deeply conscious of their common bondage to frailty, and makes a heroic resolve to emulate the firm Roman who has left her alone; but in what she says there is more than one tremulous recognition that it will not be easy to do that:

> No more but e'en a woman, and commanded
> By such poor passion as the maid that milks
> And does the meanest chares . . .
> . . . Then is it sin
> To rush into the secret house of death
> Ere death dare come to us? How do you women?
> What, what! good cheer! Why, how now, Charmian!
> My noble girls! Ah, women, women, look,
> Our lamp is spent, it's out! Good sirs, take heart.
> We'll bury him; and then what's brave, what's noble,
> Let's do it after the high Roman fashion,
> And make death proud to take us . . .
> Ah, women, women! Come; we have no friend
> But resolution and the briefest end. (IV xv 73–91)

Caesar himself is well aware that feminine frailty is his trump card in the game for 'eternal . . . triumph' (V i 66).[30] In framing his persuasions, Thyreus is to have in mind that whereas 'women are not/In their best fortunes strong . . . want will perjure/The ne'er touch'd vestal' (III xii 29–31); and Proculeius is to remember that Antony is dead and that grieving women are susceptible to comfort from any quarter: 'Give her what comforts/The quality of her passion shall require' (V i 62–3). But the very strength of Cleopatra's grief – her perception of just how weighty her loss has been – helps her to become a queen over her passion. Her desolation begins to make a better life in the sense that it teaches her the paltriness of that luck or good fortune which is now embodied in

Caesar, and the greatness of that deed which shackles accidents and bolts up change – puts an end to all games of chance, all tricks of fast and loose. Her final change, effected by courage, is from levity to gravity, from weakness into unchanging nobility, from bondage to liberty, from concubine to wife, from becoming into being :

>   What poor an instrument
> May do a noble deed ! He brings me liberty.
> My resolution's plac'd, and I have nothing
> Of woman in me. Now from head to foot
> I am marble-constant ; now the fleeting moon
> No planet is of mine . . .
>   Husband, I come.
> Now to that name my courage prove my title ! (V ii 235–40,
>   285–6)

Cleopatra ceases to resemble in any way the maid that milks and does the meanest chores. If she is a lass, she is 'a lass unparallel'd', one who was 'bravest at the last' and, 'being royal, took her own way' (V ii 314, 332–3). And Charmian's weakness is similarly gilded. Having stood 'tremblingly' by her mistress's side until she had trimmed up the crown that had gone 'awry' (a wonderfully symbolic detail), she 'on the sudden dropp'd' ; hearing of which, Caesar exclaims : 'O noble weakness !' (V ii 338–41).

As the crown should remind us, Cleopatra's transfiguration into 'something of great constancy' (*Midsummer Night's Dream,* V i 26) presupposes not only courage but a hatred of degradation and public shame which is royal as well as Roman. It is not infrequently suggested that her decision to join Antony in death loses some or most of its value as a moral choice because it is complicated by her fears of humiliation in Rome. 'Fear', however, is quite the wrong word to designate the emotion which that destiny excites in her : what she experiences is an emotion which dignifies, a feeling of disgust and horror which is at bottom moral (that the morality means little to us is beside the point). And far from reducing her claims to spiritual indentification with Antony, this feeling actually enhances them, since it was he who – in his attempt to prove he did not 'lack the courage of a woman', had not 'less noble mind than Cleopatra' – first evoked the horrid image of absolute disgrace :

Eros,
Wouldst thou be window'd in great Rome and see
Thy master thus with pleach'd arms, bending down
His corrigible neck, his face subdu'd
To penetrative shame, whilst the wheel'd seat
Of fortunate Caesar, drawn before him, branded
His baseness that ensued? (IV xiv 71–7)

To speak thus to 'valiant Eros' is to speak to the absent Queen of Love, and so she, too, becomes imbued with the Stoic conviction that we defeat Fortune's wheeling caprice by choosing death. But the high Roman fashion of death is 'high' for her not least because it allows her to retain the dignity of a queen. In her imagination there are two possible triumphs, spectacles or dramatic actions. There is 'th' imperious show/Of the full-fortun'd Caesar' (IV xv 23–4) in which Fortune's knave will play the all-conquering monarch and she the beggar-strumpet. Her scenes with Thyreus, Proculeius, and Caesar are all little previews of it; and no courtly audience watching a commoner playing the part of a king, no countess seeing a boy got up as a great queen and impudently exploiting her frailties for a few guffaws from the pit, could be more oppressed by a sense of shameful impropriety than Cleopatra is by the thought of that Roman show. With marvellous assurance and winning audacity, Shakespeare allows his own theatre and art – indeed this tragedy itself – to stand as an image of the degradation the prospect of which gives Cleopatra and her women the strength to choose death rather than life. Mr. Wm. Shakespeare (in whom all ill shows well) could hardly be expected to offer a more gracious apology to the Countess of Pembroke and her fastidious friends:

Cleo. Now, Iras, what think'st thou?
  Thou an Egyptian puppet shall be shown
  In Rome as well as I. Mechanic slaves,
  With greasy aprons, rules, and hammers, shall
  Uplift us to the view; in their thick breaths,
  Rank of gross diet, shall we be enclouded,
  And forc'd to drink their vapour.
Iras The gods forbid!

Cleo. Nay, 'tis most certain, Iras. Saucy lictors
  Will catch at us like strumpets, and scald rhymers
  Ballad us out o' tune ; the quick comedians
  Extemporally will stage us, and present
  Our Alexandrian revels ; Antony
  Shall be brought drunken forth, and I shall see
  Some squeaking Cleopatra boy my greatness
  I' th' posture of a whore.
Iras O the good gods ! (V ii 206–20)

The other show which Cleopatra has in mind is enacted immediately after this vision of disgrace. It is of the triumphant and
faultless kind desired by the Prologue of *Henry V* :

O for a muse of fire, that would ascend
The brightest heaven of invention,
A kingdom for a stage, princes to act,
And monarchs to behold the swelling scene !

In it, Cleopatra is shown 'like a queen', is arrayed in her most
regal attires, puts on her crown, and has immortal longings. She
is all fire and air and transcends the baser elements which momentarily intrude (the theatrical metaphor expands brilliantly here)
in the person of the earthy clown and his extemporal, untimely
jests. We must not view this interlude as Shakespearian audacity
for its own sake, or as a sign that Cleopatra can jest as easily in
death as she did in life. She is not at all in the mood for levity. Her
reaction to the clown's jokes and quibbles about women's dying
is a fine blend of detachment, mild impatience and forbearance.
She does not say, as the irritably grave Antony said to Enobarbus
in a dialogue on the very same subject, 'No more light answers' ;
but her tone and manner say the same thing with equal expressive-
ness and much more confidence : quietly, she mends what is
awry :

Get thee hence ; farewell . . .
Farewell . . .
Ay, ay, farewell . . .
Well, get thee gone, farewell. (V ii 257–76)

Antony will not rage at this audience, but will rouse himself to praise her 'noble act' (V ii 283). Then, having called 'great Caesar ass unpolicied', they will unarm, 'untie the knot intrinsicate of life', and enjoy a sleep 'as sweet as balm, as soft as air, as gentle' (V ii 302–8). Even Caesar, who arrives 'to see perform'd the dreaded act' which he so sought to hinder (V ii 329–30), applauds what is done and finally shares in the decorum of it all by asking for 'high order' and 'solemn show' in the burial of the lovers. The universal landlord thus sets his seal of approval on the answer calmly given by Charmian to the nervous soldier who discovered that his charge was dead :

> *First Guard.* What work is here ! Charmian, is this well done?
> *Char.* It is well done, and fitting for a princess
>   Descended of so many royal kings. (V ii 323–5)

Notes

CHAPTER I

1. Shakespeare's conscious mastery of the figures of speech and forms of reasoning has been abundantly demonstrated by Sister Miriam Joseph in *Shakespeare's Use of the Arts of Language* (New York, 1947).

2. Cicero, *De Oratore*, ed. and trans. G. L. Hendrickson and H. M. Hubbell (Loeb Classical Library; London and Cambridge, Mass., 1942) I 31–5; *De Officiis*, ed. and trans. W. Miller (Leob Classical Library; London and Cambridge, Mass., 1947) I 50–1; *De Inventione*, ed. and trans H. M. Hubbell (Leob Classical Library; London and Cambridge, Mass., 1949) I 5. Quintilian, *Institutio Oratoria*, ed. and trans. H. E. Butler (Loeb Classical Library; London and Cambridge, Mass., 1926) I x 7, II xvi 9–19. Roger Ascham, *The Scholemaster*, ed. E. Arber (London, 1897) p 118. George Puttenham, *The Arte of English Poesie* (Menston: Scolar Press Facsimile Rept., 1968) p. 118. Sir Thomas Elyot, *The Book Named the Governor*, ed. S. E. Lehmberg (Everyman's Library; London, 1962) pp. 45–6. C. H. Herford and P. & E. Simpson (eds), *Ben Jonson* (Oxford, 1925–52) VI 620–1.

3. Cicero, *De Officiis*, II 48; Quintilian, II xvi 8; Thomas Wilson, *The Arte of Rhetorique*, ed. G. H. Mair (Oxford, 1919) sig. Aii.

4. Henry Peacham *The Compleat Gentleman*, ed. G. S. Gordon (Oxford, 1906) p. 8. Cf. Cicero, *De Inventione*, I 6; *De Oratore*, I 34, 60.

5. Baldassare Castiglione, *The Book of the Courtier*, trans. Sir Thomas Hoby (Everyman's Library; London, 1928; rept. 1966) pp. 261–94; Cicero, *De Oratore*, II 115; Quintilian, II xvi 9–10, II v 2.

6. Quintilian, XI i 30; Puttenham, p. 124; Herford and Simpson (eds), VIII 625; Peacham, p. 42.

7. Cicero, *De Oratore*, I 30; Cicero, *Brutus and Orator*, ed. and trans. G. L. Henrickson and H. M. Hubbell (Loeb Classical Library; London and Cambridge, Mass., 1939) §§ 329–32; Castiglione, pp. 54–5; Bacon, *Works*, ed. J. Spedding (London, 1857–74) III 302; Quintilian, VIII iii 45; Ascham, pp. 28–9, 117–18; Herford and Simpson (eds), VI 593.

8. Wilson, Preface.

9. John Hoskyns, *Directions for Speech and Style*, ed. H. Hudson (Princeton, 1935) p. 2. Cf. Herford and Simpson (eds), VI 628; Pierre de la Primaudaye, *The French Academie*, trans. T. Bowes *et al.* (London, 1618) II ii 379.

10. Peacham, p. 8. Cf. F. Watson, *Vives on Education: A Translation of the 'De Tradendis Disciplinis' of Juan Luis Vives* (Cambridge, 1913) p. 177; Cicero, *De Oratore*, III 55, *De Inventione*, I 4–5.

11. Cicero, *De Oratore*, III 60–1, 66. See also Quintilian, II xvi 1–6.

12. The image of slander and flattery as a poison which enters the heart

through the ear was traditional (see, for example, Elyot, pp. 234–6). We shall confront it in a later chapter.

13. Elyot, pp. 180–1. Cf *The Civile Conversation of M. Steeven Guazzo,* trans. G. Pettie and B. Young, ed. Sir Ed. Sullivan, Tudor Translations, Second Series VII (1925) I 59–60; Thomas Becon, 'The Invective Against Swearing', *Early Works,* ed. J. Ayre (Cambridge; Parker Society Publications, 1843) pp. 357–61.

14. Elyot, pp. 172, 181; de la Primaudaye, I xxix 170; J. Griffiths (ed.), *The Two Books of Homilies Appointed to be Read in Churches* (Oxford, 1859) pp. 73–80. Cf. Cicero, *De Officiis,* I 23.

15. G. Gregory Smith (ed.), *Elizabethan Critical Essays* (Oxford, 1904) I 335. Cf. de la Primaudaye, p. 380.

16. Cicero, *De Officiis,* I 98, 145–6; Giovanni della Casa, *Galateo, or the Book of Manners,* trans. R. S. Pine-Coffin (London, 1958; first Engl. trans. 1576), pp. 76–81; Puttenham, pp. 218–19.

17. Puttenham, p. 220. Cf. Watson, p. 187.

18. Aristotle, *The Art of Rhetoric,* ed. and trans. J. H. Reese (Loeb Classical Library; London and Cambridge, Mass., 1926) III xii 6, *Ethics,* II ii–ix; Cicero, *De Officiis,* I 89, 129–31; Castiglione, pp. 47, 132–3.

19. De la Primaudaye, p. 74.

20. Elyot, pp. 3, 5.

21. Guazzo, I 192.

22. Cicero, *De Officiis,* I 96. Cf. de la Primaudaye, p. 74; Shakespeare, *Romeo and Juliet,* III iii 109–14.

23. Castiglione, p. 189 (cf. pp. 192–3). Cf. *Romeo and Juliet,* III iii 112.

24. Castiglione, pp. 102, 296–303, 307; Guazzo, I 173.

25. Puttenham, p. 232.

26. Quintilian, VIII ii 1.

27. Elyot, pp. 105, 165. Cf. Guazzo, I, 176, 197; Castiglione, p. 29.

28. Elyot, pp. 102–3; Castiglione, pp. 115–18, 194; Puttenham, p. 237; Griffiths, pp. 308, 315, 319.

29. Quintilian, II xiii 2; Castiglione, pp. 121, 133. Cf. Guazzo, I 168.

30. See, for example, Castiglione, p. 92. Renaissance reverence for the virtue of timeliness is abundantly illustrated and subtly analysed in Edgar Wind's *Pagan Mysteries in the Renaissance* (2nd ed., London, 1967) pp. 97–112. (No mention, however, is made of decorum.)

31. Elyot, pp. 80, 87. Cf. Cicero, *De Officiis,* I 142–4; Puttenham, pp. 223, 235.

32. Cicero, *De Officiis,* I 107–20; Castiglione, pp. 61–3, 110, 117–18, 128.

33. Shakespeare, *Two Gentlemen of Verona,* V iv 110–11.

34. Quintilian, I vi 40, VIII iii 27–30, 57–8, etc.; Castiglione, pp. 45–9, 65–7, etc.; Guazzo, I 27, 134–5, etc.

35. Castiglione, p. 59; Wilson, p. 165.

36. Puttenham, pp. 216–17, 222–5, 228–9. Cf. Quintilian, VIII iii 17, 48; della Casa, pp. 75–8; Joseph, pp. 67–8, 301.

37. Puttenham, pp. 210–11, 215. Cf. Castiglione, p. 49; Guazzo, I 132–6, 143.

38. Guazzo, I 11–12; Annibale Romei, *The Courtiers Academie,* trans.

J. Kepers (1598), cited in R. F. Jones, *The Triumph of the English Language* (Stanford, Calif., 1953) p. 210.

39. Guazzo, I 135. See also Erasmus, *Opera Omnia* (Leiden, 1703) I 3–6 (*De Copia Verborum*, cap. i–vi); Wilson, pp. 162–3; Ascham, pp. 154–5.

40. Herford and Simpson (eds.), VIII 574. Cf. Guazzo, I 136.

41. Puttenham, p. 114. Cf. Castiglione, p. 59.

42. Puttenham, pp. 124–8. Cf. Quintilian, XI i 1–3.

43. Cicero, *De Oratore*, III 99, 100–1; Quintilian, VIII vi 14; Ascham, pp. 112–13; Puttenham, p. 115; Peacham, p. 90.

44. Puttenham, pp. 216–17. Cf. Quintilian, II iii 9; [Cicero], *Rhetorica ad Herennium*, ed. and trans. H. Caplan (Loeb Classical Library; London and Cambridge, Mass., 1954) IV 15.

45. Quintilian, II xii 9–10. Cf. Wilson, p. 220; Castiglione, pp. 56–7; Guazzo, I 130–2; Peacham, p. 42.

46. Smith, I xli–xlv; V. Hall, *Renaissance Literary Criticism: A Study of its Social Content* (New York, 1945) pp. 174–89.

47. D. Klein, *The Elizabethan Dramatists as Critics* (London, 1963), p. 199.

48. Smith, I 199.

49. Shakespeare, *Midsummer Night's Dream*, I ii 11–12, V i 57–65. Cf. Spenser, *The Shepherd's Calendar*, Epistle Dedicatory: 'Oftimes we fynde ourselues . . . take great pleasure in that disorderly order . . . oftentimes a dischorde in Musick maketh a comely concordaunce'.

CHAPTER 2

1. Compare with the last two lines of the play which immediately precedes *Richard II* in the First Folio – *King John*: 'Nought shall make us rue,/If England to itself do rest but true.' Also with *III Henry VI*, IV i 40.

2. See A Schmidt, *Shakespeare-Lexicon*, rev. G. Sarrazin, *s.v.* 'constancy' and above pp. 11–12.

3. Yeats' interpretation of *Richard II* forms the basis of his essay 'At Stratford-on-Avon' (written 1901).

4. 'Grace' was the standard humanist term for beauty and so was identified with decorum. Thus, Puttenham (p. 219) describes decorum as 'the good grace of euery thing in his kinde', and Edward Phillips in his *New World of English Words: or a General Dictionary* (1658) defines it as 'good grace, order, decency'. See also della Casa, pp. 93–4; Castiglione, pp. 33, 43–9, 93; E. Garin, *Italian Humanism: Philosophy and Civic Life in the Renaissance*, trans. P. Munz (Oxford, 1965) pp. 117–22.

5. The assumption that names should be examined in relation to other linguistic phenomena and to the general question of decorum in speech and behaviour distinguishes my study of names in *Richard II* from that contained in James Winny's excellent book *The Player King: A Theme of Shakespeare's Histories* (London, 1968) pp. 48–85.

6. See Mark Van Doren, *Shakespeare* (London, 1941) p. 85.

7. *The French Academie*, I xii 53, II xiv–xv 380–5. See also above p. 6 (and n.15).

8. For a vivid example of the Elizabethan–Jacobean attitude to Bolingbroke, see Spedding, *Letters and Life of Francis Bacon*, V 145.

9. E. M. W. Tillyard *Shakespeare's History Plays* (London, 1944) pp. 247, 248, 251–2. For Pater's comments on Richard, see the essay 'Shakespeare's English Kings' in his *Appreciations* (London, 1889).

10. The oyster-wench would have been enormously flattered by Bolingbroke's gesture: 'The hat was a great asset in a well-dressed man's attire: he fought in it, and with it, using it as a parry; he sat at church and at meals with it on, and only removed it with most profuse ceremony on meeting a lady, instantly replacing it: he remained uncovered only at court and in the presence of royalty'. – *Shakespeare's England. An Account of Life and Manners of his Age*, 2 vols. (Oxford, 1916), II 109.

11. For his use of the word in speaking to York, see II iii 82, 85, 106, 163.

12. For further comments on Richard's abuse of time, see R. J. Dorius, 'A Little More than a Little', *S.Q.* XI (1960) 16–20.

13. For the association of 'degrading' and 'disgracing' in Shakespearian thought, see *I Henry VI*, IV i 43; *III Henry VI*, II ii 81, IV iv 34.

14. On the significance of the concept of excess in this play (and in *Henry IV*), see Dorius, loc. cit. Dorius argues that prudence or economy is the virtue or norm abused by those guilty of excess in these plays; but he also remarks that 'the unrealized possibility in both man and state of a kind of Aristotelian norm, an ideal of moderation or of equilibrium among opposing forces', is everywhere implicit in this tetralogy (p. 15).

15. Peter Ure (ed.), *Richard II* (The Arden Shakespeare, 5th edn.; London, 1961) pp. li–lvii.

16. M. C. Bradbrook, *Shakespeare and Elizabethan Poetry* (London, 1951) p. 37. See Puttenham, pp. 253–4, 256–7.

17. Puttenham, pp. 129, 163–5, 185.

18. Compare Quintilian, IX iv 5–6, 8. 'What art was ever born full grown? What does not ripen with cultivation? Why do we train the vine? Why dig it? We clear the fields of brambles, and they too are natural products of the soil . . . No, that which is most natural is that which nature permits to be done to the greatest perfection. How can a style which lacks orderly structure be stronger than one that is welded together and artistically arranged? . . . the truth is that nothing can attain its full strength without the assistance of art, and that art is always productive of beauty.' (See also Quintilian VIII v 26 and Castiglione, p. 63.) It might be added that 'The Garden of Eloquence' was a familiar notion in the Renaissance: Henry Peacham (the Elder), for example, made it the title of his popular rhetorical treatise (1577, 1593); Castiglione (p. 58) expressed the hope that the Italian language would one day be 'a delicious garden full of sundrie flowers and fruites'; and Carew complimented Donne thus:

The Muses garden with Pedantique weedes
O'erspread, was purg'd by thee; The lazie seeds

Of servile imitation throwne away,
And fresh invention planted, Thou didst pay
The debts of our penurious bankrupt age.

19. See p. 12, 14.

20. Cicero, *De Officiis*, I 120.

CHAPTER 3

1. By this last phrase Hamlet may mean that Claudius should be wearing the attire of a fool or Vice rather than that of a king, 'shreds and patches' being (probably) an allusion to the fool-Vice's motley. See J. D. Wilson (ed.), *Hamlet* (2nd amplified ed.; Cambridge, 1954) p. 213 (note on III iv 102).

2. Schmidt, *Shakespeare-Lexicon, sub verbum*.

3. 'Do you consent we shall acquaint him with it,/As needful in our loves, fitting our duty?' (I i 172–3); 'it us befitted/To bear our hearts in grief . . . these mourning duties' (I ii 2–3, 88); 'In that and all things we will show our duty' (I ii 40); 'I came to Denmark/To show my duty in your coronation' (I ii 52–3); 'We did think it writ down in our duty/To let you know of it' (I ii 222–3); 'Our duty to your honour' (I ii 253); etc.

4. Quintilian, XI iii 177 ('praecipue in actione spectetur decorum'). See also above, p. 15.

5. Shakespeare here quotes Quintilian's well-known axiom on the foundations of language in order to enhance his dramatic point. Says Quintilian (I vi 1): 'Sermo constat ratione vel velustate, auctoritate, consuetudine'. Cf. Herford and Simpson (eds.) VI 622.

6. For the witchcraft of the tongue, see also *Henry V*, V ii 271–3; *Henry VIII*, III ii 18; *Lucrece*, l. 1411.

7. 'It is also . . . a good pollicie in pleading or perswasion to make wise as if we set but light of the matter, and that therefore we do passe it ouer slightly when in deede we do then intend most effectually . . . to remember it'. – Puttenham on 'Paralepsis or the Passenger' (p. 194). Presumably the ghost reinforces its words with 'piteous action' (as at III iv 128).

8. For Osric's attire, see Wilson (ed.), *Hamlet*, pp. 243, 248. See also p. 180 for a plausible suggestion (based on II ii 386) that there may be 'something comical in the costume or figure of Polonius' – it would be very surprising if Polonius did not fail to practise what he preaches in dress as well as in verbal art.

9. Cf. Puttenham, p. 223: 'Prowde speeches and too much finesse and couriosite is not commendable in an Embassadour. And I haue knowen in my time such of them, as studied more vpon what apparell they should weare, and what countenaunces they should keepe at the times of their audience, then they did upon th' effect of their errraunt or commission.'

10. New Variorum *Hamlet*, ed. H. H. Furness (1873) I 344.

11. In Aeneas' tale to Dido as told by Marlowe and Nashe there is one strained hyperbole which Shakespeare transferred to the player's speech: '[Priamus] Forgetting both his want of strength and hands,/Which he disdaining whiskt his sword about,/*And with the wind thereof the King fell*

downe' [my italics] (ll 547–50). Cf. *Hamlet*, II ii 467–8. But apart from this figure the Marlowe-Nashe version is distinctly chaste and wholesome in style.

12. Puttenham, p. 159. Cf. Quintilian, VIII vi 57, IX ii 47.

13. Claude Levi-Strauss, *The Scope of Anthropology*, trans. S. O. and R. A. Paul (London, 1967) pp. 34–9. M. Levi-Strauss will find further evidence for his theory not only in *Hamlet* but in (1) the late Greek romance *Apollonius of Tyre* and its Shakespearian offspring *Pericles* (see esp. I i and note the firm identification of incest and 'unfitness'); (2) the two incest situations (father-daughter and father-daughter-in-law) described by Quintilian in his discussion of ambiguity (IX ii 69–71); (3) Seneca's *Hippolytus* and *Oedipus*. Seneca (who, unlike Sophocles, dramatises the causal connection between riddling and incest) undoubtedly influenced this aspect of Shakespeare's dramatic art.

14. 'Defende for offende' – one of a list of howlers compiled in 1570 as evidence of what happens when 'the rude doe endeavour to imitate the learned, though it be in a contrary sense'. See Jones, pp. 107–8. On *se offendendo*, see Wilson, p. 231. Verges and Dogberry use 'salvation' and 'redemption' for 'damnation' (*Much Ado*, III iii 4, IV ii 52).

15. 'Picked' was an epithet widely used to describe affected diction. See Jones, pp. 98–9; T. W. Baldwin, *William Shakspere's Small Latine and Lesse Greeke* (Urbana, Illinois, 1944) II 225; Shakespeare, *Love's Labour's Lost*, V i 11.

16. On the faults of reasoning and style in the speech of Troilus and Paris, see my article, 'Language, Style, and Meaning in *Troilus and Cressida, P.M.L.A.*, LXXIV (1969) 29–43.

17. On 'relative', see Hardin Craig, 'Shakespeare and Formal Logic', in *Studies in English Philology: A Miscellany in Honor of Frederick Klaeber*, ed. Kemp Malone and M. B. Rund (Minneapolis, 1929) p. 392.

18. Joseph, p. 195.

19. See further, E. Prosser, *Hamlet and Revenge* (Stanford, Calif., 1968).

20. Craig, p. 394. Cf. Quintilian, V iii 3; [Cicero], Rhetorica ad Herennium, ed. and trans. H. Caplan, II 41, IV 35.

21. New Variorum *Hamlet*, I 401.

22. First Folio stage direction. Note that Fortinbras does not suit the action to the word: he was given 'quiet pass' through Denmark (II ii 77) and dutifully ordered his men to 'go softly on' (IV iv 8).

23. See above p. 16.

CHAPTER 4

1. Van Doren, p. 236.

2. The phrase quoted refers to Othello, but as William Empson has remarked: 'The real murderous coxcomb, the clown who did kill out of vanity, was Iago'. *The Structure of Complex Words* (London, 1951) p. 227.

3. A. C. Bradley *Shakespearian Tragedy* (Oxford, 1904) p. 55.

4. See III iii 249, 400; IV i 75, 87-9; V i 87.

5. For the use of the terms Opportunity and Importunity in the teaching on timeliness, see above p. 10, and Puttenham, p. 223. Occasion (also frequently personified) was synonymous with Opportunity: see Cicero, *De Officiis*, I 142 and Schmidt, *Shakespeare-Lexicon, s.v.* 'Occasion' (2).

6. 'Again, in suing for others, he shall discretely observe the times, and his sute shall bee for honest and reasonable matters, and he shall so frame his sute, in leaving out those points that he shall knowe will trouble him . . . making easie after a comelie sort the lettes, that his Lorde wil evermore graunt it him.' Castiglione, p. 107.

7. see II iii 137; III iii 158; III iv 99; IV i 36.

8. In the First Folio (1623) and Second Quarto (1630) editions of the play, Cassio's 'Zounds' is omitted and his 'Fore God' (ll. 60, 70) is diluted to 'Heaven' and 'Why'. Iago's and Othello's oaths are similarly dealt with. These alterations were dictated by the Act Against Swearing of 1605 ('to restrain abuses of players'). It is difficult to appreciate the dramatic significance of the original oaths, or to gauge the responsiveness of Shakespeare's audience to them, without taking such facts into account.

9. In iconographic tradition, Occasion was represented with hair in front and as bald behind; hence the proverb that one must 'take Occasion by the front [or forelock]' if one wishes to act opportunely.

10. Said Desdemona (ll. 63-4). 'I prithee name the time; but let it not exceed three days'.

11. This whole passage was probably inspired by the vow of the heroine in Seneca's *Medea* to turn the marriage feast of her faithless husband (now wed to Creusa) into a funeral: the stylistic parallels are considerable. See *Seneca's Tragedies*, trans. F. J. Miller (London and New York; Loeb Classical Library, 1927) I 261-2.

12. Quintilian, III v 17-18; *N.E.D.* 'Cause', 7 ('The matter about which a person goes to law; the case of one party in a suit').

13. On the association of Time and Justice, see S. D. Chew, *The Virtues Reconciled* (Toronto, 1947) pp. 90ff.

14. See I i 104; I ii 11-14; I iii 51.

15. Compare *Richard II*, I iii 215-48, and above pp. 29-30.

16. M. R. Ridley's gloss on 'sanctimony' is pertinent: 'I think here near to "ritual"; "the rites are solemnised with great sanctimony" (Purchas)'. Arden edition (London, 1959; corrected rept. 1962) p. 43.

17. H. Granville-Barker, *Prefaces to Shakespeare IV* (London, 1930) p. 136 (quoting *Romeo and Juliet*, II vi 9).

18. Ridley, p. 34. But there can be no doubt about 'accommodation' – consider Elyot, p. 99: 'language . . . accommodate to time, place and company'; and Puttenham, p. 248: 'apt and accommodate'.

19. See Ridley, pp. 131-2.

20. Spenser, 'Epithalamion', ll. 353-6. (This whole section of the poem is relevant – ll. 315ff.) Cf. *A Midsummer-Night's Dream*, V i 360-409.

21. Ridley's note on 'propriety' (p. 77) reads: 'natural temper (of quiet decorum); "it is the baseness of thy fear/That makes thee strangle thy propriety" (*Tw.N.*, V i 150)'.

22. J. D. Wilson and Alice Walker (eds.), *Othello*, New Cambridge Shakespeare (Cambridge, 1957) p. 205.

23. There is a long section on the courtly art of composing 'praises' for a lady in Guazzo's *Civile Conversation* (II 186–93). The gentleman usually amplifies the idea that his lady is 'faire, gracious, honest and worthie'.

24. Wilson, p. 138.

25. The quotation from Quintilian was first spotted by Steevens, but it was Baldwin who recognised that Quintilian's principles were being applied in the oration (*William Shakspere's Small Latine and Lesse Greeke*, II 198–200). The relevant passages in Quintilian are IV i 42, 44, 76.

26. [Cicero], *Rhetorica ad Herennium*, IV 15.

27. Hamlet uses his name only twice – and on both occasions he is posturing – V i 252; V ii 225–31.

28. IV v 7–11.

29. I quote *N.E.D.*

30. Puttenham, p. 217; Joseph, pp. 66, 300.

31. See, for example, Wilson, *Arte of Rhetorique*, pp. 130–2 ('Of mouing affections'), pp. 133–4 ('Of mouing pitie'), pp. 134ff. ('Laughter mouing').

32. On which, see the detailed analysis in Empson, pp. 218–49 ('Honest in *Othello*').

33. I follow Schmidt, *Shakespeare-Lexicon*.

34. Granville-Barker, p. 198.

35. *Richard III*, III ii 37–8. This, too, is a tragedy where chaos is reflected in the villain's inclination to 'moralize two meanings in one word' (III i 83).

36. The clown promises 'to ask the given questions and return the correct answers'. Wilson and Walker, *Othello*, p. 191.

37. 'The kissing of his hand was quite a normal courteous gesture from a gentleman to a lady; "To see him walk before a lady, and to bear her fan! To see him kiss his hand" (*LLL.*, IV i 148)'. Ridley, p. 59.

38. 'Wretched, wily, wandering vagabonds calling and naming themselves Egyptians, deeply dissembling and long hiding and covering their deep, deceitful practices, feeding the rude common people, wholly addicted and given to novelties, toys, and new inventions; delighting them with the strangeness of their attire, and practising palmistry to such as would know their fortunes . . .' Thomas Harman, *A Caveat or Warning for Common Cursitors, Vulgarly Called Vagabonds* (1566), in A. V. Judges, *The Elizabethan Underworld* (London, 1930) p. 64. See also ibid., pp. xxiv–xxvi, 346.

CHAPTER 5

1. Since Macbeth has contemplated usurpation before the action of the play begins (see I vii 47–52), the process of word corruption is apparent from the first scene – although it is only fully understood retrospectively.

2. See above pp. 7–8, 20. Cf. Hooker *Ecclesiastical Polity*, I viii 1, 9 ('the Law of Nature . . . comprehendeth all those things which men by the

light of their natural understanding evidently know . . . to be *beseeming or unbeseeming, virtuous or vicious, good or evil* for them to do' [my italics].

3. Cicero, *De Officiis*, II 23–6; Elyot, p. 127.

4. *III Henry VI*, I iv 137.

5. See Cicero, *De Officiis*, I 81; Elyot, III viii–ix. See also L. B. Campbell, *Shakespeare's Tragic Heroes: Slaves of Passion* (Cambridge, 1930) pp. 208–12. The whole discussion of *Macbeth* in this book (Ch. xv: 'Macbeth: A Study in Fear') is of obvious relevance here.

6. W. G. Boswell-Stone, *Shakespeare's Holinshed. The Chronicle and the Historical Plays Compared* (London, 1896) pp. 18–19, 20–1.

7. Cf. pp. 87–8.

8. L. B. Campbell (ed.), *The Mirror for Magistrates* (Cambridge, 1938) p. 419.

9. It was pointed out by Caroline Spurgeon (*Shakespeare's Imagery and What It Tells Us* [Cambridge, 1935] pp. 187–90) that 'martin' (= 'marlet') was an Elizabethan slang term for 'dupe' and that Shakespeare must have had this meaning in mind here.

10. Cf. Holinshed, p. 25: 'Wherevpon Mackbeth reuoluing the thing in his mind, began euen then to deuise how he might atteine to the kingdome: but yet he thought with himselfe that he must tarie a time, which should aduance him thereto (by the diuine prouidence) as it had come to passe in his former preferment.'

11. Kenneth Muir (ed.), *Macbeth* (The Arden Shakespeare, 9th ed.; London, 1962) p. 50, citing Craig's interpretation of II i 54.

12. Schmidt, *Shakespeare-Lexicon*.

13. The Folio has 'thick as tale', which Peter Alexander accepts. I follow Rowe's emended reading.

14. 'He that's coming must be provided for; and you shall put/This night's great business into my dispatch.' Cf. Macbeth to Banquo's murderer. 'Is he dispatch'd?' (III iv 15).

15. The phrase quoted is from Elyot's account of order and 'seemliness' in *The Governor*, Ch. I.

16. See Spurgeon, pp. 325–7; Cleanth Brooks, *The Well Wrought Urn* (New York, 1947) pp. 22–49 ('The Naked Babe and the Cloak of Manliness'); Muir, pp. xxviii, 61–2.

17. See Elyot, pp. 105, 165; Peacham, p. 3.

18. See p. 5.

19. In the first scene of *I Henry IV*, the quibbling and irreverent Falstaff plays on 'grace' as a royal title and as a term meaning (1) divine aid, (2) royal (or paternal) favour, and (3) a prayer before meals (ll. 16–20). Cf. *Love's Labour's Lost* IV ii 146–50, where the association of ideas is similar to that in Ross' invitation to Macbeth: 'Wherefore, if before repast, it shall please you to *gratify* the table with a *grace*, I will, on my privilege I have with the parents of the foresaid child or pupil, undertake your *ben venuto* . . . I beseech your *society*' [my italics]. As well as showing that he knows the Italian for 'welcome', Holofernes (as becomes a pedant) implicitly recalls that 'gratify' and 'grace' both derive from the Latin 'gratia'. See also *Measure for Measure*, I ii 4–26.

20. Castiglione, *The Courtier*, p. 42. See also above p. 25, n.4; p. 37.
21. See Schmidt and *N.E.D.*
22. See *Richard III*, V iii 97–102.

CHAPTER 6

1. See Act V, Scene iv.
2. Compare with Desdemona, who refuses (though politely) to 'be left behind,/A moth of peace, and he go to the war' (*Othello*, I iii 255–6.)
3. Puttenham, p. 248.
4. A. B. Grosart (ed.), *The Complete Works in Prose and Verse of Samuel Daniel* (London, 1885–1896) III 24 (Epistle Dedicatory of *Cleopatra*, addressed to the Countess of Pembroke). The Countess's translation (*The Tragedie of Antonie*) is reprinted, together with *Cleopatra*, in G. Bullough, *Narrative and Dramatic Sources of Shakespeare*, V (London and New York, 1964).
5. A cheating game. Sir I. Hawkins' description of it in the 1821 Variorum edition is reprinted in the Arden edition, Ridley, p. 168. On the gipsy-Egyptian equation see also Ridley, p. 168 (note on IX xii 28) and above p. 128.
6. Pompey is similarly identified with the pristine virtues of a now degenerate Rome in *The False One* (see especially I i and II i).
7. Said Caesar in his first conversation with Lepidus: 'You are too indulgent' (I iv 16).
8. This nice point I owe to Mr. David Palmer.
9. Bullough, p. 275.
10. Plutarch, *Moralia*, ed. and trans. F. C. Babbit (Leob Classical Library; London and Cambridge, Mass., 1936) V 61, 65.
11. Bullough, p. 269.
12. Ibid., pp. 274–5.
13. Ibid., p. 274.
14. Ibid., p. 274. Cf. pp. 271–2. In 'Isis and Osiris' (*Moralia*, V 85) Plutarch identifies Osiris with Dionysus and Bacchus – and Osiris' wife Isis was another goddess in whose attire Cleopatra aparelled herself (Bullough, p. 259; *Antony and Cleopatra*, III vi 17).
15. Bullough, p. 257.
16. *Antony and Cleopatra*, ed. Ridley, p. 130.
17. *The Tragedie of Antonie*, ll 1221–3.
18. *Moralia*, V. 116–17 ('Isis and Osiris'). See also Wind, *Pagan Mysteries in the Renaissance*, pp. 87–96.
19. Fletcher understood Shakespeare's intention here and for that reason changed the name of Cleopatra's waiting-woman ('Eras' in Plutarch, 'Iras' in Shakespeare) into 'Eros'.
20. 'Friend' is here used in the sense of 'lover, paramour, sweetheart'. See Schmidt, *Shakespeare-Lexicon*.
21. Cf. Seneca, *Hercules Oetaeus*, ll 1453–6: 'Give me my club and bow, let my right hand be defiled, let me put stain upon my glory, and let a

woman be chosen as the last toil of Hercules.' *Seneca's Tragedies*, ed. and trans. Miller, II 301–3. The analogies between Antony and Hercules have been sensitively examined by E. M. Waith in his *The Herculean Hero in Marlowe, Chapman, Shakespeare and Dryden* (London, 1962) pp. 112–21.

22. *Venus and Adonis*, ll 709–10. See also ll 98–114, where Venus tells Adonis how she 'overcame the stern and direful god of war' – 'strong temper'd steel his stronger strength obeyed', yet he proved 'servile' to her.

23. No doubt one is expected to recall here the red sword of Ventidius (honour by lieutenantry).

24. De Selincourt (ed.), *Poetical Works of Spenser*, p. 434. It should perhaps be added that in his prefatory epistle E. K.'s chief aim is to prove that the author of *The Shepheardes Calender* is to be commended for 'his dewe obseruing of Decorum euerye where, in personages, in seasons, in matter, in speach', and for showing too that 'oftentimes [in poetry as in music] a dischorde . . . maketh a comely concordaunce' (pp. 416–17). On the Graces, see further Wind, Ch. II.

25. Bullough, p. 314.

26. *The Faerie Queene*, VI i 2; VI ii 2.

27. Compare Caesar's soldier on Antony's bounty: 'Your emperor/Continues still a Jove' (IV vi 28–9).

28. Because of inattention to the precise significance of the words and details noted here (all additions to Plutarch), the whole passage has been interpreted by some critics as saying the exact opposite of what Shakespeare intended.

29. The dialogue of the Player Queen and her dying husband in *Hamlet* (III ii 150–225) is, of course, very relevant here. Is 'purpose but the slave to memory,/Of violent birth, but poor validity'? Does the lady protest too much?

30. See IV xiv 19–20 ('Pack'd cards with Caesar . . . an enemy's triumph'): Warburton was the first to see a quibbling allusion to the trump card in 'triumph'.

Index